# Administering Programs
# for Young Children

# Administering Programs for Young Children

Janet Brown McCracken, Editor

National Association for the Education of Young Children
Washington, D.C.

Cover photograph: Betty C. Ford

**National Association for the Education of Young Children**
**1509 16th Street, N.W.**
**Washington, DC 20036-1426**
**202-232-8777 or 1-800-424-2460**

The National Association for the Education of Young Children (NAEYC) attempts through its publications program to provide a forum for discussion of major issues and ideas in our field. We hope to provoke thought and promote professional growth. The views expressed or implied are not necessarily those of the Association. NAEYC wishes to thank the author, who donated much time and effort to develop this book as a contribution to our profession.

Library of Congress Catalog Card Number: 84-61999
ISBN Catalog Number: 0-912674-90-3
NAEYC # 307

**Printed in the United States of America.**

*To Abbey Griffin*
*Director of Broadcasters' Child Development Center*
*Washington, D.C.*
*a dedicated advocate*
*for teachers, young children, and their families*

# About the Editor

**Janet Brown McCracken**, M.Ed., has worked for more than 20 years with, and on behalf of, early childhood teachers and children from birth through sixth grade in a variety of capacities, including child care program director, instructor for home-bound children, teacher, speaker, workshop leader, parent, advocate, photographer, editor, consultant, writer, and board member.

Ms. McCracken's educational publishing career was launched while working at the American Association of Elementary/Kindergarten/Nursery Educators with the National Education Association. In 1974 she joined the staff of the National Association for the Education of Young Children, where she edited the professional journal *Young Children* and served as publications director for more than a decade.

In 1986 Ms. McCracken became a national consultant in early childhood education. She writes and edits thought-provoking materials for parents and professionals and specializes in photography of diverse young children. She is the author or editor of more than 100 books and brochures published by NAEYC and other professional associations and agencies.

# Contents

# Plan for Quality

New challenges and exciting possibilities await directors of programs for young children each day! If we step back from our immediate concerns—locating a substitute, arranging field trip transportation, or soothing a parent on the waiting list—we can measure our progress as early childhood professionals who plan high quality programs for young children.

- Excellence is our goal as we urge staff to develop their skills in working with children and parents.

- Child development research gives us clearer direction to select effective and appropriate program activities and teaching techniques.

- Findings about health care for children in groups guide how we handle our daily routines to protect everyone's health.

- Busy families rely on us to provide original ways to involve them in their children's care and education.

- Computers help us manage our limited resources and maintain our burgeoning records.

As early childhood program administrators, we are responsible for our own professional development as well as the growth of our co-workers. *Administering Programs for Young Children* can help us set and achieve our goals for excellence in supporting staff, building a good program, protecting healthy development, strengthening families, and managing our resources wisely.

*You* play an important role in the progress we will continue to make in the field of early childhood education. Whether your program is just starting or is firmly established, you can build on and adapt the ideas in *Administering Programs for Young Children*. Just as other directors share their experiences through this book, you may be encouraged to present workshops at conferences or write for professional publication. We must all work together to meet the challenges and expand the knowledge base for our profession.

You can also demonstrate your commitment to high quality by engaging in a self-study of your program through the National Academy of Early Childhood Programs. This book centers around the Academy's Criteria for High Quality Early Childhood Programs. These Criteria form the basis for this new voluntary accreditation system. Developed with the expertise of early childhood educators including many program directors, these Criteria set goals that *can* be accomplished—and that *are* already being met in programs around the country. We invite you to join your professional colleagues in this promising effort to improve the quality of early childhood education!

\* \* \*

*Administering Programs for Young Children* follows in the tradition established by Dorothy W. Hewes, who edited *Administration: Making Programs Work for Children and Families* in 1979. Since that time, many changes have taken place in our field, as reflected in this new compilation of articles from *Young Children*. Membership in NAEYC will ensure that you continue to keep up with the most recent developments in early childhood education.

*Janet F. Brown*
October 1984

# Criteria for High Quality Early Childhood Programs

*These Criteria for High Quality Early Childhood Programs were approved in July 1984 by NAEYC's Governing Board as the basis for self-study by programs seeking accreditation through the National Academy of Early Childhood Programs. Administering Programs for Young Children is designed to assist you in meeting these criteria in your program.*

## A. Interactions among Staff and Children

**Goal:** *Interactions between children and staff provide opportunities for children to develop an understanding of self and others and are characterized by warmth, personal respect, individuality, positive support, and responsiveness. Staff facilitate interactions among children to provide opportunities for development of social skills and intellectual growth.*

A- 1. Staff interact frequently with children. Staff express respect for and affection toward children by smiling, touching, holding, and speaking to children at their eye level throughout the day, particularly on arrival and departure, and when diapering or feeding very young children.

A- 2. Staff are available and responsive to children, encouraging them to share experiences, ideas, and feelings, and listening to them with attention and respect.

A- 3. Staff speak with children in a friendly, positive, courteous manner. Staff converse frequently with children, asking open-ended questions and speaking individually to children (as opposed to the whole group) most of the time.

A- 4. Staff equally treat children of all races, religions, and cultures with respect and consideration. Staff provide children of both sexes with equal opportunities to take part in all activities.

A- 5. Staff encourage developmentally appropriate independence in children. Staff foster independence in routine activities—picking up toys, wiping spills, personal grooming (toileting, washing hands), obtaining and caring for materials, and other self-help skills.

A- 6. Staff use positive techniques of guidance, including redirection, anticipation of and elimination of potential problems, positive reinforcement, and encouragement rather than competition, comparison, or criticism. Staff abstain from corporal punishment or other humiliating or frightening discipline techniques. Consistent, clear rules are explained to children and understood by adults.

A- 7. The sound of the environment is primarily marked by pleasant conversation, spontaneous laughter, and exclamations of excitement rather than harsh, stressful noise or enforced quiet.

A- 8. Staff assist children to be comfortable, relaxed, happy, and involved in play and other activities.

A- 9. Staff foster cooperation and other prosocial behaviors among children.

A-10. Staff expectations of children's social behavior are developmentally appropriate.

A-11. Children are encouraged to verbalize feelings and ideas.

# B. Curriculum

**Goal:** *The curriculum encourages children to be actively involved in the learning process, to experience a variety of developmentally appropriate activities and materials, and to pursue their own interests in the context of life in the community and the world.*

B- 1. The curriculum is planned to reflect the program's philosophy and goals for children.

B- 2. Staff plan realistic curriculum goals for children based on assessment of individual needs and interests.

B- 3. Modifications are made in the environment when necessary for children with special needs. Staff make appropriate professional referrals where necessary.

B- 4. The daily schedule is planned to provide a balance of activities on the following dimensions:
   a. indoor/outdoor
   b. quiet/active
   c. individual/small group/large group
   d. large muscle/small muscle
   e. child initiated/staff initiated

B- 5. Developmentally appropriate materials and equipment which project heterogeneous racial, sexual, and age attributes are selected and used.

B- 6. Staff members continually provide learning opportunities for infants and toddlers, most often in response to cues emanating from the child. Infants and toddlers are permitted to move about freely, exploring the environment and initiating play activities.

B- 7. Staff provide a variety of developmentally appropriate activities and materials that are selected to emphasize concrete experiential learning and to achieve the following goals:
   a. foster positive self-concept
   b. develop social skills
   c. encourage children to think, reason, question, and experiment
   d. encourage language development
   e. enhance physical development and skills
   f. encourage and demonstrate sound health, safety, and nutritional practices
   g. encourage creative expression and appreciation for the arts
   h. respect cultural diversity of staff and children

B- 8. Staff provide materials and time for children to select their own activities during the day. Children may choose from among several activities which the teacher has planned or the children initiate. Staff respect the child's right to choose not to participate at times.

B- 9. Staff conduct smooth and unregimented transitions between activities. Children are not always required to move from one activity to another as a group. Transitions are planned as a vehicle for learning.

B-10. Staff are flexible enough to change planned or routine activities according to the needs or interests of the children or to cope with changes in weather or other situations which affect routines without unduly alarming children.

B-11. Routine tasks are incorporated into the program as a means of furthering children's learning, self-help, and social skills. Routines such as diapering, toileting, eating, dressing, and sleeping are handled in a relaxed, reassuring, and individualized manner based on developmental needs. Staff plan with parents to make toileting, feeding, and the development of other independent skills a positive experience for children. Provision is made for children who are early risers and for children who do not nap.

## C. Staff-Parent Interaction

**Goal:** *Parents are well-informed about and welcome as observers and contributors to the program.*

C- 1. Information about the program is given to new and prospective families, including written descriptions of the program's philosophy and operating procedures.

C- 2. A process has been developed for orienting children and parents to the center which may include a pre-enrollment visit, parent orientation meeting, or gradual introduction of children to the center.

C- 3. Staff and parents communicate regarding home and center child-rearing practices in order to minimize potential conflicts and confusion for children.

C- 4. Parents are welcome visitors in the center at all times (for example, to observe, eat lunch with a child, or volunteer to help in the classroom). Parents and other family members are encouraged to be involved in the program in various ways, taking

into consideration working parents and those with little spare time.

C- 5. A verbal and/or written system is established for sharing day-to-day happenings that may affect children. Changes in a child's physical or emotional state are regularly reported.

C- 6. Conferences are held at least once a year and at other times, as needed, to discuss children's progress, accomplishments, and difficulties at home and at the center.

C- 7. Parents are informed about the center's program through regular newsletters, bulletin boards, frequent notes, telephone calls, and other similar measures.

## D. Staff Qualifications and Development

**Goal:** *The program is staffed by adults who understand child development and who recognize and provide for children's needs.*

D- 1. The program is staffed by individuals who are 18 years of age or older, who have been trained in Early Childhood Education/Child Development, and who demonstrate the appropriate personal characteristics for working with children as exemplified in the criteria for Interactions among Staff and Children (Component A) and Curriculum (Component B). Staff working with school-age children have been trained in child development, recreation, or a related field. The amount of training required will vary depending on the level of professional responsibility of the position (see Table 1). In cases where staff members do not meet the specified qualifications, a training plan, both individualized and center-wide, has been developed and is being implemented for

## Table 1. Staff qualifications.

| Level of professional responsibility | Title | Training requirements |
|---|---|---|
| Pre-professionals who implement program activities under direct supervision of the professional staff | **Early Childhood Teacher Assistant** | High school graduate or equivalent, participation in professional development programs |
| Professionals who independently implement program activities and who may be responsible for the care and education of a group of children | **Early Childhood Associate Teacher** | CDA credential or associate degree in Early Childhood Education/Child Development |
| Professionals who are responsible for the care and education of a group of children | **Early Childhood Teacher** | Baccalaureate degree in Early Childhood Education/Child Development |
| Professionals who supervise and train staff, design curriculum, and/or administer programs | **Early Childhood Specialist** | Baccalaureate degree in Early Childhood Education/Child Development and at least three years of full-time teaching experience with young children and/or a graduate degree in ECE/CD |

those staff members. The training is appropriate to the age group with which the staff member is working.

D- 2. The chief administrative officer of the center has training and/or experience in business administration. If the chief administrative officer is not an early childhood specialist, an early childhood specialist is employed to direct the educational program.

D- 3. New staff are adequately oriented about goals and philosophy of the center, emergency health and safety procedures, special needs of individual children assigned to the staff member's care, guidance and classroom management techniques, and planned daily activities of the center.

D- 4. The center provides regular training opportunities for staff to improve skills in working with children and families and expects staff to participate in staff development. These may include attendance at workshops and seminars, visits to other children's programs, access to resource materials, in-service sessions, or enrollment in college level/technical school courses. Training addresses the following areas: health and safety, child growth and development, planning learning activities, guidance and discipline techniques, linkages with community services, communication and relations with families, and detection of child abuse.

D- 5. Accurate and current records are kept of staff qualifications including transcripts, certificates, or other documentation of continuing in-service education.

# E. Administration

**Goal:** *The program is efficiently and effectively administered with attention to the needs and desires of children, parents, and staff.*

E- 1.  At least annually, the director and staff conduct an assessment to identify strengths and weaknesses of the program and to specify program goals for the year.
E- 2.  The center has written policies and procedures for operating, including hours, fees, illness, holidays, and refund information.
E- 3.  The center has written personnel policies including job descriptions, compensation, resignation and termination, benefits, and grievance procedures. Hiring practices are nondiscriminatory.
E- 4.  Benefits for full-time staff include at least medical insurance coverage that is provided or arranged, sick leave, annual leave, and Social Security or some other retirement plan.
E- 5.  Records are kept on the program and related operations such as attendance, health, confidential personnel files, and board meetings.
E- 6.  In cases where the center is governed by a board of directors, the center has written policies defining roles and responsibilities of board members and staff.
E- 7.  Fiscal records are kept with evidence of long range budgeting and sound financial planning.
E- 8.  Accident protection and liability insurance coverage is maintained for children and adults.
E- 9.  The director (or other appropriate person) is familiar with and makes appropriate use of community resources including social services; mental and physical health agencies; and educational programs such as museums, libraries, and neighborhood centers.
E-10.  Staff and administrators communicate frequently. There is evidence of joint planning and consultation among staff. Regular staff meetings are held for staff to consult on program planning, to plan for individual children, and to discuss program and working conditions. Staff are provided paid planning time.
E-11.  Staff members are provided space and time away from children during the day. When staff work directly with children for more than four hours, they are provided breaks of at least 15 minutes in each four-hour period.

# F. Staffing

**Goal:** *The program is sufficiently staffed to meet the needs of and promote the physical, social, emotional, and cognitive development of children.*

F- 1.  The number of children in a group is limited to facilitate adult-child interaction and constructive activity among children. Groups of children may be age-determined or multiage. Maximum group size is determined by the distribution of ages in the group. Optimal group size would be smaller than the maximum. Group size limitations are applied indoors to the group that children are involved in during most of the day. Group size limitations will vary depending on the type of activity, whether it is indoors or outdoors, the inclusion of children with special needs, and other factors. A *group* is the number of children assigned to a staff member or team of staff members occupying an individual classroom

## Table 2. Staff-child ratios within group size.

| Age of children* | Group size | | | | | | | | | |
|---|---|---|---|---|---|---|---|---|---|---|
| | 6 | 8 | 10 | 12 | 14 | 16 | 18 | 20 | 22 | 24 |
| Infants (birth–12 mos.) | 1:3 | 1:4 | | | | | | | | |
| Toddlers (12–24 mos.) | 1:3 | 1:4 | 1:5 | 1:4 | | | | | | |
| Two-year-olds (24–36 mos.) | | 1:4 | 1:5 | 1:6** | | | | | | |
| Two- and three-year-olds | | | 1:5 | 1:6 | 1:7** | | | | | |
| Three-year-olds | | | 1:5 | 1:6 | 1:7 | 1:8** | | | | |
| Three- and four-year-olds | | | | | 1:7 | 1:8 | 1:9 | 1:10** | | |
| Four-year-olds | | | | | | 1:8 | 1:9 | 1:10** | | |
| Four- and five-year-olds | | | | | | 1:8 | 1:9 | 1:10** | | |
| Five-year-olds | | | | | | 1:8 | 1:9 | 1:10 | | |
| Six- to eight-year-olds (school age) | | | | | | | | 1:10 | 1:11 | 1:12 |

&ast; Multi-age grouping is both permissible and desirable. When no infants are included, the staff–child ratio and group size requirements shall be based on the age of the majority of the children in the group. When infants are included, ratios and group size for infants must be maintained.

&ast;&ast; Smaller group sizes and lower staff-child ratios are optimal. Larger group sizes and higher staff-child ratios are acceptable only in cases where staff are highly qualified (see Staff Qualifications, Component D).

or well-defined space within a larger room (see Table 2).

F- 2. Sufficient staff with primary responsibility for children are available to provide frequent personal contact, meaningful learning activities, supervision, and to offer immediate care as needed. The ratio of staff to children will vary depending on the age of the children, the type of program activity, the inclusion of children with special needs, the time of day, and other factors. Staffing patterns should provide for adult supervision of children at all times and the availability of an additional adult to assume responsibility if one adult takes a break or must respond to an emergency. Staff-child ratios are maintained in relation to size of group (see Table 2). Staff-child ratios are maintained through provision of substitutes when regular staff members are absent. When volunteers are used to meet the staff-child ratios, they must also meet the appropriate staff qualifications unless they are parents (or guardians) of the children.

F- 3. Each staff member has primary responsibility for and develops a deeper attachment to an identified group of children. Every attempt is made to have continuity of adults who work with children, particularly infants and toddlers. Infants spend the majority of the time interacting with the same person each day.

## G. Physical Environment

**Goal:** *The indoor and outdoor physical environment fosters optimal growth and development through opportunities for exploration and learning.*

G- 1. The indoor and outdoor environments are safe, clean, attractive, and spacious. There is a minimum of 35 square feet of usable playroom floor space indoors per child and a minimum of 75 square feet of play space outdoors per child.

G- 2. Activity areas are defined clearly by spatial arrangement. Space is arranged so that children can work individually, together in small groups, or in a large group. Space is arranged to provide clear pathways for children to move from one area to another and to minimize distractions.

G- 3. The space for toddler and preschool children is arranged to facilitate a variety of small group and/or individual activities including block building, sociodramatic play, art, music, science, math, manipulatives, and quiet book reading. Other activities such as sand/water play and woodworking are also available on occasion. Carpeted areas and ample crawling space are provided for nonwalkers. Sturdy furniture is provided so nonwalkers can pull themselves up or balance themselves while walking. School-age children are provided separate space arranged to facilitate a variety of age-appropriate activities.

G- 4. Age-appropriate materials and equipment of sufficient quantity, variety, and durability are readily accessible to children and arranged on low, open shelves to promote independent use by children.

G- 5. Individual spaces for children to hang their clothing and store their personal belongings are provided.

G- 6. Private areas are available indoors and outdoors for children to have solitude.

G- 7. The environment includes soft elements such as rugs, cushions, or rocking chairs.

G- 8. Sound-absorbing materials are used to cut down on excessive noise.

G- 9. The outdoor area includes a variety of surfaces such as soil, sand, grass, hills, flat sections, and hard areas for wheel toys. The outdoor area includes shade; open space; digging space; and a variety of equipment for riding, climbing, balancing, and individual play. The outdoor area is protected from access to streets or other dangers.

## H. Health and Safety

**Goal:** *The health and safety of children and adults are protected and enhanced.*

H- 1. The center is in compliance with the legal requirements for protection of the health and safety of children in group settings. The center is licensed or accredited by the appropriate local/state agencies. If exempt from licensing, the center demonstrates compliance with its own state regulations for child care centers subject to licensing.

H- 2. Each adult is free of physical and psychological conditions that might adversely affect children's health. Staff receive pre-employment physical examinations, tuberculosis tests, and evaluation of any infection. Hiring practices include careful checking of personal references of all potential new employees. New staff members serve a probationary employment period during which the director or other qualified person can make a professional judgment as to their physical and psychological competence for working with children.

H- 3. A written record is maintained for each child, including the results of a complete health evaluation by an approved health care resource within six months prior to enrollment, record of immunizations, emergency contact information, names of people authorized to call for the child, and pertinent health history (such as allergies or chronic conditions). Children have received the necessary immunizations as recommended for their age group by the American Academy of Pediatrics.

H- 4. The center has a written policy specifying limitations on attendance of sick children. Provision is made for the notification of parents, the comfort of ill children, and the protection of well children.

H- 5. Provisions are made for safe arrival and departure of all children which also allow for parent-staff interaction. A system exists for ensuring that children are released only to authorized people.

H- 6. If transportation is provided for children by the center, vehicles are equipped with age-appropriate restraint devices.

H- 7. Children are under adult supervision at all times.

H- 8. Staff is alert to the health of each child. Individual medical problems and accidents are recorded and reported to staff and parents.

H- 9. Suspected incidents of child abuse and/or neglect by parents, staff, or others are reported to appropriate local agencies.

H-10. At least one staff member, who has certification in emergency first aid treatment and cardiopulmonary resuscitation (CPR) from a licensed health professional, is always in the center.

H-11. Adequate first aid supplies are readily available. A plan exists for dealing with medical emergencies.

H-12. Children are dressed appropriately for outdoor activities. Extra clothing is kept on hand for each child.

H-13. The facility is cleaned daily to disinfect bathroom fixtures and remove trash. Infants' equipment is washed and disinfected at least twice a week. Toys which are mouthed are washed daily. Soiled diapers are disposed of or held for laundry in closed containers inaccessible to the children. The cover of the changing table is either dis-

infected or disposed of after each change of a soiled diaper.

H-14. Staff wash their hands with soap and water before feeding and after diapering or assisting children with toileting or nose wiping. A sink with running hot and cold water is adjacent to the diapering area.

H-15. All equipment and the building are maintained in a safe, clean condition and in good repair (for example, there are no sharp edges, splinters, protruding or rusty nails, or missing parts). Infants and toddlers' toys are large enough to prevent swallowing or choking.

H-16. Individual bedding is washed once a week and used by only one child between washings. Individual cribs, cots, or mats are washed if soiled. Sides of infants' cribs are in a locked position when occupied.

H-17. Toilets, drinking water, and hand washing facilities are easily accessible to children. Soap and disposable towels are provided. Children wash hands after toileting and before meals. Hot water temperature does not exceed 110° F (43°C) at outlets used by children.

H-18. All rooms are well-lighted and ventilated. Stairways are well-lighted and equipped with handrails. Screens are placed on all windows which open. Electrical outlets are covered with protective caps. Floor coverings are attached to the floor or backed with non-slip materials. Nontoxic building materials are used.

H-19. Cushioning materials such as mats, wood chips, or sand are used under climbers, slides, or swings. Climbing equipment, swings, and large pieces of furniture are securely anchored.

H-20. All chemicals and potentially dangerous products such as medicines or cleaning supplies are stored in original, labeled containers in locked cabinets inaccessible to children. Medication is administered to children only when a written order has been submitted by a parent, and the medication is consistently administered by a designated staff member.

H-21. All staff are familiar with primary and secondary evacuation routes and practice evacuation procedures monthly with children. Written emergency procedures are posted in conspicuous places.

H-22. Staff are familiar with emergency procedures such as operation of fire extinguishers and procedures for severe storm warnings. Smoke dectectors and fire extinguishers are provided and periodically checked. Emergency telephone numbers are posted by phones.

## I. Nutrition and Food Service

**Goal:** *The nutritional needs of children and adults are met in a manner that promotes physical, social, emotional, and cognitive development.*

I- 1. Meals and/or snacks are planned to meet the child's nutritional requirements as recommended by the Child Care Food Program of the United States Department of Agriculture in proportion to the amount of time the child is in the program each day.

I- 2. Menu information is provided to parents. Feeding times and food consumption information is provided to parents of infants and toddlers at the end of each day.

I- 3. Mealtimes promote good nutrition habits. Toddlers and preschoolers are encouraged to serve and feed themselves. Chairs, tables, and eating utensils are suitable for the size and developmental levels of the children. Mealtime is a pleasant social and learning experience for chil-

dren. Infants are held in an inclined position while bottle feeding. Foods indicative of children's cultural backgrounds are served periodically. At least one adult sits with children during meals.

I- 4. Food brought from home is stored appropriately until consumed.

I- 5. Where food is prepared on the premises, the center is in compliance with legal requirements for nutrition and food service. Food may be prepared at an approved facility and transported to the program in appropriate sanitary containers and at appropriate temperatures.

## J. Evaluation

**Goal:** *Systematic assessment of the effectiveness of the program in meeting its goals for children, parents, and staff is conducted to ensure that good quality care and education are provided and maintained.*

J- 1. The director (or other appropriate person) evaluates all staff at least annually and privately discusses the evaluation with each staff member. The evaluation includes classroom observation. Staff are informed of evaluation criteria in advance. Results of evaluations are written and confidential. Staff have an opportunity to evaluate their own performance. A plan for staff training is generated from the evaluation process.

J- 2. At least annually, staff, other professionals, and parents are involved in evaluating the program's effectiveness in meeting the needs of children and parents.

J- 3. Individual descriptions of children's development are written and compiled as a basis for planning appropriate learning activities, as a means of facilitating optimal development of each child, and as records for use in communications with parents.

# Bibliography

*Specified Criteria are reprinted with permission from the following sources:*

Auerbach, S. *Choosing Child Care: A Guide for Parents.* New York: Dutton, 1981. (Criterion A-8.)

Community Coordinated Child Care in Dane County. "Dane County Early Childhood Program Standards." Madison, Wis., 1975. (Criteria A-11, B-20, C-4b, C-5, F-3b, G-2, G-9, H-10, H-21, H-22, I-3, I-4, and I-5.)

Comprehensive Community Child Care of Cincinnati. "Child Care Performance Standards." Cincinnati, Ohio. (Criteria A-2, E-10, and I-3.)

Missouri Department of Elementary and Secondary Education. "Standards and Procedures for Voluntary Accreditation of Early Childhood Programs: State of Missouri." Jefferson City, Mo., 1983. (Criteria A-1, A-3, A-5, A-6, B-2, C-1, C-2, E-5, E-7, and J-2.)

Texas Department of Human Resources. "Day Care Quality Evaluation/Validation Criteria." Austin, Tex., 1981. (Criteria B-7, D-3, and D-4.)

*The following instruments and sets of standards were used as resources in the development of the Criteria:*

Action for Children. "Quality Child Care: What It Is . . . and How to Recognize It." Columbus, Ohio, n.d.

American Academy of Pediatrics. "Standards for Day Care Centers for Infants and Children." Evanston, Ill., 1980.

Aronson, S.; Fiene, R.; and Douglas, E. "Child Development Program Evaluation: Child Care Centers—Center Instrument." Harrisburg, Pa.: Bureau of Child Development Programs of the Pennsylvania Department of Public Welfare, 1978.

Bergstrom, J. M. and Joy, L. *Going to Work? Choosing Care for Infants and Toddlers.* Washington, D.C.: Day Care Council of America, 1981.

California State Department of Education. "Child Development Program Quality Review." Sacramento, Calif., 1982.

Child Care Coordinating and Referral Service. "How to Choose a Good Child Care Center." Ann Arbor, Mich., n.d.

Child Day Care Association of St. Louis. "Standards for Day Care Service." St. Louis, Mo., 1982.

Child Development Associate National Credentialing Program. *CDA Competency Standards and Assessment System.* Washington, D.C., 1983.

Children's Home Society of Minnesota. "Children's Home Society Day Care Programs Quality Control Checklist." Mimeo. St. Paul, Minn., n.d.

Children's World. "Children's World, Inc., Quality Control Checklist." Evergreen, Colo., 1978.

Child Welfare League of America. "Child Welfare League of America Standards for Day Care Service." New York, 1973.

City of Madison Day Care Unit, Department of Human Resources. "Guidelines for Certification/Recertification." Madison, Wis., 1981.

Community Coordinated Child Care for Central Florida. "Program Audit Assessment Tool." Orlando, Fla., n.d.

Comprehensive Community Child Care. "Selecting Quality Child Care for Parents of Young Children." Cincinnati, Ohio, 1979.

Day Care Evaluation Task Force of the United Way of Greater Rochester. "Day Care Center Evaluation Process." Rochester, N.Y., 1982.

Day Nursery Association of Cleveland Consultation Service. "Preschool Center Evaluation Scale." Cleveland, Ohio, 1963.

Endsley, R. C. and Bradbard, M. R. *Quality Day Care: A Handbook of Choices for Parents and Caregivers.* Englewood Cliffs, N.J.: Prentice-Hall, 1981.

Familiae, Inc. "Standards for Accreditation by Familiae, Inc." Columbus, Ohio, 1981.

Fiene, R.; Douglas, E.; and Kroh, K. "Child Development Program Evaluation: Center Licensing Instrument." Harrisburg, Pa.: Pennsylvania Department of Public Welfare, 1980.

Gold, J. R. and Bergstrom, J. M. *Checking Out Child Care: A Parent Guide.* Washington, D.C.: Day Care and Child Development Council of America, n.d.

Harms, T. and Clifford, R. M. *Early Childhood Environment Rating Scale.* New York: Teachers College Press, 1980.

Hartman, B. "The Hartman Assessment." Mimeo. Santa Ana, Calif., n.d.

KCMC Child Development Corporation. "Agency Assessment/Self-Assessment." Mimeo. Kansas City, Mo., n.d.

Kendrick, R.; Williamson, E.; and Yorck, J. "Finding Quality Child Care." Eugene, Oreg.: Lane County 4-C Council, n.d.

Mattick, I. and Perkins, F. *Guidelines for Observation and Assessment: An Approach to Evaluating the Learning Environment of a Day Care Center.* Mt. Rainier, Md.: Gryphon House, 1980.

Missouri Department of Elementary and Secondary Education. "Choosing the Right Early Education Program for Your Child: A Checklist for Parents." Jefferson City, Mo., n.d.

National Association for the Education of Young Children. "How to Choose a Good Early Childhood Program." Washington, D.C., 1983.

National Association for the Education of Young Children. "How to Plan and Start a Good Early Childhood Program." Washington, D.C., 1984.

New Jersey State Department of Education. "Self-Study Process for Preschool Programs." Trenton, N.J., 1980.

Oregon Association for the Education of Young Children. "Assessment Criteria Checklist for Criteria for Assessing Early Childhood Programs." Portland, Oreg., 1981.

Oregon Association for the Education of Young Children. "Criteria for Assessing Early Childhood Programs." Portland, Oreg., 1979.

Upgrading Preschool Programs. "The Book of UPP." Mimeo. Phoenix, Ariz., n.d.

U.S. Department of Health and Human Services. *A Parent's Guide to Day Care.* Washington, D.C., 1980. (DHHS Publication No. 80–30254)

U.S. Department of Health and Human Services. *Comparative Licensing Study: Profiles of State Day Care*

Licensing Requirements, Rev. Ed. Vols. 1–6. Washington, D.C., 1981.

U.S. Department of Health and Human Services. "Head Start Performance Standards Self-Assessment/Validation Instrument." Washington, D.C., 1981. (DHHS Publication No. 81-31132)

U.S. Department of Health and Human Services. "Head Start Program Performance Standards." Washington, D.C., 1981. (DHHS Publication No. 81-31131)

U.S. Department of Health, Education and Welfare. "Federal Interagency Day Care Requirements." Washington, D.C., 1968. (DHEW Publication No. 78-31-081)

U.S. Department of Health, Education and Welfare. "Guides for Day Care Licensing." Washington, D.C., 1973. (DHEW Publication No. 73-1053)

U.S. Department of Health, Education and Welfare. "HEW Day Care Regulations." Federal Register 45, no. 55 (March 19, 1980).

Washington Child Development Council. "Child Development Center Self-Assessment." Washington, D.C., 1980.

The Criteria were developed from a thorough review of the research, theoretical, and practical literature on the effects of various components of an early childhood program on children. The following is a selected bibliography of those sources which were most applicable in developing the Criteria:

Bronfenbrenner, U. The Ecology of Human Development. Cambridge, Mass.: Harvard University Press, 1979.

Caldwell, B. M. and Freyer, M. "Day Care and Early Education." In Handbook of Research on Early Childhood Education, ed. B. Spodek. New York: Free Press, 1982.

Falender, C. A. and Mehrabian, A. "The Effects of Day Care on Young Children: An Environmental Psychology Approach." Journal of Psychology 101, no. 2 (1979): 241–255.

Fiene, R. "Child Development Program Evaluation: Weighing Consensus of Individual Items: What Are the Major Risks to Children in Day Care Centers?" Harrisburg, Pa.: Office of Children and Youth, 1979.

Golden, M. and Rosenbluth, L. The New York City Infant Day Care Study. New York: Medical and Health Research Association of New York City, 1978.

Kendall, E. D. "Child Care and Disease: What Is the Link?" Young Children 38, no. 5 (July 1983): 68–77.

Kilmer, S. "Infant-Toddler Group Day Care: A Review of Research." In Current Topics in Early Childhood Education, ed. L. Katz. Vol. 2. Norwood, N.J.: Ablex, 1979.

McCartney, K.; Scarr, S.; Phillips, D.; Grajek, S.; and Schwarz, C. "Environmental Differences among Day Care Centers and Their Effects on Children's Development." In Day Care: Scientific and Social Policy Issues, ed. E. F. Zigler and E. W. Gordon. Dover, Mass.: Auburn House, 1982.

Meyer, W. J. "Staffing Characteristics and Child Outcomes." Washington, D.C.: U.S. Department of Health, Education and Welfare, 1977. (ERIC Document Reproduction Service No. 156 341)

Phyfe-Perkins, E. "Children's Behavior in Preschool Settings: A Review of Research Concerning the Influence of the Physical Environment." In Current Topics in Early Childhood Education, ed. L. Katz. Vol. 3. Norwood, N.J.: Ablex, 1980.

Phyfe-Perkins, E. Effects of Teacher Behavior on Preschool Children: A Review of Research. Washington, D.C.: National Institute of Education, 1981. (ERIC Document Reproduction Service No. 211 176)

Pizzo, P. and Aronson, S. S. "Concept Paper on Health and Safety Issues in Day Care." Mimeo. Washington, D.C.: U.S. Department of Health, Education and Welfare, 1976.

Prescott, E. "Relations Between Physical Setting and Adult/Child Behavior in Day Care." In Advances in Early Education and Day Care, ed. S. Kilmer. Vol. 2. Greenwich, Conn.: JAI Press, 1981.

Prescott, E.; Jones, E.; and Kritchevsky, S. Day Care as a Child-Rearing Environment. Washington, D.C.: National Association for the Education of Young Children, 1972.

Ruopp, R.; Travers, J.; Glantz, F.; and Coelen, C. Children at the Center, Final Report of the National Day Care Study. Vol. 1. Cambridge, Mass.: Abt Associates, 1979.

Smith, P. K. and Connolly, K. J. The Ecology of Preschool Behaviour. Cambridge, England: Cambridge University Press, 1980.

U.S. Department of Health, Education and Welfare. Appropriateness of the Federal Interagency Day Care Requirements. Washington, D.C., 1978.

# How to Plan and Start a Good Early Childhood Program

Are you thinking about opening a child care center? A preschool? An employer-supported child care facility? An after-school program? High quality early childhood programs are urgently needed in almost every community. This brochure lists the major steps involved in planning and starting programs that will benefit children, their families, and your community.

## Explore the market

**1. Find out what the child care needs are in your community.**

What programs are available now? What ages do they serve? Are parents satisfied with the quality of the care?

Which families need good early childhood programs? What are the ages of the children? When is the care needed? What locations would be most convenient for parents?

Many communities have child care resource and referral agencies that can provide valuable assistance in this regard. Local government planning offices may also be an information source.

**2. Obtain a copy of all licensing requirements.**

What state or local regulations (child care, education, zoning, fire, building, health) apply to the type of service you are planning? How will these regulations affect funding? Opening date projections? The children and families served? Facility planning? Staff selection? Community relations?

**3. Observe a variety of local programs for young children.**

How do the programs seem to meet the needs of the children? Their families? The staff? Are the programs accredited by the National Academy of Early Childhood Programs? What can you learn from their experiences?

How are the programs supported? How could a new service be coordinated with existing programs?

## Plan the business

**1. Decide how the program will be funded and governed.**

Will the program be nonprofit, employer-supported, funded by state or local agencies, or a profit-making corporation?

Who will determine policies and budgets? A board comprised of parents or agency/employer representatives? The proprietor(s)? A director?

What items will be included in the program budget? Mortgage or rent? Staff salaries and benefits? Utilities? Supplies? Taxes? Insurance? Which items will be contributed/funded by other sources?

**2. Secure the services of specialists.**

Will an early childhood specialist be needed as a consultant for planning? Will a lawyer be needed to file for incorporation? For purchase or lease of property?

Should an accountant set up a record-keeping system for income and expenditures, including worker's compensation, social security, unemployment compensation, and taxes?

What insurance is needed? Liability? Health and accident for children and staff? Fire and theft?

Will architects or contractors be needed to build or renovate a facility? Do they have expertise in designing environments for young children?

**3. Identify funding sources.**

Where will start-up funds be obtained? How much money will realistically be needed to cover fees for professional services? Purchase or lease of land and a building? Construction or renovation expenses? Classroom, office, and food-service furniture, equipment, and supplies? Publicity about the program? Initial staff training and services?

How much working capital is available to cover operating expenses until the program income is sufficient to do so? Have opportunities for local grants, partnerships, and venture capital been explored? What level of enrollment is necessary to meet expenses?

What fundraising efforts can be used for start-up costs? For operating expenses? As a basis of regular program support? For improvements, repairs, and replacement of equipment in the future?

**4. Prepare an annual budget.**

What portion of income will be from parent fees? Other sources?

What are anticipated expenditures? Salaries? Substitutes? Staff benefits? Taxes? Licensing fees? Marketing? Fees for other professional services? Mortgage or rent? Supplies? Utilities? Fundraising expenses? In-service training? Transportation?

**5. Secure a facility.**

Is the area zoned for this type of facility?

Is the location convenient to family neighborhoods, major employers, schools, or transportation centers? How will location affect the services provided? Should transportation be provided?

What renovations will be necessary to meet all state and local regulations and assure a high quality program?

## Plan the program

**1. Write program objectives.**

How will the program serve families? Children? The community? What ages of children will be served? How will groups be determined? Do program goals represent the best current knowledge about how young children grow and learn? About the roles of early childhood teachers and families? What long-term goals will the program strive for?

**2. Prepare job descriptions and schedules.**

What will be the responsibilities of the director? Teachers? Assistant teachers? Nutritionist? Social worker? Maintenance staff? Cook? Drivers? Office personnel? Others?

Will staffing patterns enable teachers to care for small groups of children? To provide the individualized attention young children need? To provide needed continuity for children? Do schedules allow paid time for staff planning and coordination? For staff breaks to keep energy levels high? How will children's arrival and departure times affect staffing and the program?

**3. Set major policies.**

What ages of children will be served? What enrollment requirements must be met? How will parents be involved? How will parent fees be collected? Will sliding fee scales or scholarships be provided? How will the program handle sick children or staff? What hours will children attend? What holidays will be observed? How will difficulties with parents or staff be resolved? How will staff be evaluated? How will the program be evaluated? What requirements will be made for transportation and field trips? How will emergencies be handled?

**4. Recruit and retain competent staff members.**

What community resources (NAEYC

Affiliate Groups or other early childhood networking organizations) can offer assistance in locating potential staff?

Do staff have the educational and work experience necessary to provide a developmentally appropriate program for children? Do staff enjoy working with young children and their families? Are they healthy and energetic?

Are staff salaries and benefit packages based upon educational qualifications and experience? Do salaries adequately reflect levels of job responsibility? Will ongoing opportunities for professional development and career advancement be provided to staff?

**5. Develop a high quality program for children.**

How will the program be designed? Will the program be appropriate for the age groups served and implemented with attention to the needs and differences of the individual children enrolled?

How will room arrangement, furniture, equipment, and play materials affect the quality of the program? Will curriculum planning reflect understanding of the ways young children learn best?

For further information about providing a high quality program, see NAEYC's resources catalog and the resources listed below.

For further information about specific procedures for starting a program in your community, contact your state licensing agency, your local resource and referral agency, the president of the nearest NAEYC Affiliate Group, or the NAEYC Information Service.

## Consider accreditation for your program

The National Academy of Early Childhood programs (a division of NAEYC) administers a national, voluntary, professionally sponsored accreditation system for preschools, child care centers, and school-age child care programs. Accreditation Criteria provide a framework for planning a high quality early childhood program. Programs must be in operation one year before receiving accreditation; however, they may use the Criteria and self-study materials at any time.

To order self-study materials, or to obtain further information about the accreditation process, contact the **Academy** at 1509 16th Street, N.W., Washington, DC 20036-1426. 202-232-8777 or 800-424-2460.

## Selected resources

Many of the resources listed below are available from NAEYC. To order, specify the publication number and send appropriate payment to NAEYC, Resource Sales, 1509 16th Street, N.W., Washington, DC 20036-1426. Orders less than $20 must be prepaid. There are no shipping charges on prepaid orders.

### General information

*Young Children*—NAEYC's bimonthly journal offers the latest information on early childhood practice, theory, and research. Subscriptions are included as a membership benefit. For more information about becoming a member, contact NAEYC.

*Child Care Information Exchange* — Excellent bimonthly magazine specifically designed for child care program directors, with regular features on finances, staffing, computers, and other administrative topics. Subscription rate is $35 per year. Contact: Exchange Press, P.O. Box 2890, Redmond, WA 98073. 206-883-9394.

*Quality in Child Care: What Does Research Tell Us?*, D. Phillips, (Ed.), 1987. NAEYC #140, $6. Monograph discusses recent research that defines quality in early childhood programs and describes how it can be measured.

*Accreditation Criteria and Procedures of the National Academy of Early Child-*

*hood Programs,* S. Bredekamp, (Ed.), 1986. NAEYC #920, $6. The Academy Criteria address all aspects of a high quality early childhood program.

*Child Care: Facing the Hard Choices,* A. J. Kahn and S. B. Kamerman, 1987. Dover, MA: Auburn House. Analysis of child care services in America today and choices for shaping the future.

### Getting started

*Developmentally Appropriate Practice in Early Childhood Programs Serving Children From Birth Through Age 8,* S. Bredekamp, (Ed.), 1987. NAEYC #224, $5. Specific guidelines on implementing developmentally appropriate practice, with chapters addressing infants, toddlers, preschool, and school-age children.

*Resource Guide on Facility Design for Early Childhood Programs.* NAEYC #789, $5. Provides contact information for organizations and experts involved with the design of early childhood learning environments, plus an extensive annotated bibliography.

*Planning Environments for Young Children: Physical Space,* S. Kritchevsky & E. Prescott with L. Walling, 1977. NAEYC #115, $2.50. See how organization of space can prevent classroom traffic jams and even diminish discipline problems.

### Administration

*The Human Side of Child Care Administration: A How-To Manual,* S. Storm, 1985. NAEYC #702, $12.50. Especially helpful to new directors. Topics include establishing personnel policies; interviewing, motivating, and evaluating staff; problem solving; and effective communication.

*Helping Churches Mind the Children,* revised edition, M. Freeman, (Ed.), 1987. $7.50. New York: National Council of Churches, Ecumenical Child Care Network. Comprehensive guide for churches and others interested in setting up and operating a child care program.

*Nursery School and Day Care Management Guide,* 2nd edition, C. Cherry, 1987. $29.95. Belmont, CA: David S. Lake Publishers. This comprehensive handbook provides all the tools needed to successfully establish and manage a full-service child care facility.

*Marketing Your Child Care Program: The Best of Exchange,* Reprint #4, 1987. $10. Exchange Press, P.O. Box 2890, Redmond, WA 98073. Collection of the most popular *Exchange* articles related to the topic.

### Finances

*Fundraising for Early Childhood Programs: Getting Started and Getting Results,* M. Finn, 1982. NAEYC #120, $3.50. An experienced fundraiser offers down-to-earth tips to increase your financial support.

*Managing the Day Care Dollars: A Financial Handbook,* G. Morgan, 1986. $7.95 plus $1.50 shipping and handling. Gryphon House, Inc., 3706 Otis Street, P.O. Box 275, Mt. Rainier, MD 20822. A basic reference for good management, specifically designed for administrators of child care programs and other human service agencies.

*Tools for Managing Your Center's Money: The Best of Exchange,* Reprint #2, 1987. $10. Exchange Press, P.O. Box 2890, Redmond, WA 98073.

### Legal

*Legal and Business Aspects of Running a Not-For-Profit Day Care Center,* Child Care Advocacy Project, Washington Lawyers' Committee for Civil Rights Under Law, 1989. $35. Contact: Ann K. Macrory, 1400 Eye Street, N.W., Suite 450, Washington, DC 20005. 202-682-5900.

*Legal Issues in Early Childhood Centers,* A. Federlein, 1986. $7.50. Child Development Designs, Inc., 3375 Buckingham Trail, West Bloomfield, MI 48033. Includes information on records and right to privacy, insurance, handicapped children, contracts, liability, and more.

## Health

*Healthy Young Children: A Manual for Programs,* A. S. Kendrick, R. Kaufmann, and K. P. Messenger, (Eds.), 1988. NAEYC #704, $12. Reflects the most current research and recommendations from experts in health and early childhood education.

*Health in Day Care: A Manual for Health Professionals,* 1987, $25. American Academy of Pediatrics, P.O. Box 927, 141 Northwest Point Blvd., Elk Grove Village, IL 60009. Primarily addressed to physicians, the information—especially checklists and forms—is helpful to those in child care centers as well.

*Resource Guide on Child Care Center Diseases and Sick Child Care.* NAEYC #785, $5. Contact information for individuals and organizations focusing on early childhood program health issues, plus an annotated bibliography.

*A Little Bit Under the Weather: A Look at Care for Mildly Ill Children,* 1987. $19 plus postage and handling. Work/Family Directions, 9 Galen Street, Suite 230, Watertown, MA 02172. An overview of ways to provide care for mildly ill children of working parents, with a summary of current literature.

## Staff development

*NAEYC Position Statement on Nomenclature, Salaries, Benefits, and the Status of the Early Childhood Profession,* NAEYC #530. Single copies are 50¢ each; 100 copies are $10.

*Developmentally Appropriate Practice: Birth Through Age 5.* NAEYC #854, ½" VHS format, $39. Training **video** depicts teachers and children in action in developmentally appropriate programs.

*A Great Place to Work: Improving Conditions for Staff in Young Children's Programs,* P. Jorde-Bloom, 1988. NAEYC #250, $5. Explores what it takes to create and maintain a healthy work climate fulfillment for adults who work with young children.

*Resources for Early Childhood Training: An Annotated Bibliography,* compiled by M. Porzel, 1987. NAEYC #790, $5. A comprehensive list of print and audio-visual training materials indexed by CDA functional areas and settings.

## Employer-assisted child care

*Information Kit on Employer-Assisted Child Care,* 1986. NAEYC #730, $12. Includes "The Child Care Market: A Newcomer's Introduction," "Investing in Quality," and "Child Care Makes It Work: A Guide to Employer Support for Child Care."

*Resource Guide on Employer-Assisted Child Care.* NAEYC #781, $5. Provides contact information for individuals and organiations with expertise in the area, plus an annotated bibliography.

*A Developer's Guide to Child Care,* 1986. $25 (6% CA sales tax) plus postage and handling. California Resource and Referral Network, 809 Lincoln Way, San Francisco, CA 94122. Information packet directed to commercial and residential developers, planners, real estate professionals, and child care providers to assess their options while planning child care services.

*Child Care Centers in Commercial Settings,* 1987. $6. Maryland-National Capital Park and Planning Commission, Information Desk, 8787 Georgia Avenue, Silver Spring, MD 20907-3760.

## Infant/toddler programs

*Setting Up for Infant Care: Guidelines for Centers and Family Day Care Homes*, A. Godwin, (Ed.), 1988. NAEYC #228, $5. These practical guidelines were developed through a project of the San Fernando Valley Child Care Consortium.

*Toddler Day Care: A Guide to Responsive Caregiving.* R. L. Leavitt and B. K. Eheart, 1985. $14.95. Lexington, MA: Lexington Books, D.C. Health and Company. A guide for providing high quality care to toddlers with focus on the distinct characteristics and needs of this age group.

## School-age care

*Activities for School-Age Child Care*, R. Blau, E.H. Brady, I. Bucher, B. Hiteshew, A. Zavitkovsky, and D. Zavitkovsky, 1989. NAEYC #214, $4. Suggests hundreds of ideas for children from 5 to 10 years, plus how to work with parents, staff, and the community.

*School-Age Child Care: Getting It Started in Your Community*, 1986. $10 plus postage and handling. California Child Care Resource and Referral Network, 809 Lincoln Way, San Francisco, CA 94122. A working guide for starting child care, with tips and protocols for site development, legal issues, model programs, resource lists, and an annotated bibliography.

## Resource groups

**American Montessori Society,** 150 5th Avenue, Suite 203, New York, NY 10011. 212-924-3209.

**Association for Childhood Education International,** 11501 Georgia Avenue, Suite 315, Wheaton, MD 20902. 301-942-2443.

**Association Montessori International,** 170 West Scholfield Road, Rochester, NY 14617.

**Child Care Law Center,** 22 Second Street, 5th Fl., San Francisco, CA 94105. 415-495-5498.

**Children's Defense Fund,** 25 E Street, N.W., Washington, DC 20001. 202-628-8787.

**Children's Foundation,** 725 15th Street, N.W., Suite 505, Washington, DC 20005. 202-347-3300.

**Council for Early Childhood Professional Recognition,** 1341 G Street, N.W., Suite 400, Washington, DC 20005. 202-265-9090 or 800-424-4310.

**Directors' Network,** Child Care Information Exchange, P.O. Box 2890, Redmond, WA 98073. 206-883-9394.

**Ecumenical Child Care Network,** 1580 N. Northwest Highway, Park Ridge, IL 60068-1456. 708-298-1500.

**High/Scope Educational Research Foundation,** 600 N. River Street, Ypsilanti, MI 48198. 313-485-2000.

**National Association of Child Care Resources and Referral Agencies,** 1319 F. Street, N.W., Suite 606, Washington, DC 20004. 202-393-5501.

**National Association of Hospital Affiliated Programs,** Shawnee Mission Medical Center CCC, 9100 W. 74th Street, Shawnee Mission, KS 66201.

**National Black Child Development Institute,** 1023 15th Street, N.W., Suite 600, Washington, DC 20005. 202-387-1281.

**National Center for Clinical Infant Programs,** 2000 14th Street, North, Suite 380, Arlington, VA 22201. 703-528-4300.

**National Coalition for Campus Child Care, Inc.,** Southern Illinois University at Edwardsville, Early Childhood Center, Box 1076, Edwardsville, IL 62026.

**Parent Cooperative Preschools International,** P.O. Box 90410, Indianapolis, IN 46290-0410.

**Resources for Child Care Management,** 16 South Street, Suite 300, Morristown, NJ 07960. 201-267-9100.

**School-Age Child Care Project,** Center for Research on Women, Wellesley College, Wellesley, MA 02181. 617-283-2547.

**Southern Early Childhood Association (formerly SACUS),** 7107 West 12th, Suite 102, Little Rock, AR 72204. 501-663-0353.

**Work/Family Directions,** 930 Commonwealth Avenue, West, Boston, MA 02215-1212. 800-346-4000.

# naeyc

National Association for
the Education of Young Children
1509 16th Street, N.W.
Washington, DC 20036-1426

# 1

# Support a Competent Staff

A competent staff is essential for a good early childhood program. If a program is housed in a perfect facility and has unlimited funding, but has an incompetent staff, the quality of care will most likely still be inferior. When staff members view themselves as part of an ever-improving team of early childhood professionals, all other aspects of a good program are sure to emerge. As director, your first priority is to hire and nurture a staff of loving professionals.

The importance of staff qualifications is highlighted in NAEYC's Position Statement, so it appears first in this section. You may find this statement helpful in convincing your board of directors or other decision makers of the need for hiring high quality personnel.

What is a professional early childhood teacher? Using a classroom dilemma, Lilian Katz identifies responses that are professional, nonprofessional, and unprofessional. You might want to look for similar responses in interviews and when observing your staff.

Have you been a teacher, or are you thinking about promoting one of your best teachers to a supervisory position?

Susan Hegland's model for assisting good teachers as they become supervisors will be especially useful to you.

One of the most important but difficult aspects of supervision is staff evaluation. Carol Catron and Earline Kendall describe a nonthreatening evaluation model that allows both staff and administrators to grow professionally.

In an effort to further expand your professional growth, you may want to participate in a mobile training program like the one described by Pearl Axelrod, Pamela Schwartz, Ann Weinstein, and Esther Buch.

Teachers and directors of programs for young children often are exhausted from the demands of their jobs. How can you and your staff cope with stress? You won't want to miss Marion Hyson's heartening suggestions.

Part 1 concludes with two NAEYC Position Statements on issues central to hiring and maintaining a competent staff: Salaries, Benefits, and Nomenclature; and Licensing. Together, we can improve the quality of our work on behalf of young children.

# NAEYC Position Statement on Staff Qualifications Related to Quality Child Care

In accordance with the purposes of the National Association for the Education of Young Children, we hereby reaffirm our commitment to promoting high quality programs for young children, especially those children and families who depend on such programs for care and education on an extended and regular basis.

Adults working with children in group programs are the key to providing high quality, consistent child care. In order to be effective in aiding and enhancing child development, these adults must have sound theoretical and practical knowledge and the skills to help children grow into responsible adults. They aid and complement parents in this task.

This knowledge base and its concomitant skills can be obtained through workshops, experience, college courses, and/or nationally recognized child development credentials. Staff members, whether paid or volunteer, are expected to demonstrate their ability to assess and meet the needs of young children and their families.

The need for high quality staff selection has been documented. For example:

(1) The primary desire of parents with children in group care is that the caregivers be reliable. Such reliability can be enhanced by an understanding, both theoretical and practical, of the needs of children.

(2) Working mothers prefer trained staff in day care centers.

(3) Quality child care benefits children, families, and communities in a variety of ways. These include improving educational skills of both child and parent, aiding in prevention of emotional and behavioral problems, enhancement of better self-image, and improving employment skills. In the long run, quality child care is cost effective since effectively functioning adults are not involved in crime and unemployment.

(4) Staff knowledge and experience in child development/early childhood education are essential to provide quality child care. Those in leadership positions need more intensive training and experience to enable them to guide other adults working or volunteering in programs serving groups of children.

The National Association for the Education of Young Children therefore acknowledges the importance of selecting qualified adults to serve groups of young children.

*Adopted on November 4, 1981*
*by the NAEYC Governing Board*

Lilian G. Katz

# The Professional Early Childhood Teacher

Betsy MacMillan

*How would you handle a situation in which two children are fighting over a tricycle? Lilian Katz holds up a mirror to our teaching in early childhood programs and urges us to reflect on the uses of professional judgment and how our teaching techniques can become more professional.*

The term *professional* means many things (Ade 1982; Hoyle 1982). This article discusses two aspects of professionalism in particular: the use of *advanced knowledge* in the formulation of *judgment* (Zumeta and Solomon 1982), and the adoption of *standards of performance* for the early childhood profession.

Advanced knowledge in early childhood education is derived from developmental psychology as well as from many other fields. Professional judgment involves diagnosing and analyzing events, weighing alternatives, and estimating the potential long-term consequences of decisions and actions based on that knowledge.

One of the major functions of a profes-

**Lilian G. Katz,** Ph.D., is Professor of Early Childhood Education and Director of ERIC Clearinghouse on Elementary and Early Childhood Education at the University of Illinois, Urbana, Illinois.

sional organization is to set standards of performance based on the best available advanced knowledge and practices. Practicing professionals are committed to performing at the same high standards consistently, without allowing personal matters or moods to affect their work or their relations with those with and for whom they work. Nonprofessionals may be very skillful, may enjoy their work, and often work very effectively as volunteers. A major difference between professionals and nonprofessionals lies in the commitment to maintain professional standards.

Professional standards are set for typical or standard situations all members of the profession can be expected to encounter, and are based on the best available knowledge and practices. In order to illustrate how a professional early childhood teacher might use advanced knowledge and judgment and apply standards of performance, let us look at a common predicament faced by early childhood teachers.

# Professional Responses to a Common Predicament

There are probably scores of ways to respond. What does a professional teacher
know that has implications for handling
such an incident?

## What can I be teaching in this situation?

Ideally a trained teacher would ask:
*What can I be teaching the children in this sit-
uation?* A professional considers the most
reliable knowledge about how children
learn plus the goals of the parents, the
school, and the community at large. The
following responses depict the kind of
judgment that might be expected of a well-
trained, experienced teacher at the stage
of "maturity" (Katz 1972).

### Social skills

*Turn-taking skills.* The teacher can help
children learn to read another's behavior
for signs of when a request for a turn is
most likely to work, when to give up,
when to come back for another try, and
similar behavioral cues that help determine the next best move. These processes
are similar to learning the turn-taking
skills required for participation in conversation (Shields 1979; Wells 1981; Frederiksen 1981). The teacher might suggest
that Robin do something else and then
ask Leslie for a turn again, or that Robin
observe Leslie for signs of weariness or
boredom with the tricycle.

*Negotiating skills.* Children during the
preschool years can begin to refine their

bargaining skills by learning to predict
what will appeal to another child (Rubin
and Everett 1982).

To help the child learn these skills, the
teacher could encourage Robin to consider
what might appeal to Leslie. Thus she
might say: "Why don't you go to Leslie
and say, 'I'll push you on the swing if you
give me a turn on the tricycle'?" The
teacher provides verbal model of how the
negotiation might go.

*Coping skills.* Teachers can help children learn to cope with having their requests rejected and to accept defeat grace-
fully.

For example, the teacher can help Robin
learn to deal with rejection by responding
matter-of-factly: "Alright. Maybe Leslie
will have a change of heart later. What
would you like to do in the meantime?"

### Verbal skills

The tricycle situation is a good one in
which to help children learn how to express their feelings and assert their wishes
more clearly and effectively.

*Assertive phrases.* Perhaps Robin simply
tugged at the tricycle, or even whined a
bit, hardly a clear statement of desire for a
turn with the tricycle. The teacher could
respond to Robin by saying "It might help
to say to Leslie, [modeling a mildly assertive tone] 'I've been waiting a long time
. . . I really want a turn'." The teacher introduces a simple phrase that the child can
use when an adult is not there, and
models a tone of moderate but firm assertiveness.

Delaine Certo

*Social perspective.* A trained teacher can help children to learn what is a tragedy and what is not. Not getting a turn to ride a tricycle is not a tragedy. The teacher helps the child put desires into perspective by responding to the complaint with gentle good-humored empathy, rather than with tragic tones or by rushing to rescue the child from distress.

The teacher might assert, "I know you're disappointed not to get a turn on the tricycle, but there are other things you like to do." Again, the tone is matter-of-fact and pleasant, without hint of reprimand.

*Rudiments of justice.* Preschoolers probably are ready to absorb some of the rudiments of justice (Johnson 1982), particularly in the form of *ground rules* that everyone is asked to observe. A professional teacher's response would be "Leslie, you have been riding the tricycle for five minutes and it is time for you to give Robin a turn now," followed by, "And when you need help getting a turn with something I will be glad to help you to."

Similarly, if the situation were to lead to combat the teacher might say to the instigator, "I won't let you hit him, *and I won't let anyone hit you either.*" This reassures aggressors that they are in a just environment in which everyone's rights are protected and everyone's needs are considered. One of the important elements of professionalism is the teacher's acceptance of responsibility for the learning and development of both the victim and the aggressor (Grusec and Arnason 1982).

If Leslie monopolizes the tricycle and refuses to give Robin a turn, when other techniques have failed, the teacher might say to Leslie, "Five more minutes, Leslie. Then I want you to let Robin have a turn. When you need help with something just let me know." And the teacher insists that Leslie yield after five minutes, removing her physically if necessary.

*Conversational phrases.* It may be that these children have few appropriate phrases and are only just learning to engage in heated conversations. Teaching the needed verbal skills can be done through what is called "Speaking-*for*-Children" (Schachter and Strage 1982) in which the adult speaks to each child on behalf of the other.

The teacher might say to Leslie, "Robin really wants a turn." If Leslie refuses, the teacher can say to Robin, "Leslie isn't ready to give up the tricycle yet." Robin might protest, in which case the teacher can paraphrase what Robin is feeling to Leslie: "Robin really would like a turn now."

### Social knowledge

Nucci and Turiel (1978) have shown that preschool children understand the distinction between social conventions and moral transgressions and thus can be helped with moral and social insights. This typical incident provides a good opportunity for children to gain social knowledge.

*Observers' understandings and skills.* Professional judgment includes taking into account what the children observing the incident might be learning. All the teacher's responses outlined so far can provide indirect instruction for the uninvolved children. They might learn techniques of negotiation and verbal strategies for use in confrontation, and are likely to feel reassured that they are in a just environment.

## Dispositional learning

In addition to teaching social skills and knowledge, the professional teacher would also consider which personal dispositions could be strengthened or weakened in this situation.

*Empathy and altruism.* Young children are capable of strengthening empathy and altruism in various ways (Grusec and Arnason 1982). For example, if Leslie resists giving up the tricycle, the teacher might say, "Leslie, Robin has been waiting for a long time . . . and you know how it feels to wait a long time . . .," thereby stimulating empathy and nurturing sharing capabilities as well. This should not be said in a tone that implies guilt, of course.

Sometimes children refuse to accede to the requests of others because *they do know what it feels like to be in the other's position. In such cases empathy exists, but charity does not.* It is not very useful for adults to say things like, "How would you like someone to do that to you?" If charitable attitudes are lacking, the teacher must judge how to respond in the long-term interests of the children. At times, confrontations like these are inevitable and benign; their significance should not be exaggerated or overinterpreted.

*Disposition to experiment.* Many situations arise in which the teacher can strengthen children's dispositions to approach social situations experimentally as problem-solving situations in which alternative solutions can be invented and tried

out, and in which a few failures will not be debilitating.

When Robin complains that Leslie won't take turns, the teacher can respond by saying something like, "Go back and say to Leslie, 'I really want a turn. I've been waiting a long time' [in a mildly assertive tone]. *If that doesn't work, come back and we'll think of something else to try."* This tag teaches a disposition to be experimental.

*Complaining and tattling.* Professional judgment may be that Robin complains too often. The trained teacher tries to assess the legitimacy of complaints and to determine which of them require action. If, in the teacher's best judgment, the complaint requires no intervention, the teacher sends Robin back to the situation with some suggested strategies for coping. If complainers do succeed often, complaining can become persistent.

Similarly, with tattling the teacher may send the child back to cope with the conflict. When children are older, perhaps after age six or seven years, the teacher can explain the conditions under which telling on another child to an adult is warranted, for example, when the consequence of some activity unknown to the teacher may be dangerous.

## Clinical judgments

*Clinical* describes the processes of taking into account the *meaning* of the children's behaviors. Professional teachers attempt to put behavior into the context of everything they know about the children. A teacher might ask questions such as the following:

■ Is this a typical day for Robin? If so, is Robin a chronic attention seeker? Are Robin's expectations for receiving attention too high to be satisfied by the teacher?

■ How much experimentation can Robin tolerate? Robin's disposition to be self-assertive may not be strong enough to risk failure yet.

■ Does Leslie's behavior reflect progress? Perhaps this is the first time Leslie has been assertive.

■ Will the children develop healthy ways of interacting if they resolve the situation themselves? For children's long term interests, the professional teacher will try to minimize the success of the bully or bossy child.

■ Will the pattern of behavior of the children cause them trouble later on if it is left unattended now?

■ Have these children's characters been defined (Leslie as selfish and a bully or Robin as weak and a complainer) so that they are matching their behavior to the traits attributed to them (Grusec and Arnason 1982)?

## Curriculum and management considerations

The professional teacher might ask these questions regarding the program.

■ Is the behavior to be expected for this age group? In the children's culture? Preaching and moralizing are ineffective methods for changing the behaviors of preschool children. However, the teacher may tell a story with a relevant moral at an appropriate level of complexity for the children.

■ Have I provided the right kind and/or quantity of equipment for children of this age, background, and culture? Are there enough suitable alternative activities? Is the curriculum sufficiently appropriate and challenging for children?

*Not only is it unethical to let one's feelings dictate the response to a situation, but the school of hard knocks is likely to provide the wrong lessons to children.*

# Nonprofessional Responses to Common Incidents

Many people without professional education work with children in groups. In many settings parents and volunteers contribute greatly to the quality of the program. The term *nonprofessional* does not imply inferiority, but is used to contrast the application of knowledge and professional experience and practices with common sense responses, and to focus attention on how training and judgment come into play in daily work with *other people's children.*

How would people without profession education and experience respond when confronted with the same hypothetical situation? Typically nonprofessionals focus on what is happening rather than on what is being learned. They may wish simply to stop the incident rather than consider which of many possible interventions is most likely to stimulate long-term development and learning. If teachers saw teaching as fire-extinguishing, they would be smoke detectors rather than teachers!

*Distraction.* Many people without professional education and experience might respond by distracting Robin. Distraction seems to make sense, very often works, and is therefore a probable technique. However, for three-or four-year-olds it is not a preferred technique. It does not *help children learn* alternative approaches to the situation. On the contrary, it may teach children that complaining gets adult attention.

*Exhortations.* Other nonprofessional responses in situations like the tricycle squabble include saying things to children such as *Cut it out!, Don't be so selfish!, Be nice!, We take turns in this school!,* and *Don't be nasty!* Such exclamations are also unlikely to help the participants develop alternative approaches.

*Removal.* A nonprofessional might respond to squabbling over equipment by putting it away or locking it up. This eliminates the situation, of course, but *it does not teach.* A professional's commitment is to teaching.

*Empty threats.* A nonprofessional may issue a threat as a means of control. For example: "If you don't let Robin have a turn you can't go to the zoo with us on Friday . . ." Will the threatener really keep Leslie away from the zoo? How does one make the sanction match the seriousness of the behavior? Sometimes threats are out of proportion to the transgression. Then when a truly serious transgression comes along, what is left to threaten?

Perhaps four-year-olds cannot yet sense that threats indicate that the adult has lost or given up control. But some four-year-olds do. Then their testing behavior is apt to increase and the relationships in the class focus on the rules, on what happens when they are broken, and on who is really in charge.

*Bribery.* Some adults resort to bribery: "If you give Robin a turn with the tricycle, I'll let you give out the raisins." The danger in using a bribe is that it tends to devalue the behavior you want. The values of generosity and concern for others are discounted as not worth engaging in for their own sake. While bribery often works, the professional question is *what does it teach?*

*Time out.* Some adults use time out in cases of persistent refusal to cooperate with other children. Time out often seems to work and, indeed, many teachers are trained to use it. The main problem is that time out does not teach new skills or desirable dispositions, although it does change behavior. If the child's mental ability is reasonably normal, it is not necessary to circumvent the mind by insisting on a time out chair. The cognitive connection between sitting on a particular chair and granting another child's request for a turn must be fairly obscure if not confusing to a four-year-old (Katz 1977).

*Preaching.* Many adults moralize or preach about the virtues of sharing, kindness, generosity, and the evils of selfishness. None of these approaches are likely to help children learn strategies to use when adults are not present.

*Sympathy.* Another common response of adults without training is to become preoccupied with the feelings and needs of the victim and to neglect the feelings, needs, and the development of the aggressor. The professional is committed to responding to the feelings, needs, and development of *all* children.

*Guilt.* Some untrained adults, when confronting situations like the tricycle squabble, would say to Leslie "What you did makes me sad" or "That makes me feel bad." Such statements draw attention to the adults' own internal states and can cause the child to feel guilty for not pleasing the adult. Again, the basic problem with guilt is that it fails to teach the participants ways of coping with and resolving the predicament.

*Other manipulative techniques.* An untrained person is apt to combine common sense with impulse, customs, folk tales, and shaming comparisons with other children in order to intimidate children so they will give in to the adult's demand.

# Unprofessional Responses to Common Incidents

One of the characteristics of a fully developed profession is that its members subscribe to a code of ethics which serves as a guide to professional conduct (Katz 1977). Conduct which violates any part of the code is unethical and therefore unprofessional. *Nonprofessional* behavior is determined by personal predeliction, common sense, or folk wisdom rather than by professional knowledge and practices. *Unprofessional* behavior is that which contravenes agreed-upon standards of performance of the society of professional practitioners and their code of ethical conduct.

In general, unprofessional behavior is the result of giving in to the temptations of the situation at hand. It could be, for instance, that Leslie and/or Robin's behavior frequently puts the teacher into this kind of predicament. The adult might be a bit weary of it, and silently hope that aggressive children will "get what they deserve." Not only is it unethical to let one's feelings dictate the response to a situation, but the school of hard knocks, although powerful, is likely to provide the wrong lessons to children.

The trained teacher is not without feelings of the kind alluded to here. What is professional is to temper one's feelings with the knowledge and insight that constitutes professional judgment, and to respond based on that judgment rather than the feelings or temptations of the moment.

Occasionally we are tempted to blame the children for creating the predicament or to blame their parents for not raising them properly. However, what is relevant is not whom to blame, but what to teach in this situation.

## Conclusion

The professional responses presented here use judgment based on the most reliable knowledge and insight available. They reflect only a sample of the potential uses of contempory knowledge about children's development and learning. They are intended to add weight to the proposition that the effective training and education of early childhood teachers can make a significant contribution to children's development and learning.

## References

Ade, W. "Professionalization and Its Implications for the Field of Early Childhood Education." *Young Children* 37, no. 3 (March 1982): 25–32.

Frederiksen, C. H. "Inference in Preschool Children's Conversations: A Cognitive Perspective." In *Ethnography and Language in Educational Settings,* ed. J. Green and C. Wallat. Norwood, N.J.: Ablex, 1981.

Grusec, J. E., and Arnason, L. "Consideration for Others: Approaches to Enhancing Altruism." In *The Young Child: Reviews of Research.* Vol. 3, ed. S. G. Moore and C. R. Cooper. Washington, D.C.: National Association for the Education of Young Children, 1982.

Hoyle, E. "The Professionalization of Teachers: A Paradox." *British Journal of Educational Studies* 30, no. 2 (June 1982): 161–171.

Johnson, D. B. "Altruistic Behavior and the Development of Self in Infants." *Merrill-Palmer Quarterly* 28, no. 3 (1982): 379–387.

Katz, L. G. "Developmental Stages of Preschool Teachers." *Elementary School Journal* 23, no. 1 (1972): 50–54.

Katz, L. G. *Ethical Issues in Working with Children.* Urbana, Ill.: ERIC Clearinghouse on Elementary and Early Childhood Education, University of Illinois, 1977.

Nucci, L. P., and Turiel, E. "Social Interactions and the Development of Social Concepts in Preschool Children." *Child Development* 49 (1978): 400–407.

Rubin, K. H., and Everett, B. "Social Perspective-Taking in Young Children." In *The Young Child: Reviews of Research.* Vol. 3, ed. S. G. Moore and C. R. Cooper. Washington, D.C.: National Association for the Education of Young Children, 1982.

Schachter, F. F., and Strage, A. A. "Adults' Talk and Children's Language Development." In *The Young Child: Reviews of Research.* Vol. 3, ed. S. G. Moore and C. R. Cooper. Washington, D.C.: National Association for the Education of Young Children, 1982.

Shields, M. M. "Dialogue, Monologue and Egocentric Speech by Children in Nursery Schools." In *Language, Children and Society,* ed. O. I. Garnica and M. L. King. London: Pergamon, 1979.

Wells, G. *Learning Through Interaction: The Study of Language Development.* London: Cambridge University Press, 1981.

Zumeta, W., and Solomon, L. C., "Professions Education." *Encyclopedia of Educational Research.* Vol. 3, 5th ed. New York: Macmillan and Free Press, 1982.

Susan M. Hegland

# Teacher Supervision
## *A Model for Advancing Professional Growth*

*How can a good teacher become a good supervisor? What techniques are most effective in helping co-workers develop as early childhood professionals? A combination of the enabler model and the CDA credentialing process can enhance the quality of teaching young children.*

Competent teachers are often promoted to supervisory positions. Good teaching techniques do not necessarily become good supervisory techniques, however, as the following example illustrates.

The position of education coordinator was vacant in a preschool program. The director was impressed by the qualifications of Sharon, a head teacher in the program, who was an excellent teacher. She related warmly to children, staff, and parents. Sharon planned and implemented a well-rounded, developmentally appropriate program with variety, stimulation, and challenge. She regularly attended professional conferences and kept abreast of current developments in early childhood education. Her recordkeeping was excellent and she was well respected by her colleagues. Although she had no experience in staff supervision, the preschool director was confident that she would quickly acquire these skills and Sharon was hired for the position.

Sharon moved into the new position with much enthusiasm and only a few misgivings. She honestly felt that she was an excellent teacher, and looked forward to the opportunity to share her ideas with others. Although concerned about evaluating her former peers, Sharon felt confident that they would soon learn to welcome her suggestions and advice

**Susan M. Hegland,** Ph.D., is Assistant Professor of Child Development, Iowa State University, Ames, Iowa.

based on her long years of teaching experience. Sharon's overriding concern was to provide a high quality early childhood program for the children.

As education coordinator, Sharon started by visiting classrooms to observe and assess the teachers' strengths and needs and to begin to provide assistance to each teacher. Sharon found the teacher assisting each child in the completion of an elaborate product-oriented craft project in the first classroom she visited. During a conference after the children left, Sharon pointed out the value of process-oriented activities for young children. The teacher responded that children need to learn to follow directions and, furthermore, that product-oriented activities help to reinforce the unit theme as well as to provide information to the parents about the child's activities. Discouraged, Sharon prepared to visit the next classroom.

In the second classroom, she observed restless children standing in lengthy lines waiting to move from the classroom to the bathroom next door, outdoors, and to the lunchroom. During their conference, Sharon pointed out the value of gradual transitions which minimize wasted time and restlessness of the children. The teacher responded that children need to learn to stand in lines in order to be ready for kindergarten. Frustrated, Sharon proceeded to the next classroom.

Sharon observed the teacher in the third classroom urging the children to clean their plates prior to dessert. Reminded that dessert was planned to be a nutritious part of the meal, this teacher responded that children need to

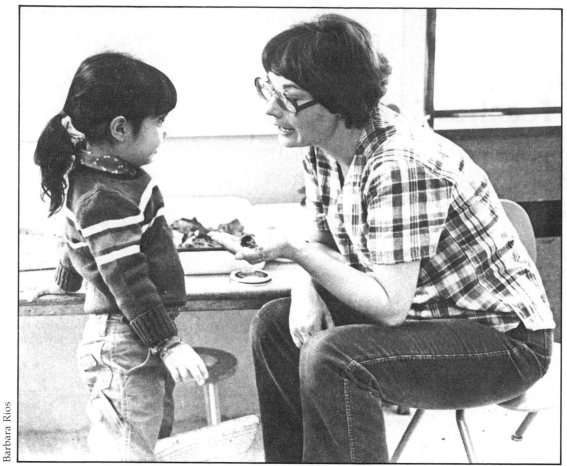

*Teachers who are assured that their strengths are recognized by their supervisor can improve their teaching by working on their own self-identified needs.*

learn to try a variety of foods. At the end of this conference, Sharon returned to her office regretting her decision to leave the classroom to take on the important role of the supervisor.

Sharon's experience is typical of other classroom staff promoted to supervisory positions. Competent, experienced teachers eager to share their ideas with others often become frustrated at the unwillingness of other staff to change. Frustration over the perceived stubbornness of the staff and/or pressure from licensing agents, funding agents, parents, and administrators may cause Sharon to resort to authoritarian procedures in an attempt to get her staff to implement the suggestions

they refused to adopt voluntarily. Sharon may become a supervisor who seeks to control rather than to facilitate the professional development of her staff.

Teachers, like children, move through stages of development at their own pace. In a climate in which teachers are assured that their strengths are recognized, they can use a resource teacher to work on their own self-identified needs. Sharon had not developed her own philosophy of supervision congruent with her philosophy of early childhood education. By ignoring teacher strengths and focusing on needs only, Sharon aroused defensive responses from resentful teachers who felt unfairly criticized.

Hegland

## The enabler model

The enabler model of supervision can help early childhood professionals as they move from the role of teacher to that of supervisor (Hegland 1982). The model assumes that teachers are professional adults who move from short-term concern with immediate self-preservation to universal concern for humanity (Loevinger 1976; Erikson 1950; and Maslow 1962).

Similarly, Katz (1977) describes stages of teacher development as moving from the early survival stage, where teachers' needs center on activities and skills to survive a day, through stages of consolidation and renewal, to maturity, in which teacher concerns revolve around more abstract issues such as motivation for learning. Glickman (1981) suggests that different supervision styles should be used with teachers in different developmental stages. The dilemma for the supervisor is to create an environment with moderate stress which enables professional growth without threatening staff competence.

The enabler model is based on a four-step model of supervision:
1. Supervisor and teacher agree on program philosophy and goals.
2. Supervisor and teacher develop mu-

tual trust and respect in an atmosphere of open communication.

3. Supervisor identifies teacher strengths relevant to program goals while teacher identifies professional needs, goals, and preferred mode of learning; both agree on a timetable for accomplishment of goals.

4. Supervisor acts as a resource person to select appropriate training resources relevant to teacher-identified needs. (Hegland 1982)

Thus, a supervisor facilitates rather than controls and directs the professional development of staff members. As staff members become more confident of their competence, they become more able to self-assess their strengths and needs and to use the supervisor as a resource to meet those needs.

## Implementing the model

### Agree on goals

Supervisor and teacher need to agree on the program philosophy and goals during the first stage of the model. These may be imposed on the program as a condition of funding and/or licensing (such as Head Start Performance Standards or state licensing standards), or developed by staff, supervisors, and parents to reflect the values of the local community. Once developed, they need to be prominently displayed and frequently reviewed with staff to assure that all program participants are aware of and attempt to meet program goals. In Sharon's situation, she could begin by integrating program goals into interviews with prospective staff members. She could also design preservice and inservice training around specific program goals to ensure that staff are aware of these goals as they plan and implement their program.

### Develop mutual respect

Secondly, the supervisor and teacher need to develop mutual respect for each other's competence. Although this may sound elementary, some beginning supervisors like Sharon feel that the way to demonstrate their competence is to point out their staff members' weaknesses and to offer suggestions to remedy these perceived weaknesses. Unfortunately, such helpful suggestions have the opposite effect on staff, who perceive the suggestions as criticisms and threats to their professional competence. Aware that their supervisor finds more to criticize than to praise in their professional skills, staff members learn to defend their strengths and to conceal their needs in the supervisor's presence. As a result, teachers avoid identifying their needs and fail to use the supervisor as a resource person. The response, "Yes, but . . ." to a suggestion from a supervisor may be a clue that a teacher is defensive about her or his competence and is too threatened to consider the suggestion seriously and accept it.

Some supervisors like Sharon take too broad a view of their responsibility to ensure a high quality program for children and leave little or no autonomy for the teacher. For example, one Head Start director sent a memo to staff specifying the placement of every table in their classrooms! In contrast to this approach are more effective supervisors who see their role as ensuring that program goals are met and leave to teachers the method and manner of their implementation. They project strong expectations that goals are being met in an atmosphere of empathy, warmth, and respect. For example, during an in-service meeting, instead of giving a lecture on how to best achieve safety goals in the classroom, Sharon could ask staff members to share successful safety activities and procedures that they have used. By actively listening, Sharon would convey her respect for their ideas.

### Identify strengths and needs

Once basic trust and respect have been established, the supervisor can move to the third step which involves helping staff members identify their own strengths and needs relative to program goals. Regular classroom visits by the supervisor, followed by supervisor-teacher conferences, are an essential component of this stage, as Sharon recognized. The presence of the supervisor scribbling notes can be very threatening to the teacher, however. A more productive strategy for supervisors like Sharon is to establish mutual respect by noting strengths relevant to program goals and relying upon the teacher to identify her or his professional needs. Because of its emphasis on self-assessment, the Child Development Associate (CDA) credentialing process may be useful for guiding the professional development of inexperienced and experienced early childhood teachers (Galler 1981). Although some supervisors use a checklist to identify staff strengths and needs, many who have served as CDA advisors prefer to use observed anecdotes that relate to specific CDA functional or program areas (see Table 1). A sample of an observation based on these areas is shown in Table 2. These observations make it possible to identify the different ways in which each staff member demonstrates professional competence. While checklists may provide examples of program goals, the very presence of unchecked statements can focus the teacher's attention on these apparent weaknesses rather than on the stengths observed. Since staff members are more likely to seek and profit from assistance in program areas they themselves identify as needs, the anecdotal approach may lead to greater success in supervision.

Supervisors may sometimes feel that needs initially identified by staff members are trivial; however, these needs may represent safe starting points for the staff member. As staff members develop trust and confidence in the supervisor, they will become more open to identifying other needs. The CDA training process, for example, requires candidates to recognize their own areas of need.

## Table 1. CDA competency goals and functional areas.

| Competency | Functional area |
|---|---|
| I. Establishes and maintains a safe and healthy environment | 1. Safe<br>2. Healthy<br>3. Environment |
| II. Advances physical and intellectual competence | 4. Physical<br>5. Cognitive<br>6. Language<br>7. Creative |
| III. Builds positive self-concept and individual strength | 8. Self-concept<br>9. Individual strength |
| IV. Promotes positive functioning of children and adults in a group | 10. Social<br>11. Group management |
| V. Brings about optimal coordination of home and center childrearing practices and expectations | 12. Home-center |
| VI. Carries out supplementary responsibilities related to programs | 13. Staff |

## Table 2. Sample anecdotal observation.

**Date:** 1–24     **Observer:** Sharon     **Teacher:** Bonnie

| Observation | Functional Area: Indicators |
|---|---|
| During free choice time, Bonnie sets up the easel with paint, a table with playdough, and low shelves with crayons, scissors, paste, and glue for children to use at a nearby table. | *Creative:* makes available a wide variety of materials to stimulate creative expression |
| Bonnie sits and eats with the children during lunchtime. While eating, Bonnie and the children talk about Stacy's dog, Heather's new baby brother, and Jeremy's new boots. | *Language:* helps children develop expressive language skills through informal conversations |
| After lunch, Bonnie gives each child her or his toothbrush and a small glass of water. After brushing, children hang their toothbrushes on pegs mounted on a board. | *Health:* helps children acquire good dental health practices |
| Bonnie takes the children outdoors. Some children build a snowman and others play in a sandbox while Bonnie supervises children sledding down a low hill. | *Physical:* provides opportunities for large motor development |

Occasionally a glaring need is immediately apparent to the supervisor who cannot wait for the teacher to notice, such as when several unsupervised children are observed using saws and hammers at the workbench in a potentially hazardous manner. To present this immediately to the teacher may be very threatening and may elicit defensive responses such as "I never wanted that dangerous workbench anyway," or "I told my aide to watch over that area." While the children are present, the supervisor can increase safety by unobtrusively supervising that area and by helping the children follow such safety precautions as using C-clamps to hold materials. After the children have gone, in order to decrease defensiveness, the supervisor can open discussion by communicating in relative rather than absolute terms: "Some teachers have found the workbench to be a difficult area to supervise." Another way to diminish the threatening nature of the situation is to begin by relating an incident from the supervisor's own teaching experience: "I found the workbench hard to supervise until someone suggested limiting its use to two children at a time."

Another way to focus attention on a teacher's potential need areas uses the behavior modification technique of shaping. In shaping behavior, the supervisor may ignore instances of inappropriate behavior and instead note as strengths the occurrences of appropriate behaviors. For example, one supervisor observed one teacher's harsh, authoritarian guidance statements but chose not to comment on them. Instead, she noted as a strength the one instance in which the teacher gave a child a reason for a particular rule. During her next several visits to the classroom, the supervisor noted that the teacher used a few more reasons when she redirected children. During each subsequent visit, the supervisor continued to comment on the times the teacher used positive guidance techniques such as approaching a child rather than shouting from across the room, using the child's name, and giving positive directions rather than negative criticisms.

In addition to identifying candidate strengths through written anecdotal observations, the supervisor may choose to identify teacher strengths with photographs or videotapes. Photographs can also be used in a classroom display to enhance children's self-concept. Videotapes are least threatening if they are used to focus on a child with behavior problems rather than on the teacher.

When the teacher and supervisor agree on the teacher's strengths and needs, they then should agree on professional goals relevant to the teacher's needs and on a mutually acceptable timetable for accomplishing those goals. Again, the CDA functional areas can be used as a starting point for training.

Setting the timetable to accomplish training goals may require a gradual shift in the balance of power toward the teacher (see Bronfenbrenner 1979). With less committed teachers, the supervisor will need to take a more active role in helping the teacher set realistic deadlines. However, in order to help the teacher develop more professional commitment and take more responsibility rather than rely on the directive supervisor, the supervisor gradually shifts more responsibility for setting and meeting deadlines to the teacher.

## Select training resources

Once the supervisor and teacher agree on a timetable for achieving training goals, the supervisor can serve as a resource person for selecting training materials for the teacher. Here again, it is vital for teachers to identify their preferred mode, location, and timing of training. As Katz (1977) points out, training needs of teachers differ according to their stage of professional development. Novice teachers may require immediate on-site consultation to deal with the many crises that often develop during the first year of teaching. More experienced teachers seek new ideas from workshops, visits to other programs, and articles relating to classroom situations. Mature teachers seek to clarify their philosophy through seminars and conferences. Some teachers may find books and articles helpful, others prefer more graphic resources such as films, filmstrips, or demonstrations.

It is unrealistic to expect professional development from staff without allowing them to engage in developmental activities during the working day (Long 1977). Preservice and in-service workshops scheduled during the workday, or release time to complete CDA portfolios, attend conferences, and observe in other programs are tangible evidence that an agency values professional development.

Supervisors might also be tempted to try demonstrations of model teaching or guidance techniques as an additional resource, especially upon request by a staff member. Although modeling can occasionally be useful, it must be done cautiously and sparingly (Katz 1979). Hunt (1963) coined the "problem of the match" and the "optimal discrepancy" to describe motivation for development in another context, but it seems appropriate here as well. A teacher who feels very uncomfortable with music may be more threatened than aided by watching Hap Palmer or Ella Jenkins work with children. On the other hand, if the model's skill and that of the teacher are only slightly different, this technique is more likely to benefit the teacher.

## Conclusion

The enabler model requires supervisors like Sharon to begin by developing a program philosophy and goals which are agreed upon by parents, staff, and directors. Sharon then works to develop an atmosphere of mutual respect by such activities as actively listening to teachers' ideas and concerns as well as noting behavioral examples of teacher strengths during regular classroom visits. She relies upon teachers to identify their own needs and facilitate their professional development during both working and nonworking hours.

Program change may appear to come more slowly using the enabler supervisory model than using more authoritarian approaches. Change, when it does occur, however, it more likely to reflect true commitment on the part of teachers and an actual advancement in level of professional understanding. It will not be merely a temporary mask grudgingly worn in the presence of the supervisor.

## Bibliography

Bronfenbrenner, U. *The Ecology of Human Development*. Cambridge, Mass.: Harvard University Press, 1979.

Carkhuff, R. "Helping and Human Relations: A Guide for Training Lay Helpers." *Journal of Research and Development in Education* 4 (1971): 17–27.

Erikson, E. *Childhood and Society*. New York: Norton, 1950.

Galler, B. "Providing CDA Training with an Interactive Model." *Young Children* 36 (1981): 25–35.

Glickman, C. *Developmental Supervision: Alternative Practices for Helping Teachers Improve Instruction.* Washington, D.C.: Association for Supervision and Curriculum Development, 1981.

Goldhammer, R. *Clinical Supervision: Special Methods for the Supervision of Teachers.* New York: Holt, Rinehart & Winston, 1969.

Hamilton, P. *Competency-Based Teacher Education.* Menlo Park, Calif.: Stanford Research Institute, 1973.

Hegland, S. M. "The Enabler Model of Teacher Supervision." Paper presented at the Annual Conference of the Iowa Association for the Education of Young Children, Des Moines, Iowa, 1982.

Hunt, J. McV. "Motivation Inherent in Information Processing Systems." In *Movtivation and Social Interaction: Cognitive Determinants*, ed. O. J. Harvey. New York: Ronald Press, 1963.

Jackson, P. "Old Dogs and New Tricks: Observations on the Continuing Education of Teachers." In *Improving In-Service Education*, ed. L. Rubin. Boston: Allyn & Bacon, 1971.

Katz, L. *Talks with Teachers*. Washington, D.C.: National Association for the Education of Young Children, 1977.

Katz, L. "Helping Others Learn to Teach." *CDA Bulletin*, no. 2 (May 1979): 1–2.

Knowles, M. *The Modern Practice of Adult Education from Pedagogy to Androgeny*. Chicago: Association Press, 1980.

Loevinger, J. *Ego Development: Conceptions and Theories*. San Francisco: Jossey-Bass, 1976.

Long, D. "Competency-Based Staff Development." In *Staff Development: Staff Liberation*, ed. C. Beegle and R. Edelfelt. Washington, D.C.: Association for Supervision and Curriculum Development, 1977.

Maslow, A. *Motivation and Personality*. New York: Harper & Row, 1962.

Rogers, C. "A Theory of Therapy, Personality, and Interpersonal Relationships, As Developed in the Client-Centered Framework." In *Psychology: A Study of a Science. Vol. 3: Formulations of the Person and the Social Context*, ed. S. Koch. New York: McGraw-Hill, 1959.

Selye, H. "The Stress Concept Today." In *Handbook on Stress and Anxiety*, ed. I. Kutash and L. Schesinger. San Francisco: Jossey-Bass, 1981.

Carol E. Catron and Earline D. Kendall

# Staff Evaluation That Promotes Growth and Problem Solving

One challenge for directors of programs for young children is to create an atmosphere that promotes growth and enables adults as well as children to develop. While child care programs are designed for the development of the children, providing for the development of adults in the program will support an atmosphere for children's growth (Katz 1977). "... We cannot have optimum environments for children in centers unless we also have optimum environments for their teachers and caretakers" (Katz 1979, p. 1).

The development of an enabling environment for adults is directly connected to the program philosophy and to the development of relationships within the program, but the management of adult relationships requires special skills from the administrator. Rogolsky (1979) found that supervision and direction of staff is often one of the greatest problems a director faces. A major challenge to the director is "instituting procedures that create an atmosphere that encourages all staff to enhance their skills . . . encouraging staff to engage in self-assessment and helping to plan experiences that result in improved functioning are critical to the development of not only the staff but the administrator as well" (Stevens and King 1976, pp. 303–304).

This article outlines an approach to staff evaluation based on Gordon's (1977) model that synthesizes the areas of relationships, development, supervision, and

evaluation. This model "strengthens the development of a relationship of mutual confidence and respect" between the director and the staff, and enables staff members to "draw on a stable source for corrections over a long period of development" (Katz 1979, pp. 3–4).

## Purpose of evaluation

Staff evaluation may serve many purposes. At its best, evaluation provides a means of growth and change for staff, management, and the organization. Directors who see this as the purpose of evaluation establish nonthreatening evaluation techniques that promote growth, provide feedback to both administrator and staff, and aid in the creation of an optimum program environment.

## A problem-solving approach

We established a regular system of monthly director-staff member evaluation

**Carol E. Catron,** Ed.D., is Assistant Professor of Early Childhood Education, Tusculum College, Greeneville, Tennessee.

**Earline D. Kendall,** Ph.D., is Associate Professor and Chairperson of the Education Department, Belmont College, Nashville, Tennessee.

conferences based on Gordon's (1977) model of the two-way problem-solving conference through which the director and the staff member work out a mutually acceptable plan for growth. The purposes of these individual conferences were to help the staff member grow to be a more effective teacher, to provide a feedback mechanism from the director to each staff member and from the staff member to the director, and to help the center progress in providing high quality care for young children.

According to Gordon, the effective administrator uses counseling skills to achieve balance between meeting the individual's needs and meeting the total program needs. Good leaders balance task and people orientation (Gordon 1977; Blake and Mouton 1972) through a no-lose conflict resolution.

## Evaluation conferences

The individual conference/staff evaluation approach follows a sequence of specific events.

### Before the conferences

Discuss the rationale for the implementation of such a procedure with the staff and *ask staff to help plan the behavior evaluation form to be used.* Figure 1 shows a sample form that worked well for us. Commit to trying this procedure for a *specific length of time* during which the director's responsibility is to make sure the conferences are scheduled.

Schedule conferences at convenient times for staff members and the director. Post a schedule for dates and times. *Establish a regular pattern of conferences.*

Elisabeth Nichols

*An evaluation procedure of the type described in this article can be an invitation to grow, can increase our potential as adults working together with young children, and can enable the creation of better program environments.*

Catron and Kendall

## Figure 1. Sample behavior evaluation form.

| No problem area: | *proactive work areas* |
| Behaviors indicating staff member has a problem (staff member owns problem): | *staff member's unmet needs* |
| Behaviors causing the organization/director a problem (director owns problem): | *director's/organization's unmet needs* |

Date: _____

Staff members: _____

In programs with more than ten staff members, arrange for monthly conferences to be held *between staff members and their immediate supervisors.* This eliminates director overload and opens communication between staff members who work most closely together.

### Conduct the conferences

Uninterrupted, focused time is essential to the effectiveness of this conference evaluation procedure. Establish *a nonthreatening atmosphere* which stresses open communication and an attitude of helpfulness, not confrontation and conflict. Both director and staff member meet to facilitate growth, to solve mutual problems, and to make the working situation a more positive one for everyone involved, by being life-givers, not life-diminishers—enablers, not squelchers.

Begin the conference with a discussion of those areas where no problem exists for either the director or the staff member using the behavior evaluation form. This focus on the positive gives both staff and director an opportunity to *take joy* in how much is being accomplished successfully and competently! The staff member's job description may be a helpful vehicle for initiating discussion of job-related behaviors. As topics are discussed, note both the director and the staff member's comments and reactions. For example, the staff member may be especially confident of an ability to foster creative dramatic play in the classroom, or the director may compliment the staff member for developing positive relationships with parents.

Next, *listen* as the staff member does a self-evaluation by identifying frustrations and problems. List concerns identified by the staff member on the second part of the form. Be supportive and nonjudgmental. There are many different levels of needs (Maslow 1954). For example, staff members who are fearful for their personal safety cannot relate to higher level needs until their security needs are met. In one large school where thefts were threatening

## Figure 2. Problem-solving form.

Behavior targeted to change:



Responsibilities of staff member:



Responsibilities of director:



Time frame agreed upon:



Date: _____

Evaluation/follow-up:



Date: _____

Staff member:

Catron and Kendall

staff security, a lock on the door and a buzzer for admission allowed staff to move to other concerns.

The final section of the behavior evaluation form focuses on needs that are unmet from the director or center's point of view. Don't attack or belittle; give "I-messages." Sending I-messages is sometimes called leveling—being open, honest, and direct with people; You-messages warn, put down, blame, or lecture and are largely ineffective in creating positive behavior changes (Gordon 1977, pp. 98–99). For example, Gordon cites this as an effective I-message to a staff program who is haphazard about attendance at staff meetings: "When you're absent from our staff meetings, I feel strongly that our effectiveness is reduced because we don't have the benefit of your experience and knowledge" (Gordon 1977, p. 99).

If neither participant identifies any problems—that's great—end the conference there. The director should *compliment* that person.

Most of the time, however, several problems are identified. *Be realistic.* Set priorities. Don't attempt to deal with ten problems at once; identify one or two areas for focus. Don't increase the level of frustration by attempting to problem solve too many areas at once. The point is to make frustrations manageable—to initiate change—to increase positive attitudes. You and the staff member are on the same side work together creatively to solve problems so that everyone benefits—increase the sense of connectedness among staff people.

When you move on to the problem-solving form (Figure 2) your first step is to *set goals*. Each person takes responsibility where appropriate. For example, frequent late arrival is clearly a problem for which the staff member must assume responsibility. Classroom discipline is one that both the director, by providing resources or modeling behavior, and the staff member, by searching for new techniques and trying them out, may assume respon-

sibility. Together, develop strategies for meeting the goal, and agree on a realistic time frame to meet the goal. Usually one month is adequate to make progress toward solving the problem.

End the conference with a positive note—with a sense of hopefulness and helpfulness—*together we can move and grow and change.*

### Reevaluation

*Reevaluate* the problem at the beginning of the next month's conference. Has the problem-solving approach outlined been effective? Talk about the progress that has been made. Again, listen to gain a sense of how the staff member is feeling. Express your own sense of the situation. Together agree on a new approach, an extended time frame, or rejoice that the problem has been solved! Note the outcome on the problem-solving form, then use the behavior evaluation form to initiate discussion of new problems.

*Repeat the process monthly.* At the end of a 12-month period, the supervisor and the staff members have a clear picture of growth that has or has not been made. File the forms in individual staff folders for reference and documentation.

## Conclusions

Over a two-year period of using this individual monthly conference procedure, we found it to be a positive technique for nonthreatening, growth-promoting evaluation. This process was an effective tool for promoting staff growth, for providing a clear evaluative measure for the director's use, and for increasing overall program effectiveness.

Responses to the process include the following:

■ The procedure was well-liked by staff members and seen as nonthreatening and helpful. The conference time was perceived as each staff member's time with the director. It provided special time for the director to listen and help staff become more effective in their jobs. Even the most timid staff member began to view these individual conferences as a time to verbalize frustrations, to receive support, and to obtain assistance in solving problems.

■ The procedure became, in practice, largely a self-assessment tool as staff members evaluated themselves and owned their own job-related problems. The procedure also lessened the burdens on the staff as they felt they received help while sharing their problems. Thus, the evaluation procedure was an effective stress-reliever for all concerned.

■ The procedure gave a clear picture of staff growth or lack of growth and documented a staff member's performance and progress.

■ The process is time consuming and may not be perceived as worth the time and effort by some staff members. Usually these individuals are won over if they see colleagues' needs and their own needs being met through this communicative process.

■ This conference format was not meant to take the place of other types of director-staff communication (such as informal, regular feedback, praise for job performance, staff meetings, and in-service training sessions), but was seen as a formalized method of aiding growth in a nonthreatening atmosphere.

■ The individual conference can be expanded to include team conferences for supervisory staff or for teachers and assistant teachers. We found this process to be effective in helping to transform individuals into a cohesive group of authentic, communicative, and supportive staff members.

Best of all, the process worked for us! This technique for evaluation increased our ability to problem solve effectively, to become better at our jobs of caring for young children, and to convey to staff members a sense of being cared for and supported. The forms suggested for use are a vehicle for facilitating this evaluation process, but the forms don't make the process effective—the people involved do. We stress individual adaptation of these ideas and staff involvement in the total process.

An evaluation procedure of the type described in this article can be an invitation to grow, can increase our potential as adults working together with young children, and can enable the creation of better program environments.

**Bibliography**

Blake, R. R., and Mouton, J. S. *Managerial Grid.* Houston, Tex.: Gulf Publishing, 1972.

Gordon, T. *Leader Effectiveness Training: L.E.T.* New York: Wyden Books, 1977.

Katz, L. *Talks with Teachers.* Washington, D.C.: National Association for the Education of Young Children, 1977.

Katz, L. "Principles of Staff Development in Programs for Younger Children." *Children in Contemporary Society* (January 1979): 1–4.

Maslow, A. H. *Motivation and Personality.* New York: Harper & Row, 1954.

Rogolsky, M. "Psychologist Views the Role of Day Care Director." *Child Care Information Exchange* 9 (September 1979): 1–5.

Stevens, J. H., Jr., and King, E. W. *Administering Early Childhood Education Programs.* Boston: Little, Brown, 1976.

Takanishi, R. "Evaluation of Early Childhood Programs: Toward a Developmental Perspective." In *Current Topics in Early Childhood Education.* Vol. II, ed. L. C. Katz. Norwood, N.J.: Ablex, 1979.

Catron and Kendall

Pearl Axelrod, Pamela M. Schwartz, Ann Weinstein, and Esther Buch

# Mobile Training for Directors of Day Care

### The Last Straw

Once upon a time . . . that's how I would like to start this story and pretend it was all make believe. It's all true.

The Center opened at 7:30 a.m. on Monday morning as usual. By 8:15 I had learned that the cook had the flu, one bus driver was ill and her back-up person (our one and only substitute bus driver) was home with her own two children who had strep throat, and I still was without a secretary since our "free" one had left the week before for a paying job. Fine, I thought, I can take care of these things. The next realization was that I had bummed a ride to the Center and was without a car myself.

Having started snack and lunch, I set about to borrow a car and/or coerce someone else to drive to four elementary schools and pick up four kindergartners (vowing that we will really have to reassess our position on transporting children), and then I was interrupted (nothing new for directors) by a mother, father, and child who wanted to tour the Center, discuss the program, and possibly enroll. In view of the fact that I now had spaghetti sauce on the yellow wall and on my pants and the phone was ringing, I tried to appear calm, collected, and capable. . . .

Monday continued on much the same with teachers giving up breaks to do dishes and answer the phone and joke about the rubbery lunch. Tuesday was more of the same. I did have my own car and the cook assured me that she only needed to be out one more day. I made several frantic calls to the local organizations that placed secretaries with us for training, and begged for anyone who could say hello and smile at the same time.

Wednesday was a woeful day. The cook made it in but wasn't strong enough for dishes. The bus driver's substitute ran the route. The noise levels in the Center rose all day since teacher staff meetings had been cancelled for Monday and Tuesday, thus removing some support for them. All in all, when I left the Center Wednesday I knew we had made it through a rough time without many difficulties to the total program. After settling my own son into bed I proceeded to lament, groan, ponder out loud, and in general look for sympathy for my previous three days when the phone rang. Knowing from high school English that Shakespeare and others use ringing phones and slamming doors to forewarn us, I still answered the phone at 8:35 p.m. It was the janitor.

I will now quote the denouement for the week . . . 'I think this is my last minute to work.'

Connie Crawley, Director
Edgewood Village
Child Care Center
East Lansing, Michigan

**Pearl Axelrod,** M.S.W., was Project Director, Mobile Training for Directors of Day Care Centers, and a former special assistant to the Dean, School of Education, University of Michigan.
**Pamela M. Schwartz,** Ph.D., is Assistant Research Scientist, School of Public Health, University of Michigan.
**Ann Weinstein,** M.A.T., is a licensing consultant, Michigan Department of Social Services.
**Esther Buch,** M.A. is Adjunct Instructor, Mercy College of Detroit.

All of the co-authors were associated with the Mobile Training for Directors of Day Care Centers.

*The director of a child care center is the head of a small business, and therefore needs to know management procedures. Most directors, however, take their jobs out of concern for children and have minimal business experience.*

This letter summarizes some of the perils involved in running a program for young children. Most directors are called on to juggle at least four jobs, any one of which probably could be full time. They are the chief financial officer, program coordinator, personnel officer, and public relations person. In addition, they function as the center trouble-shooter. In the confusion of roles it would be easy to forget that the true purpose of the director's job is to provide a happy, safe developmental experience for young children. But before attention can be given to the program, immediate pressing issues need to be resolved.

The director of a child care center is the head of a small business, and therefore needs to know management procedures. Most directors, however, take their jobs out of concern for children and have minimal business experience. The Mobile Training for Directors of Day Care Centers

(MTDDC) Program was created to provide directors with information to improve their administrative and organizational skills.

## The Program

The MTDDC Program grew out of a course offered through the University of Michigan Extension Service called "Preschool and Child Care Administration." The staff of the course realized the importance of acquiring administrative skills for the many day care directors who enrolled. It also became apparent that the need for this training was larger than could be met through a course offered at a single site, so a mobile weekend plan for administrative training was devised. Funding was obtained from the Department of Health, Education and Welfare under Section 426 of the Social Security Act—Child Welfare

Axelrod, Schwartz, Weinstein, and Buch

Training Grant. The state was divided into six areas. Project staff and selected instructors from relevant fields traveled to an area and offered a consecutive series of three weekend workshops. These were available without charge to all of the directors located within a 100-mile radius. During the first year, the staff went to all areas except Detroit. In the second year, two series were held in Detroit and an advanced series was given in Ann Arbor for the entire state. The Friday-Saturday workshop made attendance possible without too much disruption to center programs.

During the early planning stages, project staff gathered workshop content ideas from a wide variety of sources including representatives of the Michigan Department of Social Services, Child Care Licensing Consultants, and 4-Cs Council members. In addition, to better understand local issues, preplanning committees were formed at each site. These committees were composed of local day care directors and Social Service representatives. We found their assistance valuable for logistics and for their suggestions about local concerns and issues that might be stressed in the workshop program.

Several principles determined the final content. First, the information had to be useful and practical for directors of nonprofit centers and directors operating a day care center on a tight budget. Second, because the workshop series was brief, the methods presented had to be ones which could be utilized with no further training, although many materials would be made available for use as future resources.

Directors of centers were viewed as crucial people in determining the quality of care in a center. Directors are more likely to be able to provide leadership if they can efficiently and effectively manage finances and business matters and have cooperative, supportive relationships with staff. They should also have a basic knowledge of good programming and administrative procedures. They should understand the role of day care as a support for families and promote parent involvement in the center.

## Business management and finance

The first workshop in the series was entitled "Business Management and Finance." Much of a director's stress relates to finances. While there is no magic way to get more money, problems can be reduced by a clear understanding of where money is coming from, where it is being spent, and where expenses can be cut. We presented systems that would promote that understanding. Directors were introduced to functional budgeting and a special accounting system for day care. A preventive maintenance system was described. In addition, lists of possible public and private resources were made available so centers could seek additional funds.

## Personnel

The workshop on personnel reiterated the obvious fact that staff is a vital ingredient in quality care. Directors complained about inappropriate behavior of staff and frequent turnover. We introduced group exercises that might help to reduce these problems. These were aimed at improving communication with staff members, increasing staff motivation, and helping to resolve conflicts. Participants indicated that this approach was very useful, and used the exercises later with their staffs. Career ladders, on-site affordable in-service training, and involvement of staff in planning were described as ways to counteract the stress of a demanding, low paying job. Fair personnel practices that included written contracts, regular staff meetings, and provision for supervision and evaluation were described and sample forms were made available.

During this weekend we gave attention to the problem of involving working parents in day care programs. Most center directors indicated that they felt such involvement was important but few had programs for parents. We suggested that center staff begin by examining their own attitudes toward parents. A parent's manual describing center philosophy and programs and delineating staff and parents' responsibilities vis-à-vis the child and the day care center was suggested as one important method to promote understanding between staff and parents.

## Program

The third workshop dealt with the issues seen as critical in the administration of a program: developing goals, observing and recording children's development, scheduling and individualizing activities, using space and equipment well, guiding children's behavior, evaluating the center, and dealing with the problems of health, safety, and child abuse.

The most frequently chosen goal of the directors attending this workshop was to design a balanced program that met the physical, social-emotional, and intellectual needs of children. They all wanted more information about dealing with children who were behavior problems and time was given to this. Examples of a medical policy that included safety issues were presented.

## Workshop materials—the MTDDC

*The Preschool and Child Care Administration* kit (1977), a compilation of annotated materials on budgeting, accounting, center management, licensing, personnel, policies, parent involvement, child development, program planning, accounting, in-service training, observing and recording children's cognitive development, children with special needs, and health and safety issues was provided for all participants. The kit provided an index of resources, state and local requirements, and methods for implementing managerial

and supervisory techniques presented in the workshops.

Instructors also prepared new materials relevant to their subject. Free materials such as the excellent series "Caring for Children" were distributed or promoted. State health departments provided pamphlets on immunization and common childhood diseases. Life insurance companies provided health and safety booklets. County Cooperative Extension Agents prepared information on nutrition and menus.

Other resources were also developed as a result of the program. A library of administration materials, including books and pamphlets collected during the program are cataloged and are housed in the media center at the University of Michigan School of Education.

## Instructors

Just as the quality of a child care program is dependent on the skill, enthusiasm, knowledge, and concern of the staff, so a training program for directors is dependent on informed, flexible, and involved instructors. We looked for professionals who had knowledge and skill in the administrative content areas, even if they did not know specifically about day care. Many such individuals were eager to apply their skills to the particular needs of day care centers and they have become new resources for centers.

The project staff served as resource people and coordinators for all the Mobile Training sessions, and as instructors in their own areas of expertise. Other instructors were chosen from the faculties and staffs of the University of Michigan, local community colleges, and other universities. Personnel from private and government agencies dealing with children in day care or their parents, spoke about issues and programs with which they were involved.

Several instructors came from the De-

Axelrod, Schwartz, Weinstein, and Buch

partment of Educational Administration at the University of Michigan. One faculty member developed the workshop on functional budgeting and another presented group exercises on values, achievement, motivation, and conflict resolution. A financial officer of the University prepared a special accounting system for day care centers. A pediatrician directed her attention to the special health problems in day care.

Participation in the workshops by Licensing Consultants for the Michigan Department of Social Services (DSS), Division of Child Care Center Licensing was sought and appreciated. The on-the-spot consultation and interpretation of regulations was beneficial, as was the more formal participation of the consultants as instructors. Directors of centers who had a particular talent were often called upon to share their knowledge with other directors.

## The advanced workshop series

At the end of the first year, directors asked for the program to be extended to deal with issues in greater detail.

The first of this in-depth weekend series dealt with preventive health care and safety. The directors indicated a number of concerns in the area of health care, including planning for children with special problems, and gaining information on preventive health and safety measures. The second weekend addressed effective business management techniques, including legal concerns, obtaining funds, and effective financial management.

The final weekend was devoted to recruiting, hiring, and in-service training of child care workers.

## Impact of the project

The MTDDC Program was funded from 1976 to 1978. During that time 409 individuals representing 211 centers attended the workshops. The majority were employed as the child care administrators of full-day centers. The program reached personnel serving 11,250 children or 16.8 percent of the children enrolled in day care in Michigan. While these figures indicate that a very small program can have a wide impact if it can be flexible and become mobile, they also point to a further need for training for other directors. The greatest number of changes reported by participants dealt with improving the accounting system and instituting functional budgeting. Table 1 lists all changes reported through our questionnaires.

Prior to workshop attendance directors reported concerns over particular center practices but were unaware of the most effective means of implementing changes. In these instances follow-up reports of change were dramatic. For instance, prior to the supervision workshop all but two centers reported using informal, unwritten staff evaluation methods. Our follow-up, however, indicated an almost immediate change to written evaluations which were shared with the staff. In contrast, another aspect of successful supervision, that of staff input into decision making, was not an area in which much change was noted. It may well be that the weekend workshop format may be most effective in introducing methods and procedures to organize administration and supervisory tasks more efficiently. Changes involving major adjustments in center organization or policy, such as allowing staff input into decision making, may be more resistant to modification.

Informal conversations and letters sent to us indicate that the workshop series provided directors with an unplanned bonus. By gathering together directors from nearby areas to meet and discuss mutual problems, the Program had served to establish a series of informal support networks to share experiences and ideas.

## Table 1
### Changes in Centers Reported by MTDDC Participants ($N = 86$)

| Change | Frequency |
| --- | --- |
| Improve accounting system and/or institute functional budgeting | 24 |
| Strengthen program development and initiate center evaluation | 12 |
| Nutrition and efficient kitchen management | 7 |
| Revise personnel policies; write job descriptions, institute grievance procedures | 7 |
| Change or initiate staff evaluations | 7 |
| Improve staff relations—accentuate the positive | 7 |
| Write handbooks for staff and parents | 7 |
| Use developmental checklists and folders for individual children | 5 |
| Increase or initiate staff training | 4 |
| Alter time usage by delegating responsibilities | 3 |
| Use preventive maintenance calendar | 3 |
| Develop new forms | 3 |
| More frequent staff meetings incorporating goal setting | 3 |
| Other changes (each mentioned only once) | 20 |

A mobile training program cannot solve problems like replacing sick staff members or volunteers who leave to take paying jobs. The roles of day care directors remain many, varied, and difficult. However, information and resources such as those offered by MTDDC can make the task less overwhelming.

### References

Axelrod, P. G., and Buch, E. R. *Preschool and Child Care Administration*. Ann Arbor, Mich.: University of Michigan, School of Education, 1977. Available from ERIC Clearinghouse on Elementary and Early Childhood Education, University of Illinois, College of Education, Urbana, IL 61801. ED 174 341.

Murphy, L., and Leeper, E. "Caring for Children." (Series) Washington, D.C.: U.S. Department of Health, Education and Welfare, Office of Child Development.

Marion C. Hyson

# "Playing with Kids All Day": Job Stress in Early Childhood Education

Teaching young children is creative, exciting, and fulfilling. It can also be exhausting and frustrating, for novice and veteran alike. The problem of teacher burnout has drawn increased attention, as more and more well-trained, idealistic educators seem to fall victims to work-related stress (Cichon and Koff 1980; Jameson 1980; Kyriacou and Sutcliffe 1977; McGuire 1979; Needle et al. 1980).

Teaching at every level, from preschool to university, has stressful dimensions. The elementary school teacher copes with increased paperwork and an unending procession of new curricula; the high school teacher copes with vandalism and violence (Cichon and Koff 1980; Jameson 1980). The impact of stress on the teacher of young children has just begun to be examined (Duncan 1980; Maslach and Pines 1977; Pines and Maslach 1980). Certainly a career in early childhood education imposes some unique pressures, perhaps less dramatic but just as significant as those associated with other areas of teaching. What are the major sources of stress for teachers of young children? What are the psychological and physical effects of stress? And, most important, how can early childhood educators cope effectively with the special challenges of their profession?

## Defining stress

*Stress* is a term whose meanings seem to multiply with every new book and magazine article. Sometimes the term refers to a list of specific events or life stresses (Holmes and Rahe 1967), while at other times it is used to describe physical responses or stress reactions (Selye 1976). Monat and Lazarus define the psychological state of stress as created by an imbalance between demands and resources:

> . . . the arena that the stress area refers to consists of any event in which environmental demands, internal demands, or both *tax* or *exceed* the adaptive resources of an individual, social system, or tissue system. (Monat and Lazarus 1977, p. 13)

This definition suggests that stress is a complex and highly subjective phenomenon. A sense of being under stress arises from a personal interpretation of and response to a potentially stress-producing event. A minor disturbance may be devastating when one's resources are depleted; conversely, the availability of support may turn a possibly stressful experience into a routine challenge.

## Causes of stress

The complexity of these factors makes each person's stress equation unique.

Marion C. Hyson, Ph.D., is Assistant Professor, Department of Individual and Family Studies, University of Delaware, Newark.

*Early childhood educators may be particularly at risk for stress caused by novelty and uncertainty since there are few other professions where the unexpected is so much to be expected.*

However, research has identified certain conditions that often set the stage for stress. Observation of classroom settings shows that these stressors form a major part of the early childhood teacher's daily routine.

### Novelty and uncertainty

Although variety makes life interesting, too much variety creates distress. A moderate amount of novelty and ambiguity encourages curiosity and exploration. However, a constant barrage of unpredictable stimuli results in physical and psychological overload. In this area, early childhood educators may be particularly at risk, since there are few other professions where the unexpected is so much to be expected.

First, young children are predictably unpredictable. They are developing faster than their older siblings, their interests shift more quickly, and their emotions may swing rapidly from joy to distress. This is part of the profession's appeal, but it is also a source of stress. Every teacher has seen a peaceful music time suddenly erupt into chaos or a smoothly running game dissolve into tearful accusations. A group that is too quiet in September may be too rowdy by Thanksgiving.

Besides this child-created uncertainty, many educators are faced with the uncertainty that they themselves have built into

Hyson

the early childhood curriculum. Most teachers of young children emphasize the importance of exploration, creativity, and spontaneous play. Therefore, the daily routine includes large segments of free time and unstructured materials such as sand, paint, blocks, and water. As many teachers in open programs know, the results, while creative, are often unpredictable. Two children may decide to take all the Styrofoam chips from the collage table and dump them into the water. Another child may decide to paint the table itself instead of the paper on the table. From the teacher's perspective, these unexpected variations are often stress producing (Maslach and Pines 1977).

Elementary and secondary classrooms usually follow an officially mandated curriculum with specific objectives and assessment procedures for each unit of work, while teachers planning early childhood programs experience relative freedom. However, without a prepackaged curriculum and without concrete measures of progress, teachers are often uncertain about just what they are supposed to be doing and how they will know if they are doing it well. Again, this ambiguity may create anxiety and stress.

## Frustrations and barriers

A state of stress often occurs when goals are blocked or thwarted. Teachers of young children may experience more than their share of barriers to their goals.

First, educators set high ideals for themselves. They often choose their profession because of the opportunity to influence children's development in the most formative years (Needle et al. 1980). Teachers impose upon themselves the responsibility for unlocking each child's potential. They often have September fantasies of creating a sensitive, stimulating, perfect classroom like those described in workshops and books.

However, many barriers stand between these ideals and their realization. First,

there are the children themselves. Teachers are reluctant to admit that children can be frustrating and infuriating—but often they are. For example, a teacher may spend hours preparing the materials for a new art activity, only to have a group of children respond by rejecting "that dumb idea."

Parents, too, may seem like roadblocks at times. A teacher may feel that a child's problems would be resolved if only the mother or father would listen to the teacher's suggestions. Yet frequently this well-intentioned advice is ignored or even angrily rejected.

Relationships with colleagues are another potential source of frustration. Many programs for young children have small staffs that must work more closely than the teachers in larger schools. The resulting atmosphere can be both supportive and stressful. In a small program there is no way to avoid an irritating teacher aide or a critical director who always arrives just in time to see the worst part of the morning.

Other barriers are less immediate but just as stress producing. Teachers today are threatened by a lack of job security and restricted mobility. Children's services are often the first victims of funding cuts. From the independent nursery school struggling to raise enough money to buy art materials to the city-wide day care plan that is expensive for the taxpayers, program planners repeatedly find their ideals punctured by the sharp edge of economic and political reality.

## Pressures to achieve

Our society is highly achievement oriented. Those who succeed in a visible way are rewarded, while those who fail are given little help in dealing with their failure. Although most professions carry with them some achievement pressure, the field of early childhood education has its own occupational hazards.

"Playing with kids all day" has never been considered a high-status profession.

Some teachers leave the classroom in order to obtain the satisfactions of more highly regarded and highly paid professions. Others may deal with their need for achievement by placing inordinate demands for perfection on themselves and the classes they teach. Their classrooms must have the most imaginative bulletin boards, the most unusual art projects, and the best-behaved children. In the long run, standards such as these are both inappropriate and stress producing.

### Separation and loss

Good teachers develop a special bond with the young children in their care. In the early years, teachers are involved with every aspect of a child's life. Especially in day care settings, teachers share in some of the most exciting moments of human development—the first step, the first word, the first friendship with another child. The attachment that grows out of these shared experiences may be deeply felt by both child and adult.

These attachments are part of what makes teaching worthwhile. However, they also make it difficult to maintain the attitude of "detached concern" (Lief and Fox 1963) that is crucial to effective professional behavior. Some teachers take on the role of surrogate parent or child saver, especially when a child's parents may not be the most loving or competent caregivers. This role may lead to a subtle competitive struggle with the children's families or with other teachers.

Even teachers who resist these competitive urges are faced with the reality that at the end of the year or as children join new groups, "their" children will be gone. Although the departure of a few children may be accompanied by a sigh of relief, teachers usually become closely identified with each group. Thus the year-end letdown may be tinged with grief and depression. Some teachers respond by actively planning for next year's group. After a few years, others shield themselves from the pain of loss by refusing to allow these attachments to develop. Their relationships with children may remain at a briskly efficient but superficial level.

## The effects of stress

For many teachers, then, the situations just described can be sources of stress. What is the impact of this state of stress—this sense that one's resources are inadequate to meet outer and inner demands? Stress has both psychological and physical consequences.

The effects of stress on psychological functioning are not always detrimental. A moderate degree of arousal or tension may actually increase problem-solving ability (Berlyne 1960). A teacher with ten years of experience may be at her best when she is being observed by visiting students. Or the challenge of being assigned a child with special needs may stimulate another teacher to develop exciting new approaches for the entire group. Even when goals are blocked, a person may react at first with constructive, persistent attempts to find ways around the barrier. However, when stress is prolonged or extreme, research shows that people react in less effective ways (Wortman and Brehm 1975). Their ability to find solutions becomes impaired. They may be overwhelmed by feelings of anger. Finally, if their efforts have no apparent effect, many people finally stop trying. Teachers and other human service professionals may burn out, drop out, or retreat into apathy or cynicism (Freudenberger 1977). At its most extreme, this helpless behavior pattern may lead to a depression that penetrates every area of life (Seligman 1975).

Because the mind and the body are so closely related, the effects of stress are physical as well as psychological. Selye (1976) has been a pioneer in analyzing the physiological changes that take place as our bodies attempt to adapt to unpleasant stimuli. He observes that although these adaptive efforts may have helped our evolutionary ancestors mobilize for "fight or flight," the world of today creates prolonged, complex stress-producing situations for which such responses may be maladaptive. The toll that these alarm reactions take is reflected in a variety of symptoms (Pelletier 1977). Muscle tension may result in chronic headaches. Immune systems may become less effective, lowering resistance to disease. For example, one formerly healthy teacher found that a year with a difficult group of children was punctuated with repeated bouts of flu. The following year, with a less demanding class, her health returned.

## Coping with stress

Despite these potentially harmful effects, human beings are not simply passive victims of stress. We are capable of an almost infinite array of active, adaptive responses to stressful events. According to White (1974), these coping behaviors can be grouped in three categories: seeking information, maintaining autonomy, and maintaining internal equilibrium. All of these strategies of adaptation may be useful additions to the teacher's antistress repertoire.

### Seeking information

We have seen the pressures that uncertainty puts on teachers of young children. As White points out, by seeking information one is able to reduce some of this uncertainty and make what is unexpected seem reassuringly familiar.

Early childhood educators need to inform themselves about children in general and about each child in their care. Although a teacher will never be able to predict what two-year-olds will do next, the teacher can become thoroughly familiar with the developmental characteristics of this age group. In addition, specific in-

Stephanie H. Meye

*The effects of stress on psychological functioning are not always detrimental. A moderate degree of arousal or tension may actually increase problem-solving ability.*

formation about a child's family, early experiences, and likes and dislikes helps to make her or his behavior more predictable and therefore less stressful for the teacher.

It is also possible to plan a curriculum that provides structure without sacrificing flexibility. Both children and adults benefit from knowing what to expect and what is expected of them (Freudenberger 1977). Sometimes simple changes in the room or materials will provide enough information about these expectations (Pines and Maslach 1980). Perhaps the children who dumped the Styrofoam chips into the water did so because the uncovered water table was temptingly close to the collage area. Perhaps the table painter needs larger sheets of paper to accommodate grandiose designs. In addition, a predictable daily schedule, definite transition routines, and clear statements of rules help reduce uncertainty without destroying the spontaneity of a good early childhood program.

Teachers of young children often experience stress because they receive little direct feedback about their performance or that of their class. This problem can be managed without imposing a regime of daily tests. Many teachers create their own informal monitoring system such as a loose-leaf notebook with sections for weekly objectives and daily plans and sections with information about each child. Each Friday this notebook is brought up to date and used as a basis for evaluation and planning. Writing it down gives teachers a sense of accomplishment and progress. A difficult three-year-old may still be hitting other children in March, but the notebook reminds the teacher that the child was biting in January.

Sometimes teachers overlook the value of their colleagues as sources of information. Novice teachers may be afraid to expose their inexperience by soliciting advice about an activity or a troublesome child, while veterans may not want to shatter their perfect image. This reluctance is understandable, yet the stress of uncertainty may be far greater than the stress of possible criticism. Teachers can give one another feedback in many ways. At one day care center, teachers regularly visit one another's classes; another school has monthly potluck lunches where staff share problems and solutions in a nonthreatening atmosphere.

## Maintaining and regaining autonomy

One of the most universal sources of stress is the feeling that we have lost control (Cichon and Koff 1980; Seligman 1975). Therefore, a great deal of effective coping must be directed toward the goal of maintaining or regaining autonomy. However, many people, especially women, have been socialized to believe that they have no right to protest. They would rather rage inside than calmly inform a superior that something is wrong.

Difficult as it may be, direct and assertive confrontation is a very powerful means of regaining control. However,

there are other less obvious paths to increased autonomy.

For example, many teachers feel like victims when a new program is imposed by their administration (Cichon and Koff 1980). Their objections may be directed less at the content than at their lack of choice about the program. However, they probably have more options than they recognize. In small ways, they can begin to make the curriculum their own. Perhaps they can choose when to schedule the activities, which to begin with, and with which children. They may also be able to vary the predetermined curriculum by using somewhat different materials or adapting the details of certain games to the interests of their own group. These kinds of changes may or may not improve the curriculum, but they will undoubtedly increase the teachers' sense of personal independence and control.

## Maintaining internal equilibrium

Seeking information and maintaining autonomy are strategies directed at the stressful event itself. However, White (1974) points out that effective coping must deal not only with the objective demands of the situation but also with the emotions (anxiety, anger, distress) often experienced under stress. Often, little can be done to change the situation—a teacher may be paired with an uncongenial coworker; budget cutbacks may have left a center with too many children in too cramped a space.

In unavoidably stressful circumstances, children often comfort themselves with the safe and familiar. One child may suck her thumb; another clings to his denim jacket and retreats to his cubby.

We often envy children their security blankets, but adults can devise their own ways to detach their minds and emotions from an impossible situation. Comfortable objects, like a favorite old sweater or a hanging plant from home, may provide a secure anchor in a new and threatening environment.

Exercise is a comfort strategy which has psychological as well as physical benefits. Even clinically depressed patients often improve when put on a regimen of daily, vigorous exercise. Although teachers may feel that running is the last thing they want to do after a day of picking up blocks and changing diapers, exercise has a way of increasing energy rather than depleting it. During the day, a jog around the yard with the children, or an indoor dance session, may make everyone feel better.

Relaxation techniques (Benson 1975; Pelletier 1977) may further diminish the effects of anxiety and tension. Some people enjoy the discipline of yoga or meditation; others find simple breathing and stretching exercises more beneficial. Even in the middle of a hectic morning, it is possible to get into the habit of body monitoring, noticing signs of stress, and making a deliberate effort to relax.

Other people may also help teachers achieve internal equilibrium not necessarily by giving advice, but by sharing and accepting feelings of anger or fear. The availability of support systems, whether family members, friends, or colleagues, has repeatedly been identified as a factor in effective coping (Caplan and Killilea 1976; Maslach and Pines 1977).

## Coping as an individual

Despite all the self-help books on the market, there is no such thing as a cookbook approach to coping. Although a flexible repertoire of resources is needed to manage stress, each person develops a distinctive coping style, based on temperament, early experiences, and personality traits. Some rely primarily on *seeking information*; they read every book and attend every meeting. Others emphasize *maintaining autonomy*; they actively try to change what exists, or substitute something better. Finally, some people rely on the maintenance of *internal equilibrium*, a kind of inner comfort, to get through the difficult stretches.

Whatever one's preferred style, the most important first step is to recognize stress when it appears. Teachers should be as sensitive to their own feelings as they are to the children's. The next step is to stop and identify the possible causes of the stress. Simply recognizing the reason for anger or fear can frequently alleviate these emotions. Finally, it is important to plan coping strategies that are appropriate to the situation and consistent with one's personal style.

Given the day-to-day demands of teaching young children, it is probably impossible to eliminate stress entirely. Nor do we want to. It is true that prolonged or extreme stress can lead to breakdown. Yet, when seen as challenges rather than as threats, stressful situations may provide unique opportunities for personal and professional growth.

### References

Benson, H. *The Relaxation Response.* New York: Morrow, 1975.

Berlyne, D. *Conflict, Arousal and Curiosity.* New York: McGraw-Hill, 1960.

Caplan, G., and Killilea, M., eds. *Support Systems and Mutual Help: Multidisciplinary Explorations.* New York: Grune & Stratton, 1976.

Cichon, D. J., and Koff, R. H. "Stress and Teaching." *NASSP Bulletin* 64 (1980): 91-104.

Duncan, C. W. "Coping with Stress." *Day Care and Early Education* 7 (1980): 18-21.

Freudenberger, H. J. "Burn-Out: Occupational Hazard of the Child Care Worker." *Child Care Quarterly* 6, no. 2 (1977): 90-99.

Holmes, T., and Rahe, R. "The Social Readjustment Rating Scale." *Journal of Psychosomatic Research* 11 (1967): 213-218.

Jameson, S. A. "Distress Signals." *School and Community* 66 (1980): 17-19.

Kyriacou, C., and Sutcliffe, J. "Teacher Stress:

A Review." *Educational Review* 29, no. 4 (1977): 299-306.

Lief, H. I., and Fox, R. C. "Training for 'Detached Concern' in Medical Students." In *The Psychological Basis of Medical Practice*, ed. H. I. Lief, V. F. Lief, and N. R. Lief. New York: Harper & Row, 1963.

McGuire, W. M. "Teacher Burnout." *Today's Education* 64, no. 5 (1979): 34-39.

Maslach, C., and Pines, A. "The Burn-Out Syndrome in the Day Care Setting." *Child Care Quarterly* 6, no. 2 (1977): 100-113.

Monat, A., and Lazarus, R., eds. *Stress and Coping.* New York: Columbia University Press, 1977.

Needle, R. H.; Griffin, T.; Svendsen, R.; and Berney, C. "Teacher Stress: Sources and Consequences." *Journal of School Health* 50 (1980): 96-99.

Pelletier, K. R. *Mind As Healer, Mind As Slayer.* New York: Delta, 1977.

Pines, A., and Maslach, C. "Combatting Staff Burn-Out in a Day Care Center: A Case Study." *Child Care Quarterly* 9, no. 1 (1980): 5-16.

Seligman, M. *Helplessness: On Depression, Development and Death.* San Francisco: Freeman, 1975.

Selye, H. *The Stress of Life.* New York: McGraw-Hill, 1976.

White, R. W. "Strategies of Adaptation: An Attempt at Systematic Description." In *Coping and Adaptation*, ed. G. V. Coelho, D. A. Hamburg, and J. E. Adams. New York: Basic Books, 1974.

Wortman, C., and Brehm, J. W. "Responses to Uncontrollable Outcomes: An Integration of Reactance Theory and the Learned Helplessness Model." In *Advances in Experimental Social Psychology. Vol. 8*, ed. L. Berkowitz. New York: Academic Press, 1975.

Hyson

# NAEYC Position Statement on Nomenclature, Salaries, Benefits, and the Status of the Early Childhood Profession

## Preamble

One of the major goals of NAEYC is to facilitate the professional growth of people working with/for young children. As a step toward professional development, NAEYC's Governing Board has formulated several recommendations toward the goal of enhancing both the self-image and public perception of Early Childhood professionals.

NAEYC's Governing Board recommends:

1) the establishment of common nomenclature for Early Childhood personnel who work in a variety of settings with children ranging in age from birth through eight, with clear definitions of the roles and responsibilities and the qualifications required to fulfill each role, and
2) the establishment of guidelines for appropriate salaries and benefits for Early Childhood personnel.

## Background information

Research during the past two decades has provided much evidence that far more social, cognitive, and emotional development occurs in the early childhood years than was previously recognized. A large knowledge base of child development now exists from which to plan appropriate environments for children.

Just as our knowledge of child development has expanded, the need for programs for young children has increased greatly. The principal environment for childrearing for all children in our society is the home, but for most children some care which supplements that which the family provides will be necessary. In rapidly increasing numbers families in a variety of circumstances are seeking child care while parents work. Currently, about half of the women with children younger than the age of 6 are in the labor force, and the number is expected to increase.

## Position Statement

In response to the tremendous need for care which supplements and complements that which the family provides, Early Childhood programs are expected to expand and multiply. As such programs increase in number, it is equally important that they reflect the knowledge that exists concerning how best to provide optimal care and education for young children.

Research clearly shows that a major factor in the quality and effectiveness of programs for young children is the specialized education of the staff. Parents have every right to assume that people who are paid to care for and educate their children have the attitudes, skills, and knowledge which will ensure not only that all children will receive safe and healthful care, but will also be helped to realize their fullest potential.

As the number of Early Childhood settings proliferates, it becomes extremely important that the individuals who staff them are adequately qualified to fulfill the roles and responsibilities assigned to them. The role of the Early Childhood staff member is more complex than the role of the traditional teacher. In addition to instructing and facilitating learning, Early Childhood personnel are expected to provide child care, emotional support and guidance, and to work with adults to a far greater extent than teachers of older children.

In actuality there is not one single role performed by Early Childhood personnel, but rather several roles, each requiring different degrees of knowledge and skills. For instance, the skills and knowledge required of an individual who assists the leader of a group of children are different from those required of the group leader. Similarly the requirements for a group leader are different from those of a program director.

Recognition of levels of qualifications is one means of assuring that appropriately qualified individuals assume the various roles in the field of Early Childhood Education. This document recommends various levels of professional responsibility, the competencies required of each level, and the means for achieving those competencies.

The field of Early Childhood Education values diversity. These recommendations reflect the concept that Early Childhood knowledge and skills can be acquired through different paths. For example, the field welcomes the pre-professional, a person without a formal credential who has been professionally screened and who will develop further skills through supervised experience with children and participation in staff development. The field of Early Childhood Education also benefits from the existence of a competency-based assessment system administered by the National Child Development Associate (CDA) Credentialing Program, which identifies and recognizes individual competencies that may have been acquired through diverse patterns of training and life experiences. At the same time, people enter the field of Early Childhood Education through college education with supervised field experiences. In view of the intensity and level of supervision involved in such programs, most states accept the completion of such training as evidence of competence.

### Definitions

**Early Childhood personnel**—adults who are employed to work with children in group settings serving children ranging in age from birth through eight

**Group of children**—the children assigned to a staff member or team of staff members, occupying an individual classroom or well-defined physical space within a larger room

# Recommendations for nomenclature and qualifications for Early Childhood Educators

The Early Childhood professional path consists of four levels. The following is a description of the knowledge and skills required for each level and the ways in which these can be acquired. See Figure 1 for a summary of this information.

# Figure 1. Early Childhood professional development paths.

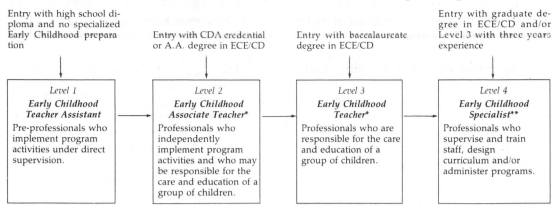

Entry with high school diploma and no specialized Early Childhood preparation

Entry with CDA credential or A.A. degree in ECE/CD

Entry with baccalaureate degree in ECE/CD

Entry with graduate degree in ECE/CD and/or Level 3 with three years experience

| Level 1 | Level 2 | Level 3 | Level 4 |
|---|---|---|---|
| **Early Childhood Teacher Assistant** | **Early Childhood Associate Teacher*** | **Early Childhood Teacher*** | **Early Childhood Specialist**** |
| Pre-professionals who implement program activities under direct supervision. | Professionals who independently implement program activities and who may be responsible for the care and education of a group of children. | Professionals who are responsible for the care and education of a group of children. | Professionals who supervise and train staff, design curriculum and/or administer programs. |

*Early Childhood Associate Teachers and Early Childhood Teachers may perform similar roles and functions. The different titles reflect the different patterns of formal education received and the extent of background knowledge of child development.

**The Early Childhood Specialist can become qualified to perform a number of optional roles (such as Program Administrator in agencies with multiple programs, Resource and Referral Specialist, Parent Educator, Researcher, Policy Analyst) with successful completion of specialized education through college courses or formal credit for life experience.

## Level 1—Early Childhood Teacher Assistant

Level 1 is an entry-level position. People at this level are pre-professionals who implement program activities under direct supervision of the professional staff. Such supervision occurs directly in the classroom by an Early Childhood Associate Teacher or Early Childhood Teacher in charge of the group of children who models professional skills and contributes to the growth of the individual serving in the assistant role.

This level requires basic and minimal personal qualities which include a potential for and willingness to improve one's skills in working with young children, mental and physical health, a genuine liking of children, ability to get along with other adults, and general dependability.

The basic educational requirement for entry at this level is a high school diploma or equivalent. No specialized Early Childhood preparation is required for entry at this level, but once employed the individual should participate in professional development programs.

## Level 2—Early Childhood Associate Teacher

Level 2 consists of Early Childhood Associate Teachers, professionals who independently implement program activities and who may be responsible for the care and education of a group of children.

To be qualified as an Early Childhood Associate Teacher, the individual must be able to demonstrate competency in six basic goals as developed by the National Child Development Associate (CDA) Credentialing Program:

- to establish and maintain a safe, healthy, learning environment
- to advance physical and intellectual competence of children
- to support social and emotional development and provide positive guidance and discipline
- to establish positive and productive relationships with families
- to ensure a well-run, purposeful program responsive to participant needs
- to maintain a commitment to professionalism

These qualifications can be achieved by successfully completing either a system of competency evaluation such as the one implemented by the CDA National Credentialing Program or an associate degree in Early Childhood Education or Child Development. The attainment of these competencies requires supervised field experiences in appropriate settings with young children.

**Level 3—Early Childhood Teacher**

Level 3 consists of Early Childhood Teachers, professionals who are responsible for the care and education of a group of children. Individuals at Levels 2 and 3 may perform similar roles and functions. The different titles reflect the different patterns of formal education received and the extent of background knowledge of child development.

The qualifications of an Early Childhood Teacher are presented in NAEYC's *Teacher Education Guidelines for Four- and Five-Year-Programs* (1982). To be qualified as an Early Childhood Teacher, the individual must demonstrate all Level 1 and Level 2 competencies and also possess theoretical knowledge and practical skills in:

- human development through the lifespan, with special emphasis on cognitive, language, physical, social, and emotional development, both typical and atypical, from birth through age eight

- historical, philosophical, psychological, and social foundations of Early Childhood Education
- curriculum for young children, including goal setting and developmentally appropriate content and methodology
- observation and recording of children's behavior for purposes of assistance in achieving goals, providing for individual needs, and appropriately guiding children
- preparation for working in settings that include atypical children: understanding the needs of developmentally diverse children, and recognizing conditions requiring assistance from other professionals
- communication and conference techniques, interpersonal and intergroup relations, and techniques for working with staff as an instructional team
- family and community relations, including communication with parents and parent involvement
- awareness of value issues and the existence of codes of ethics in professional life
- comprehension of cultural diversity and its implications
- legislation and public policy as it affects children, families, and programs for children

Completion of a baccalaureate degree in Early Childhood Education or Child Development from an accredited college or university is used to predict the existence of the competencies required of an Early Childhood Teacher. The attainment of these competencies requires supervised field experiences in appropriate settings with young children. The requirements specified for this level do not exclude people who wish to enter Level 3 primarily on the basis of experience in the field, as colleges are increasingly accepting relevant experiences as evidence of partial fulfillment of degree requirements.

## Level 4—Early Childhood Specialist

Level 4 consists of professionals who supervise and train staff, design curriculum, and/or administer programs. Every Early Childhood program should have at least one qualified Early Childhood Specialist, who in small programs may also be the Director or Master Teacher. Larger programs should have more than one Early Childhood Specialist.

To qualify as an Early Childhood Specialist, an individual must be able to demonstrate all Level 1, Level 2, and Level 3 competencies as well as competency in the following areas:

- designing and supervising the implementation of developmentally appropriate program content and curriculum
- designing and implementing appropriate staff development activities and adequate supervision of personnel and volunteers

Completion of the following education and experience is used to predict the existence of the qualifications required of an Early Childhood Specialist: baccalaureate degree in Early Childhood Education or Child Development from an accredited college or university plus successful completion of at least three years of full-time teaching experience with young children and/or an advanced degree.

The Early Childhood Specialist role requires expertise in the areas of curriculum design, supervision of adults, and staff development. This expertise may be obtained through specific administrative coursework within the baccalaureate program or may require additional training and experience beyond the baccalaureate degree.

***Optional roles for Early Childhood Specialists.*** The Early Childhood Specialist can acquire additional competencies to qualify for a variety of optional roles. Most frequently, Early Childhood Specialists act as Administrators or Curriculum Specialists.

However Early Childhood Specialists may also serve as Resource and Referral Specialists, Parent Educators, Researchers, or Policy Analysts.

## Salary recommendations

Salaries in the Early Childhood field should be on a par with other professional groups with comparable training and responsibilities.

*Level 1—Early Childhood Teacher Assistant*—should receive at entry at least a salary no less than the U.S. Department of Labor minimum wage, and there should be regular increments offered for continuous service and for participation in internal and external staff development activities.

*Level 2—Early Childhood Associate Teacher*—should receive at entry at least a salary equal to others with comparable degrees and supervised experience, with increases based on performance and participation in additional educational opportunities.

*Level 3—Early Childhood Teacher*—should receive at entry at least a salary equal to others with comparable degrees and supervised experience, with increases based on performance and participation in additional education opportunities.

*Level 4—Early Childhood Specialist*—should receive entry salary at least equal to other human service professionals with comparable degrees and supervised professional experience. Additional increments should be based on performance and participation in additional educational opportunities.

## Benefits recommendations

All professional and pre-professional staff working full time should receive the following benefits, in addition to mandatory Social Security and workmen's compensation benefits. All professional and pre-professional staff working less than full time should receive the following benefits on a pro-rated basis:

1) health benefits (medical coverage) offered by the employer, and paid or co-paid by the employee
2) regular breaks during the work day, paid time for preparation and for work with parents
3) staff development opportunities
4) vacation time, sick leave, and personal/professional days should be available for all full-time employees on a schedule that increases with length of time employed

The employer is encouraged to also offer additional employee benefits:

1) child care
2) additional retirement plan
3) life insurance

*Adopted in July 1984*
*by the NAEYC Governing Board*

# NAEYC Position Statement on Child Care Licensing*

## Rationale

Findings from the 1980 census show that more than 50 percent of mothers of young children in the United States are employed outside the home. Therefore an increasing number of parents are seeking child care settings within their communities which will nurture, protect, and educate their children. Child care licensing is an official acknowledgment of the public responsibility to maintain healthy, safe, and developmentally appropriate conditions for children during the time they spend in child care. Licensing is a form of consumer protection for parents and personal protection for children.

Child care is provided in a variety of settings reflecting the diverse needs of today's families. These settings can be grouped into three major categories— center care, group home care, and family day care. In most states, centers usually provide care for 12 or more children, group homes for 7 to 12 children, and family day care homes for 6 or fewer children. States without group home care provisions generally define centers as settings for the care of 7 or more children.

Each of these settings may provide care for infants, toddlers, preschool children, school-age children, and/or children with special needs. All three types of settings may provide full-day or part-day care on either a regular or flexible basis. Standards are needed for all three types of care to ensure that children are protected and educated in a nurturing environment.

The goal of child care licensing should be to assure a level of good quality care while taking into account the different types of settings and the numbers of children served in each. Agencies charged with enforcing licensing standards should be publicly visible so that individuals caring for children know about them and can seek technical assistance from them. The standards represented in the licensing statutes should be widely disseminated so that parents will be in a better position to locate and monitor licensed child care settings. In addition to licensing statutes, health, building, and fire safety codes must also be met. The inspection, monitoring, and enforcement of all applicable statutes should be coordinated to ensure that personnel and fiscal resources are wisely used.

## Position

The National Association for the Education of Young Children affirms the importance of child care licensing as a vehicle for controlling the quality of care for children in settings outside their own homes. NAEYC supports licensing standards that:

- take into account the nature of the child care setting and the number of children to be served
- set standards for centers, group homes, and family homes
- include care of children from infancy through school age

*The governing board of NAEYC has adopted a more recent position statement on this subject entitled *NAEYC Position Statement on Licensing and Other Forms of Regulation of Early Childhood Programs in Centers and Family Day Care*; it is available as a brochure (NAEYC order #535). See p. 66 for more details.

- cover full-time, part-time, and drop-in care arrangements
- include facilities serving children with disabilities
- reflect current research demonstrating the relationship between the quality of care provided and such factors as group size, staff-child ratio, and staff knowledge and training in early childhood education or child development
- are clearly written, enforceable, and vigorously enforced
- are administered by agencies which are known about and accessible to parents and the individuals providing care for children
- include written policies describing processes for initial licensing, renewal inspections, revocation, and appeals

Because licensing requirements stipulate the basic necessary conditions for protecting children's well-being, NAEYC firmly believes that all forms of supplementary care of young children should be licensed and that exemptions from licensing standards should not be permitted. Whenever a single program or group of programs is exempted or given special treatment, the entire fabric of licensing is weakened.

It is a public responsibility to ensure that child care programs promote optimal development in a safe and healthy environment. All parents who need child care have the right to choose from settings which will protect and educate their children in a nurturing environment.

*Adopted on November 2, 1983*
*by the NAEYC Governing Board*

## For more information

For further information about the licensing requirements in your state, contact your state licensing agency or the NAEYC Information Service, 1834 Connecticut Avenue, N.W., Washington, DC 20009. NAEYC distributes information on the regulation of early childhood programs through a collaborative effort with Work/Family Directions, a joint venture of Rodgers & Associates and Wheelock College, formed in 1983 to create a national network of community-based resource and referral agencies for employer clients.

Single copies of the more recent brochure *NAEYC Position Statement on Licensing and Other Forms of Regulation of Early Childhood Programs in Centers and Family Day Care* are 50¢ each or $10 for 100 copies. Order NAEYC #535. Copyright © 1987 by the National Association for the Education of Young Children. All rights reserved.

# 2

# Build a Good Program

*Curriculum Is What Happens* was the title of a popular NAEYC book, and with good reason, because young children learn *every* minute of the day. The best curriculum, therefore, is built around high quality teachers; an environment filled with potential for learning; and warm, respectful interactions between all adults and children. As an administrator, you are responsible for ensuring that you and your staff consider all these elements in program planning.

Millie Almy succinctly describes why play is so important in the lives of all young children.

Further evidence of the kinds of everyday activities that foster children's learning are described by Joseph Stevens. He cites research which clearly documents children's need for challenging intellectual experiences.

Play and intellectual experiences are combined when good learning materials are offered. *Toys: Tools for Learning* shows how toys contribute to development and offers suggestions for toys appropriate for children from ages two through six. You may want to obtain copies of the borchure on choosing good toys to distribute to parents as well.

Christine Cataldo suggests how the best facets of several approaches can be blended in programs for infants and toddlers. Her examples include techniques and materials that are especially suited to the learning needs of very young children.

Transitions between activities are just as important as all other times of the day. Harriet Alger demonstrates how scheduling teachers and children, room arrangements, and other considerations must be carefully selected and monitored to maintain a high quality program.

# Reaffirmations: *Speaking Out for Children*

In response to today's retrogressive attitudes toward human needs, the U.S. National Comm ee for Early Childhood Education of the Organisation Mondiale pour L'Education Prescolaire (OMEP), th Association for Childhood Education International, and the National Association for the Education of You g Children urge child advocates to speak out about public responsibility for assuring children's basic ights. This series of statements, compiled by Monroe Cohen, Director of the Queens College Institute for Family and Community Life, is not copyrighted, and may be freely reproduced with credit to the authors.

## A Child's Right to Play
### *by* Millie Almy

*University of California*
*Berkeley, California*

Why play?

Children's play is often depreciated by adults who think of it as a mere time filler rather than an essential component of healthy development. Were these adults to follow the lead of an increasing number of researchers and teachers, examining closely what children do when they play, they might understand why play is so essential to the child's well-being and competence.

Play is a very special activity with distinctive features that set it apart from other behaviors.

*When children play* their interest is self-directed. They are intrinsically motivated to solve problems that stem from either the physical or the social world and are important to them.

*When children play* they are not as concerned with particular goals or ends as they are with the variety of ways a goal may be achieved. In play they experiment with possibilities and become more flexible in thinking and problem solving.

*When children play* their behavior is not literal. Much of what they do stands for something else. They represent their experiences symbolically. Their ability to conceive objects and situations as if they were something else is thought by researchers to contribute to later skill in hypothetical reasoning and the understanding of abstract symbols and logical transformations.

*When children play* they free themselves from external rules, from the restrictions imposed by adult regulations, and from the realities imposed by time and space. Paradoxically, however, children generate rules for their play situations and establish roles and plots. Close study of such play reveals that children's negotiations with one another are complex. They make longer utterances and use more varied vocabulary than in other situations.

*When children play* with objects they discover what they can do with them. Increasing their own repertoire of behaviors in this way contrasts with the exploration of objects in which they establish what properties the objects have. Both play and exploration, involving on the one hand the familiar, and on the other the novel, are essential to children's understanding of the world and of their own powers.

Finally, *when children play* they are actively engaged. Their attention is not easily distracted. Children who are unable to so involve themselves in play signal that something has gone seriously amiss in their development.

Adults who give serious consideration to these distinctive features of children's play will recognize that play is as essential to the child's all-around development as adequate food and rest. They will understand why those who wrote the United Nations' *Declarations of the Rights of the Child* set the right to play parallel to such rights as special protection, adequate nutrition, housing, health care, and education.

Children realize their right to play when the adults around them appreciate and respect their playfulness and provide ample time and space for them to play. Materials and equipment are also important, although they need not be elaborate. The crucial role that parents and teachers have in responding to and supporting children's play ideas, while not overwhelming them, becomes increasingly evident.

Play, the child's way of coming to terms with personal experience in and knowledge of the physical and social world, is never sufficient in itself. Adults must also provide ever-expanding opportunities for children to learn from their own actions and observations, as well as from being told, the nature of the people and of the things that surround them. But it is in play that children come to terms with those realities, comprehend them more, and more effectively create new possibilities for dealing with them.

# research in review

## Everyday
## Experience and
## Intellectual Development

### by Joseph H. Stevens, Jr.

What types of everyday experiences are most critical for young children's intellectual development? Are language-mastery experiences more important than other types for intellectual development? Are experiences that children structure for themselves more strongly related to the development of intelligence than are adult-structured experiences?

Studies by Carew (1980) have provided data about some of these important questions. Carew conducted naturalistic observations of home-reared and day care children in the second and third years of life to record their everyday experiences, and then examined the relationship of these experiences to children's test performance.

Children were observed in their ongoing activities in a 10-minute cycle of a 15-second observation period followed by a 15-second period when the observer dictated a narrative description of what had happened. Usually four 10-minute observations were made during frequent visits beginning when infants were 12 months old and continuing until their 33-month birthday. The data collected were a sampling of the children's moment-to-moment experiences and not a continuous record of the ebb and flow of experience that would be obtained from systems such as those used by ecological psychologists (Scott 1980).

Observations were then coded according to their intellectual value, their content, and the roles of the principal actors. Four types of presumably intellectually valuable experiences were coded: language-mastery; spatial, fine-motor; concrete reasoning and problem-solving; and expressive-artistic. Language-mastery activities were ones in which the child was encouraged to engage in or practiced describing, classifying, comparing, defining, or where vocabulary expansion or grammatical improvement was the focus. Spatial and fine-motor experiences involved the discrimination or ordering of objects by perceptual characteristics or fitting, stacking, matching, or building. Experiments involving concepts like gravity, volume, trajectory, or reflection were coded as reasoning and problem-solving experiences. Expressive-artistic experiences were ones that emphasized the refinement of representational abilities, be they in activities like construction or in role play. Activities considered to be less intellectually valuable were coded either as play-exploration; execution of simple routines like chores, routine talk, gross-motor activities; or basic care. Socio-emotional experiences included attention seeking, social games, preparation for an activity, or restriction. Average inter-observer agreement between both coders

This is one of a regular series of columns edited by Joseph H. Stevens, Jr., Ph.D., Professor, Department of Early Childhood Education, Georgia State University, Atlanta.

and observers was high, and ranged from .76 to 1.00.

Children were administered the Stanford-Binet Test of Intelligence, a spatial abilities test, and a language test. The spatial measure assessed the ability to match shapes and complete wholes by replacing missing pieces or putting pieces together. The language measure assessed picture vocabulary, as well as understanding of grammatical forms, such as plurals, possessives, comparatives, prepositions, and action agents. Children were tested at 12, 24, and 36 months of age.

The 23 children observed in the home study had varied socioeconomic backgrounds, and came from families of unskilled, skilled, managerial, and professional workers. Fifteen of the children were female and all were White. Parents identified themselves as Catholic, Protestant, Jewish, or unaffiliated. The day care sample was similar in other dimensions but less diverse socioeconomically; all families had middle or high socioeconomic status.

## The nature of everyday experience

Along major dimensions of activity and interaction patterns, the nature of children's activities, whether in day care or at home, was remarkably similar during the period studied. For the children at home, 36 percent of their time was spent in solitary activities; 46 percent in interaction with others; 12 percent in watching others; and 6 percent in watching television. In the day care group 38 percent of the children's time was spent in solitary activities; 48 percent in interaction with others; and 5 percent watching others; no time was spent watching television.

Similar parallels in experience were revealed when time in specific types of activities was examined. Across the entire 12- to 23-month period, the home-reared children spent about 19 percent of their time in intellectually valuable experiences; 21 percent in simpler, exploratory play; 10 percent in basic care activities; 4 percent in gross-motor activities; and 9 percent in routine talk. For the day care children, across the entire period, children devoted 27 percent of their time to intellectually valuable experiences; 18 percent to exploratory play; 10 percent to basic care; 8 percent to gross-motor activities; and 6 percent to routine talk. Whether any differences that did occur in the everyday experiences of the home care and the day care children were significant was not reported.

The amount of time that children devoted to these types of activities did change across the time period. Such changes were reported only for the home-reared group. There was a significant increase in the amount of time devoted to intellectually valuable activities and a decrease in time spent in exploratory play. This increase in intellectual activities was due primarily to more time spent in language, spatial, and expressive activities. There was no accompanying increase in the amount of time children devoted to concrete reasoning experiences. There were significant increases in time spent in routine talk and in preparatory experiences. Decreases across this period were noted for time spent in basic care, attention seeking, as well as in exploratory play.

## Types of home experiences related to intelligence

Significant relationships were found between specific types of experiences and children's intellectual development. The more intelligent 3-year-olds were those observed to spend more time in intellectually valuable activities and in preparatory activities between 12 and 33 months. The types of intellectually valuable experiences that they participated in were more likely to be language-focused, rather than ones which emphasized spatial, expressive, or reasoning abilities. These high-scoring children were more likely to have experienced a higher proportion of language-focused, intellectually valuable activities in which the adult (usually the parent) played a central role, ones in which the parent in the 15-second interval adopted the lead role or was jointly responsible with the child for the intellectual richness of the episode. It was not until around 30 months that the proportion of language episodes in which the child adopted a decisive role in the interaction predicted IQ scores.

These correlational data seem to suggest that providing children with language-focused activities in which the parent or adult actively participates is critical for the development of intelligence. The nature of this parent participation may change across the 12- to 33-month period observed. Early in the period when children's expressive abilities are just emerging as one- and two-word utterances, the parent's responsiveness through expansion and elaboration provides critical new information as well as further models of expressive language. During this period, rich language stimulation appears to be very important. As children's expressive abilities grow, opportunities to practice oral language in a task situation in interaction with an adult takes on increasing importance. But during either period both actors (adult and child) play important roles; yet the relative contribution that the child makes to the interaction and its intellectual value increases as the child matures.

The research about maternal teaching style and that about parent training programs is supportive of this central role of the parent as a language model. Recall Hess and Shipman's study (1965) in which the degree to which the parent used abstract and task-specific language was related to children's success in learning to perform the tasks. Gray and Wandersman (1980) suggest that the programs that trained parents to use verbal stimulation strategies were particularly powerful in enhancing children's intellectual development.

What types of experiences between 12 and 24 months were predictive of children's ability to design and generate their own intellectually valuable activities at 30–33 months? Surprisingly, these were not the experiences generated by toddlers. More predictive was the proportion of activities in which an adult assumed an active role in sharing information, and in labeling objects and relationships, and in which the child was an active observer.

Carew's data seem to support a transactional model of development. On the one hand the types of experiences adults helped to structure for toddlers appeared to significantly influence their intellectual development. Yet these children's own characteristics (in this case, their mental development) also appeared to shape how adults interacted with them. Bright, more verbal children appeared to elicit experiences led by an adult that emphasized language mastery. Twelve-month-old infants scoring higher on the Bayley were more likely to have intellectually valuable experiences at 18–21 months and at 24–27 months—experiences that were led by the adult. Similarly those 12-month-olds scoring higher on the language test were more likely to be provided intellectually valuable experiences led by or shared with the adult. While the present study provides neither clear nor direct support for such a model, the pattern of the results seems to fit with this perspective best.

## Everyday day care experiences and intellectual development

Comparable relationships emerged when data gathered on the children in the day care centers were analyzed. The observational data gathered in this study did

*Intellectually valuable experiences that involve the teacher and/or parents as active participants in the task with the child in labeling, describing, comparing, classifying, and questioning, support intellectual development.*

not cover as extensive a period as in the study of children at home. Nine of the children were observed beginning at 18 months, and 13 were observed beginning at 24 months. The final observation was conducted at 34 months.

Examination of the correlations between IQ and the 13 types of different everyday experiences coded, showed that only intellectually valuable experiences were significantly and positively related to Binet IQ scores. Involvement in intellectually less valuable experiences and socioemotional activities was uncorrelated or negatively correlated with intelligence. Yet, not all intellectually valuable experiences were predictive of IQ scores. Surprisingly, time spent in spatial, in problem-solving, or in expressive-artistic activities, was uncorrelated with IQ scores. These middle socioeconomic status day care children's IQ at three years of age was predicted by the amount of language-focused activities that was provided by an adult who assumed a leadership role in the interaction. While such language activities (in which the adult engaged in extensive labeling and information sharing) were strongly predictive of intelligence, two other types of language-mastery situations were also predictive: interactions in which the child dominated the verbal interchange, and situations in which the child simply observed others who were actively engaged in intellectually valuable pursuits. Thus, it appears that while participation in

language-focused instructional activities is most supportive, the opportunity the early childhood center provides the child to observe others engaged in stimulating activities also facilitates the development of intelligence.

When the performance of children on the language tests and on the spatial tasks was examined in relation to previous everyday experience, a comparable, though slightly different, picture emerged. Children obtaining higher scores on the receptive language test were more likely to participate in language activities led by an adult, and to engage in independent expressive-artistic experiences. Neither time spent in spatial nor problem-solving experiences was related to children's performance on receptive language tests. Performance on spatial abilities tests was related to participation in language, spatial, and artistic experiences, but not to concrete reasoning or problem-solving experiences. The opportunity to engage in such tasks (that might have included experiments about speed/velocity of objects, or weight or measurement) was not predictive of intelligence as measured by the Stanford-Binet Test.

## Implications

Everyday experiences judged to be intellectually valuable were predictive of children's IQ, spatial abilities, language abilities, and ability to generate their own such activities. The greater the proportion of preparatory activities observed, the more likely the child was to obtain high scores on IQ and language tests. The proportion of time spent in routine talk, gross-motor activities, basic care, and social games, was either unrelated or negatively related to development. Providing children with challenging everyday activities is essential to the development of intelligence.

*Intellectually valuable experiences that involve the teacher and/or parents as active participants in the task with the child in labeling, describing, comparing, classifying, and questioning, support intellectual development.* This relationship was a strong one for both the home-reared and the day care children.

Carew concluded that effective caregivers, whether parents or teachers, were successful in integrating a variety of interactional strategies; one such strategy for the development of children's intellectual competence was information-giving and teaching. Thus it also is important for adults to include a proactive, generative role with other important teacher and parent roles.

Certainly children's own characteristics shape adult behavior in home and in school. Moreover, children acquire and master important cognitive abilities, social skills, as well as attitudes about people and situations when they work alone or interact with peers. Yet it is the quality of the frequent teacher-child or parent-child interchanges and learning episodes that is a central factor in the growth of cognitive competence. Between 12 and 33 months, the teacher or the parent can determine if these interactions are intellectually valuable ones. The results of this study place the responsibility for designing an intellectually stimulating environment squarely on the adults, both parent and teacher.

Proper balance in objectives, interactional strategies, and activities is an appropriate goal. Not only do programs need to systematically support language and cognitive development, but other objectives as well, like curiosity, helpfulness, achievement motivation, cooperativeness, persistence, and aesthetic abilities. As planners of children's environments, we continuously examine whether an instructional activity is best for achieving given objectives. We scrutinize to assure that a fitting blend of experiences is implemented. The development of intelligence is one such important objective.

What Carew's work says to us is that *we cannot expect the child to build intelligent behavior in an environment devoid of stimulating human interchange.* Appropriate language-focused adult-child interaction is required.

Cazden (1981) and Mattick (1981) identify several guidelines for teachers of young children to foster effective communication and the development of language skills. Cazden and Mattick underscore the potency of talking with children in situations where they are working avidly, and where the interchange is pertinent to that work. Concept-rich, action related, and purposeful communication in the context of problem-solving tasks promotes intellectual development.

Let us examine some of the types of language-mastery episodes that Carew found to be supportive of intellectual development.

Sara looks at a worm crawling on the ground. Teacher. "It's a worm. It's long and brown, sort of like a stick. See, it's littler than your finger."

Sonja (24 months old) says something about a circus. Mother: "No, you didn't go to the circus—you went to the parade." Sonja: "I went to the parade." Mother: "What did you see?". . .Sonja: "Big girls." Mother smiles. "Big girls and what else?". . .Sonja: "Trumpets." Mother: "Yes, and fire engines. Do you remember the fire engines?" Sonja: "You hold my ears a little bit." Mother smiles. "Yes, I did, just like this," and puts her hands on

Sonja's ears. Sonja laughs. (Carew 1980, pp. 73–74)

These data provide information about the role of experience in the development of psychometric intelligence. Whether intelligence tests and Piagetian tasks measure the same construct is debatable. Humphreys (1980) presents data suggesting the correlations between the two types of measures are quite high, reflecting considerable common factor variance. Kohlberg and DeVries' analyses of similar data led them to conclude that Piagetian tasks measure factors in addition to those that are measured by an intelligence test (Kohlberg and DeVries 1980). Whatever their shortcomings and misuses, intelligence tests do provide one useful way to assess intellectual development.

The relationships outlined in the Carew study are based on correlational analyses and as a consequence we cannot conclude with certainty that frequent adult-child interchanges that were both intellectually valuable and language-focused brought about enhanced intellectual competence of some children. Yet substantial other correlational and some experimental research is consonant with this view. In an experimental study, Mann (1970) found that training lower socioeconomic status parents to use elaboration and extension to help children describe, label, make predictions, define relationships, and make associations resulted in increases in the amount and diversity of mothers' verbal stimulation and improved children's concept development. Levenstein's (1970) parent education program that emphasized improved verbal interaction skills produced significant improvement in low-income children's intellectual functioning across several different groups of participants. These data and other (Streissguth and Bee 1972) lend support to the plausible causal relationship between verbal stimulation and the development of intelligence.

*The critical comments made by Ruth Hough on an earlier draft of this review are greatly appreciated.*

**References**

Carew, J. V. "Experience and the Development of Intelligence in Young Children at Home and in Day Care." *Monographs of the Society for Research in Child Development* 45 (1980). Serial No. 187.

Cazden, C. "Language Development and the Preschool Environment." In *Language in Early Childhood Education. Revised ed.* ed. C. B. Cazden. Washington, D.C.: National Association for the Education of Young Children, 1981.

DeVries, R., and Kohlberg, L. "Relations Between Piagetian and Psychometric Assessments of Intelligence." In *Current Topics in Early Childhood Education. Vol. 1.* Norwood, N.J.: Ablex, 1977.

Gray, S. W., and Wandersman, L. P. "The Methodology of Home-Based Intervention Studies: Problems and Promising Strategies." *Child Development* 51 (1980): 993–1009.

Hess, R. D., and Shipman, V. C. "Early Experience and the Socialization of Cognitive Modes in Children." *Child Development* 36, no. 4 (1965): 869–886.

Humphreys, L. G. "Methinks They Do Protest Too Much." *Intelligence* 4 (1980): 179–183.

Kohlberg, L., and DeVries, R. "Don't Throw Out the Piagetian Baby with the Psychometric Bath: Reply to Humphreys and Parsons." *Intelligence* 4 (1980): 175–177.

Levenstein, P. "Cognitive Growth in Preschoolers Through Verbal Interaction with Mothers." *American Journal of Orthopsychiatry* 40 (1970): 426–429.

Mann, M. "The Effects of a Preschool Language Program on Two-Year-Old Children and Their Mothers." Final Report, ERIC Document No. D 045 224, 1970.

Mattick, I. "The Teacher's Role in Helping Young Children Develop Language Competence." In *Language in Early Childhood Education. Revised ed.* ed. C. B. Cazden. Washington, D.C.: National Association for the Education of Young Children, 1981.

Scott, M. "Ecological Theory and Methods for Research in Special Education." *Journal of Special Education* 14 (1980): 279–294.

Streissguth, A. P., and Bee, H. L. "Mother-Child Interactions and Cognitive Development in Children." In *The Young Child: Reviews of Research, Vol. 2,* ed. W. W. Hartup. Washington, D.C.: National Association for the Education of Young Children, 1972.

# Toys: Tools for Learning

When your children are engrossed in play, what are they doing? Many infants squeal with delight when they drop their spoon to the floor over and over again. Toddlers usually love to stack plastic bowls or bang lids together. Preschoolers often build elaborate constructions with blocks or sand. Puppet shows or art projects can consume hours for older children.

If you think about the types of activities your children enjoy, you can choose good toys to appeal to them. Toys are expensive and there are hundreds from which to choose. Toys are also your children's tools for learning. These tips will help you make wise toy choices for your children.

## Children learn through play

Play is essential for children to grow and learn. What do children learn while they play? Watch them concentrate as they

- figure out how things work
- pick up new words and ideas
- build strong muscles they can control
- use their imagination
- solve problems
- learn to cooperate with others

Children outgrow their clothes rapidly because their bodies are growing. In much the same way, children's play changes as their minds and bodies develop. Let's look at what kinds of toys will grow with your children.

## Match toys to the child

Every child is different, yet children are similar in many ways. Inside this brochure is a chart showing what to expect of children at each age. It will help you select a toy that will fit your child's thinking, language, physical skills, feelings, and friendships. Product labels are no substitute for what you know about your child.

## Spend wisely on toys

Children need good toys, just as we need good tools to do our work well. Good toys are not necessarily expensive, and children do not need very many. In fact, many favorite activities involve what seem not to be toys at all. For examples, interacting with magazine pictures, mirrors, plastic cups, yarn, water, cardboard boxes, or singing songs!

Some good toys, such as blocks and books, are fairly expensive. *But* these usually appeal to children for many years and last for generations. Brothers and sisters, neighbors, and even your grandchildren may play with these! And library books are free!

Other toys are so perfect for children they are still good investments, even if they get used up or appeal to children for only a brief period. Art materials such as fingerpaint and watercolor markers, stacking toys, and simple puzzles are examples of this type of toy.

How do you know if a toy is a good investment? Take the checklist in this brochure along when you shop. Look for the types of toys suggested here, keeping in mind your child's interests and development.

## Select various types of toys

Toys affect what children learn and how they feel about themselves and others. For example, when children play with baby dolls, they are practicing what it is like to be a parent. Select different types of toys to help your children become well-rounded people. Then let your children decide which toys to use and how to play with them. What are children learning as they play with different types of toys?

*Hands-on toys* such as rattles, squeeze toys, balls, puzzles, beads, and board or card games build hand-eye coordination, encourage ideas about how things work, and foster cooperation and problem solving. Kitchens contain many great hands-on toys. Measuring cups and spoons, pans and lids, trays to sort utensils, and muffin cups and tins, are good examples.

*Books and recordings* are sources of joy for children and adults. Choose some to build on children's interests such as animals or silly words. Infants enjoy bright pictures and can soon turn the pages of board books. Look for stories and poems for other children. Share fingerplays, songs, and nursery rhymes you recall from your childhood.

Your choices help children appreciate words, literature, and music. To vary the selection, buy inexpensive paperback books, use pictures from magazines or drawn by your child to create yor own books, and visit your local library. Children who are read to in their early years usually become better readers.

*Art materials* also foster creativity and build skills that lead to reading, writing, and seeing beauty in life. Infants who can grasp a marker will delight in the motion of scribbling! Preschool children enjoy painting, pasting, and cutting. Offer large sheets of blank paper, wide brushes, and dress your child in washable clothes. The mess is half the fun!

Children learn the most and gain confidence when their art is all their own—so avoid coloring books and models to copy. Ask children to tell you about their art, rather than demand, "What is it?" Children enjoy the *doing* and are not concerned about the end result. We cannot expect adult representations from children under six.

*Construction items* such as blocks, building sets, and woodworking supplies are excellent ways to help children learn about science and number ideas. They contribute to muscle strength and coordination, too.

Few toys are as durable as hardwood unit blocks. Children enjoy them from their first year, when they feel and taste them, through the elementary years. Cardboard blocks, table blocks, and other building sets also lead to hours of constructive play.

Young children can safely enjoy woodworking if they have lightweight *real* tools, nails with large heads, and soft woods. Once again, make sure the child does the creating with your supervision—avoid kits or models. Ask at a lumberyard for scraps for children to nail or glue together.

*Experimental materials* Such as sand, water, clay, and musical instruments are ideal learning tools because children have so much control over them—they relish their feel and sound. Sand and water never break or wear out, but can bring hours of pleasure as children pour, measure, and combine them. They will soon pour without spilling, too! Children can help make dough clay with the recipe here. They love to roll, pound, and poke it. Through all these activities children begin to understand more about math and science.

Children can create their own music with real instruments. Babies love to shake bells mounted on an elastic band around their ankles or wrists. Harmonicas, maracas, and triangles are relatively inexpensive and can be handled by young children.

*Active play equipment* builds strong muscles and confidence to meet physical challenges. Make sure your child is safe, but at the same time don't be too overprotective or your child will be reluctant to try new skills.

Old tires and climbing frames are great to balance, jump, climb, and play on with other children. Swings, slides, and rocking toys challenge children's balance and viewpoint. Wagons and riding toys should be matched to your child's size. Make sure the steering mechanism works so your child can control it. Visit a nearby playground or park frequently, too.

*Pretend play objects* such as dolls, stuffed animals, dramatic figures, and dress-up clothes give children a chance to try new behaviors and use their imaginations. This type of play also helps children understand the world and how we can work together. Children like to imitate adults at work or at play.

Cuddly companions can be made with fabric scraps and stuffed with hosiery. Puppets can be made from socks, paper bags, or fabric. Your infant will enjoy a small, soft doll and a puppet face drawn on a paper plate. Look in your closet for dress-up clothing—your worn shoes will clunk just right for a preschooler. Hats, briefcases, and jewelry are some other suggestions for items children can use for pretend play.

## How to get the most from toys

Toys arranged on low, open shelves are easy for young children to locate, reach, and return. Toys get lost and broken in toy chests or boxes, and falling lids are dangerous.

Children need time, space, and some child and adult companionship to enjoy their toys. Infants especially need a responsive, verbal adult to introduce them to the world. As children grow, they play with other children in more complex ways. You set the stage for how and what your children will learn with the toys and materials you select—choose them carefully.

### For more information

Burtt, K. G., & Kalkstein, K. (1981). *Smart toys for babies from birth to two: 77 easy-to-make toys to stimulate your baby's mind.* New York: Harper & Row.

Gordon, I. J. (1970). *Baby learning through baby play: A parents' guide for the first two years.* New York: St. Martin's.

Hirsch, L. (Ed.). (1984). *The block book.* Washington, DC: NAEYC.

Isenberg, J. P., & Jacobs, J. E. (1982). *Playthings as learning tools: A parents' guide.* New York: Wiley.

Lasky, L., & Mukerji, R. (1980). *Art: Basic for young children.* Washington, DC: NAEYC.

McCracken, J. B. (1987). *Play is FUNdamental.* Washington, DC: NAEYC.

Sawyers, J. K., & Rogers, C. S. (1988). *Helping young children develop through play.* Washington, DC: NAEYC.

Schickedanz, J. (1983). *Helping children learn about reading.* Washington, DC: NAEYC.

# Some good toys & activities for young children*

| Approximate age | What children are like | Types of good toys and worthwhile activities |
|---|---|---|
| Birth to 3 months | Begin to smile at people, coo<br>Follow moving person or object with eyes<br>Prefer faces and bright colors<br>Reach, discover hands, kick feet, lift head<br>Suck with pleasure<br>Cry, but often are soothed when held<br>Turn head toward sounds | Rattle, large rings, squeeze or sucking toys<br>Lullabies, nursery rhymes, poems<br>Bright pictures of faces hung so baby can see them<br>Bells firmly attached to baby's wrist, ankle, booties<br>Cardboard or vinyl books with high-contrast illustrations to stand in baby's view<br>Brightly patterned crib sheets<br>Mobile with parts visible from baby's position |
| 4 to 6 months | Prefer parents and older siblings to other people<br>Repeat actions that have interesting results<br>Listen intently, respond when spoken to<br>Laugh, gurgle, imitate sounds<br>Explore hands and feet, put objects in mouth<br>Sit when propped, roll over, scoot, bounce<br>Grasp objects without using thumbs, bat at hanging objects<br>Smile often | Soft doll, texture ball, socks with bright designs<br>Toys that make noise when batted, squeezed, or mouthed<br>Measuring spoons, teething toy<br>Cloth, soft vinyl books with bright pictures to grasp, chew, & shake<br>Pictures of faces covered in plastic, hung at child's level; unbreakable mirror<br>Fingerplays, simple songs, peek-a-boo<br>Socks with bright designs or faces |
| 7 to 12 months | Remember simple events, form simple concepts<br>Identify themselves, body parts, voices of familiar people<br>Understand own name, other common words<br>Say first meaningful words<br>Explore, bang, or shake objects with hands<br>Find hidden objects, put objects in and out of containers<br>Sit alone<br>Creep, pull themselves up to stand, walk<br>May seem shy or become upset with strangers | All of the above *plus*<br>Rag and baby dolls, stuffed animals, puppets<br>Container for large beads, blocks, balls<br>Nesting toy or plastic containers<br>Board books to read, old magazines to tear<br>Recordings of voices, animal sounds, music<br>Wooden blocks, large soft blocks<br>Water toys that float<br>Rubber or large plastic balls<br>Soft plastic or wood vehicle with wheels<br>Games like peek-a-boo |
| 1 to 1½ years | Imitate adult actions<br>Speak and understand more words and ideas<br>Enjoy stories<br>Experiment with objects<br>Walk steadily, climb stairs<br>Assert independence, but strongly prefer familiar people<br>Recognize ownership of objects<br>Develop friendships, but also play alone<br>Are beginning to understand what adults want them to do, but do not yet have the ability to control themselves | All of the above *plus*<br>Surprise or music box<br>Puzzles, 2 to 6 large pieces with knobs<br>Books/recordings with songs, rhymes, simple stories, & pictures<br>Wide watercolor markers, nontoxic fat crayons, large blank paper<br>Geometric, unit, or cardboard blocks<br>People and animals, vehicles: wood or rubber<br>Pounding bench<br>Sand & water play: plastic measuring cups, boats, containers, washable doll<br>Large cardboard box to crawl in<br>Toys that jingle or move when used<br>Kitchen cupboard of *safe* pots, pans, lids, and utensils. |
| 1½ to 2 years | Solve problems<br>Speak and understand even more<br>Show pride in accomplishments, like to help with tasks<br>Exhibit more body control, run<br>Play more with others<br>Begin pretend play | Self-help toys: sorting box, holes with pegs<br>Large spools or beads to string<br>Books with large colorful illustrations, short stories<br>Soft dough clay, bells, drum<br>Small broom, sponge, camera, pots & pans<br>Shopping cart, wagon, steerable riding toy; toy telephone, washable doll |
| 2 to 3½ years | Enjoy learning new skills<br>Learn language rapidly<br>Are always on the go<br>Have some sense of danger<br>Gain more control of hands and fingers<br>Frustrated easily<br>Act more independent, but are still dependent, too<br>Act out familiar scenes | Wood puzzles with 4 to 20 pieces<br>Pegboard, sewing cards, stacking toys, picture lotto, dominoes<br>Picture/story books, poems about familiar things<br>Classical, folk, children's music<br>Finger or tempera paint, ½" brushes, blunt scissors, white glue<br>Unit blocks & accessories, wood train set with large pieces<br>Hammer (13 oz steel shanked), soft wood, roofing nails, nailing block<br>Triangle, wood block; texture- & sound-matching games |

*Each child develops at a different pace, so most suggestions overlap age groups.

| Approximate age | What children are like | Types of good toys and worthwhile activities |
| --- | --- | --- |
| 2 to 3½ years | | Wagon or wheelbarrow, large rubber ball, riding toy |
| | | Washable doll with a few clothes, doll bed |
| | | Dress-up clothes: hats, shoes, shirts; hand puppet |
| 3½ to 5 years | Have a longer attention span | Puzzles with more pieces, simple card or board |
| | Act silly, boisterous, may use shocking language | games |
| | Talk a lot, ask many questions | Smaller beads, parquetry blocks, small objects to |
| | Want real adult things, keep art projects | sort |
| | Test physical skills and courage with caution | Flannel board with pictures, letters; sturdy |
| | Reveal feelings in dramatic play | numbers & letters |
| | Like to play with friends, do not like to lose | More detailed books, simple science books |
| | Share and take turns sometimes | Sturdy record/tape player, book & record sets |
| | | Potter's clay, easel, narrower brushes, thick |
| | | crayons, chalk, paste, tape & dispenser, collage |
| | | materials |
| | | More unit block shapes & accessories & realistic |
| | | model vehicles |
| | | Construction set with smaller pieces |
| | | Woodworking bench, saw, sandpaper |
| | | Sand & water play: egg beater, muffin tin, |
| | | vehicles |
| | | Xylophone, maracas, tambourine |
| | | Roller skates, plastic bat & balls, balance board |
| | | Bowling pins, ring toss, bean bags & target |
| | | Planks, boxes, old tires |
| | | Child-sized stove or sink, toy telephone, play |
| | | food, cardboard cartons, more dress-up clothes, |
| | | dolls, carriage, & accessories |
| | | Airport, doll house, other miniature settings; |
| | | finger or stick puppets |
| 5 to 8 years | Grow curious about people and how the world works—by 7, are beginning to understand other people's feelings and that varying viewpoints and lifestyles exist | All the toys for 3s and 4s *plus* |
| | | More complex puzzles |
| | | More difficult games, including board and card |
| | | games |
| | Show an increasing interest in numbers, letters, reading, and writing—by 7, most understand adding and subtracting if real objects and real situations are often used, can really read, and can draw/write/spell stories (in their own ways) | Yarn, big needles, mesh fabric, weaving |
| | | Magnets, balance scales, magnifying glass, math games made for 5s through 7s with pieces to handle |
| | | Books with chapters, favorite stories children can read and books adults can read *to* children (even 7s and 8s), children's recipe books, diaries for the older children to write in privately |
| | Become more and more interested in a final product as they move toward 7 | |
| | Gain more confidence in physical skills | |
| | Like grown-up activities—by 7, show interest in jobs admired adults do | Watercolors, stapler, hole punch, chalkboard, oil crayons, paint crayons, charcoal, simple camera, film |
| | Use words to express feelings and to cope but still may need adult help to calm down—by 7, many children are able to help others plan group activities and solve social problems | More unit blocks, props; hollow or attribute blocks |
| | Become more outgoing, play cooperatively, need to make many choices and decisions and to initiate independent activities; also need time to play alone | Brace & bits, screwdriver, screws, metric measure |
| | | Sand & water play: food coloring, pump, funnel, containers |
| | | Harmonica, kazoo, guitar, recorder |
| | Still need reassurance and affection | Outdoor toys: playground ball, tetherball, jump rope, Frisbee, bicycle, roller skates |
| | Need protection from the competitive stress-producing world many of today's children find themselves in, and warmly enthusiastic adult support for what they *can* do and *do* do "right" | Cash register, typewriter, other dramatic play props |
| | | Nature activities |
| | | 7s and 8s are beginning to be interested in hobbies, group and team games, clubs, and time to "hang out" and talk with friends |

*Tools For Learning*

Christine Z. Cataldo

# Infant-Toddler Education
## Blending the Best Approaches

*What and how should babies learn? Parents and professionals have recently been overwhelmed with information about various programs for teaching infants and toddlers—much of it contradictory and confusing. Some programs are based on sound research and child development theory, while others neglect or overemphasize some aspects of growth and learning. How can we blend the best attributes from each good program approach?*

Helping babies thrive is a special challenge for parents and early childhood educators. While infant, preschool, and early elementary education share many of the same views about children, families, and learning, there are also vital differences in how children learn during their first eight years. An understanding of how infants and toddlers differ from children older than age three is a prerequisite for making decisions about what kinds of teaching and learning experiences are best for such young children.

## What is different about infants and toddlers?

Information about how infants and toddlers can be expected to grow and develop is readily available. We know that infants and toddlers
■ have unique physical, emotional, social, and intellectual needs, skills, and styles
■ grow and change rapidly
■ are especially vulnerable to inadequacies in their environments

Because of these differences, their care must be more personal, intense, and family-centered. While retaining an understanding of the continuity of learning throughout early childhood, adults who care for infants and toddlers must develop special skills to balance the unique needs of this age group. Some programs are based on sound philosophies and practice. Others neglect or overemphasize particular elements. This article will explore several good approaches and offer suggestions for developing an effective, blended program that reflects the best of what we know about how infants and toddlers grow and learn.

## Approaches to infant-toddler programming

There are many models available for designing programs for infants and toddlers

**Christine Z. Cataldo**, Ed.D., is Assistant Professor of Early Childhood Education and Director of the Early Childhood Research Center, State University of New York at Buffalo, Buffalo, New York.

*An understanding of how infants and toddlers differ from children older than age three is a prerequisite for making decisions about what kinds of teaching and learning experiences are best for such young children.*

(Cataldo 1983). Each program model overlaps the others, especially in recommendations to encourage play activities, attend to emotional needs, nurture developmental progress, facilitate peer relationships, provide responsive toys, monitor development, and work with parents. Yet each also highlights particular elements of the program through suggestions for training or descriptions of principles, content, and organization.

### High quality caregiving

One basic and important approach to infant-toddler programming is to provide good home-style care in such a way that growth is nurtured during typical daily experiences. This approach highlights the value of naturally occurring learning opportunities, flexibility in working with babies' schedules and interests, and a general respect for the child's developing sense of self. Gonzalez-Mena and Eyer (1980), Keister (1977), and Willis and Ricciuti (1977) have all presented strong models that enhance the development of infants and toddlers through loving and thoughtful caregiving. Each child in these programs encounters individual affection and learning opportunities during caregiving routines. Self-esteem and autonomy are encouraged. Play materials and social exchanges provide additional enrichment. Peer experiences are seen as similar to those in a preschool where a comfortable daily schedule includes social play and activities spread out in various areas of the room.

> **Some examples of this caregiving approach are**
>
> - using words for clothes and body parts during dressing
> - providing soft blocks and activity centers in cribs
> - singing songs during feedings
> - looking at books in a quiet area of the room
> - making playthings available throughout the day

## Babies' needs

Infants' and toddlers' needs mediate much of their feelings and behavior. Attention to these needs is nearly always tied to caregiving, but in this approach special attention is placed on the range of developmental, interpersonal, and environmental requirements known to be important for the early years. Needs of children form the basis for encouraging particular staff behaviors and making program provisions (Caldwell and Rorex 1977; Huntington, Provence, and Parker 1971). In meeting babies' physical, emotional, and social requirements, the program is seen as contributing to growth and development. Adults' awareness of and planning for these needs are cornerstone elements to this approach. Children's interests in sensory, exploratory, and toy play activities, and in peer interactions are also considered. Through focusing on such areas of need, the program is seen as a means for supporting and educating infants and toddlers. Needs and interests have long served as sources of traditional preschool curriculum practices.

> **Some examples of the needs approach are**
>
> - holding and hugging fussy babies
> - providing self-feeding foods
> - playing pat-a-cake with an alert child
> - supplying new rattles and pictures regularly
> - clearing floor areas for wobbly walkers

## Adult roles

Teacher-caregivers are seen as the critical element in some infant programs. Their comfort, guidance, language modeling, playing participation, and knowledge about child development are the children's assurance of love and learning. The training and continued support of adults who work with babies is emphasized in this approach. Their understandings and techniques with infants and toddlers are seen as the basis of personal growth and developmental progress. Two of the most important responsibilities for adults who work with infants are to provide interesting activities for babies and to interact positively with them (Honig and Lally 1981). Others include the use of the theories of Piaget and Erikson as guides to interaction and play. This model is readily extended to the teacher in the preschool classroom who is also viewed as the essential organizer, guide, and consultant.

> **Examples of the adult roles approach are**
>
> - remembering the baby's abilities and interests
> - using praise and affection often
> - providing tasks that build thinking
> - explaining events and using new vocabulary
> - giving one-to-one attention to each child each day

Cataldo

## Play and learning

In this model the focus is on the belief that the business of babies is to play and interact. Infants and toddlers gain concepts and develop skills during their own changes with people and objects, and in the context of enjoyable, playful experiences. Playing and learning are therefore inseparable in this approach to programming (Adcock and Segal 1979; Fowler 1980; Gordon 1970). Games, materials, and activities are described in terms of how adults and children can be involved with each other in the context of play. Social and intellectual learning occur along with pleasure and mastery of the environment. Both the caregiver and the baby appreciate the fun they have while information and skills are being acquired. Play continues to be a major element throughout early childhood education, especially in the peer group. The children's fanciful, but intellectually and socially valuable activities with their friends using blocks, vehicles, dramatic roles, games, and creative materials are seen as primary learning modes at all ages.

---

**Some examples of the play and learning approach for very young children are**

- using dishes and dolls for pretend play
- joining two to three sitting babies using a toy assortment
- creating games with balls, music, or puppets
- helping two toddlers play together at the sand table
- modeling sharing and turn-taking with toys

---

## The environment

This program model views babies as explorers whose investigations are limited only by their surroundings and materials. Their curiosity and delight propel them into educational encounters using playthings and equipment within their reach. Materials are selected and arranged to facilitate learning and play. Thus, the baby's environment, in both the physical and interpersonal senses, is highlighted in this approach to infant-toddler programming. The child actively manipulates and explores materials in several play areas with adult monitoring and participation. The interesting setting and attentive caregiver-teacher fulfill roles in organizing and mediating babies' experiences so that learning occurs. The result is developmental progress and social growth (Cataldo 1983; Harms 1970). Such creative use of the program setting is also important at the preschool level, where design of the classroom is considered to be part of the teacher's skill in teaching.

---

**Examples of the environmental approach are**

- organizing simple activity centers in the room
- providing varied, multilevel toys
- using textured natural objects and materials
- changing some playthings each month
- using water, sand, and dough to explore

---

## Tasks and activities

The curriculum in other programs for very young children is essentially seen as planned independent and guided activities. The developmental sequence of predictable early milestones of growth and learning is used as a basis for designing activities to enhance observable skills and understandings in ways thought to be common for most infants and toddlers. Toys and games aimed at these growth markers are made available to the babies, either with some demonstration or supervision, or as self-selected activities. Enrichment activities are also designed and conducted for the children's gain and enjoyment, often with the adults as leaders. These may be special experiences that can add spice to the child's week or help accomplish new skills.

The conscious planning by teachers and caregivers, often as a result of using resources such as Karnes (1979), Meier and Malone (1979), and Sparling and Lewis (1979), is characteristic of this approach. It resembles the early childhood program in the use of independent and guided play and specially planned activities that can be a part of the children's free play times. This approach is also common in programs for handicapped infants and toddlers.

> **Some examples of the tasks and activities approach are**
>
> - helping babies to use shape sorters and nesting blocks
> - providing seasonal resources such as pumpkins and flowers
> - using developmental checklists to spot needs
> - arranging a sequence of easy to difficult toys
> - encouraging persistence in finishing a simple puzzle

## Administration

Another way of designing and conducting the infant-toddler program could be called the organizational or administrative approach (Herbert-Jackson et al. 1977; O'Brien et al. 1979). Procedures, forms, charts, and specific management strategies are described for infant and toddler caregivers to help them monitor children's progress and manage the center. Caregiving activities are described in detail and the smooth functioning of the center is seen as the means by which very young children are provided with safe, appropriate experiences supportive of developmental growth.

This approach resembles the emphasis in early child care on establishing clear program policies, maintaining records that document progress, and helping teachers to manage the classroom and center. Observation as a tool for understanding and enhancing developmental and personal well-being is also valued in early education.

> **Some examples of the administrative approach are**
>
> - recording babies' play activities and interactions
> - noting changes in abilities and interests
> - using suggested health and daily report forms
> - creating flexible schedules for routines
> - comparing actual to recommended care practices

## Parent-family

The last approach to be included here is one of the most important for infant and toddler programs. Since mothers and fathers are babies' primary loved ones, teachers, and lifelong advocates, it is the responsibility of professionals to provide families with information, emotional support, and shared activities with other families. Several developmental resources for the first years of life have been created for use primarily by parents in the home setting (Brazelton 1969, 1974; Caplan 1971, 1977; Church 1973; Leach 1976; Stein 1976). The orientation of most is to provide descriptions of the growing infant and toddler along with guides for parents in reacting to the child's growth and building appropriate childrearing skills. Often these materials are used by caregivers to familiarize themselves with the stages they will encounter during this period.

For programs involving high-risk families, there are resources containing specific intervention strategies (Badger 1977;

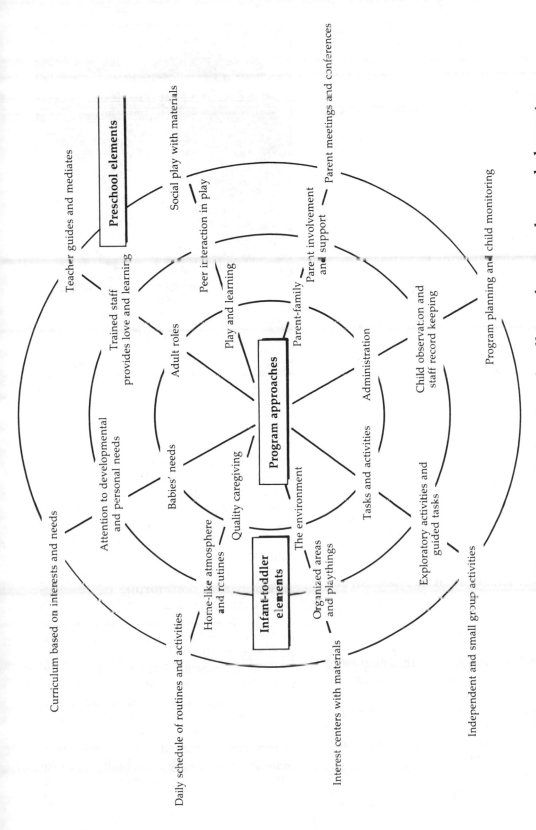

**Figure 1. Infant-toddler-preschool education: A collage of approaches and elements.**

Bromwich 1980; Levenstein 1977) that promote positive relationships and help parents to establish a learning environment in the home.

This emphasis upon including mothers and fathers as part of the program and as learners in meetings and related projects is tied to the child study origins of early education and to recent efforts toward preventing problems in children (Cataldo 1980).

---

**Some examples of the parent-family approach are**

■ helping parents to play with babies
■ providing ideas for home activities
■ demonstrating educational uses of toys
■ describing the goals of program activities
■ pointing out changes in babies' development

---

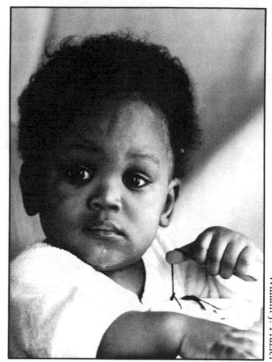

*Good programs for babies are enriching without being formal or concentrating too much on a single group of skills.*

## The program collage

A collage has been designed to tie together these approaches to infant and toddler programming (Figure 1). The continuity and balance contributed by all eight elements and their links to traditional early childhood education programs are presented. It should be reemphasized that none of these approaches exists in a vacuum, and a good quality infant-toddler program integrates aspects of each approach in its operation. The collage can be used to help determine the degree to which a program addresses itself to each element. What are the program's major strengths? Are there gaps? Are there appropriate differences in the child's experiences during the earlier and later years? Where is continuity maintained?

The blended program that can result from use of this collage is educational in the broadest sense. Good programs for babies are enriching without being formal or concentrating too much on a single approach at the expense of others. Child care programs, early intervention projects, preschools, family day care, and playgroups in homes can all achieve a balance among elements.

The educational focus helps to maintain an emphasis upon nurturant, developmental care provided by skilled adults. A foundation of love and learning ties the enrichment and satisfaction of present experiences to the child's future. Education is a lifelong process that begins very early, is guided by maturation and experience, and has unique challenges at each stage. Good infant-toddler programs are one of the first links in this chain, a link that is comfortably embraced by basic early childhood principles with their high regard for personal growth and meaningful learning.

Cataldo

# References

Adcock, D., and Segal, M. *Two-Years-Old: Play and Learning*. Rolling Hills Estates, Calif.: B. L. Winch and Associates, 1979.

Badger, E. "The Infant Stimulation/Mother Training Project." In *Infant Education: A Guide to Helping Handicapped Children in the First Three Years*, ed. B. Caldwell and D. Stedman. New York: Walker, 1977.

Brazelton, T. B. *Infants and Mothers*. New York: Dell, 1969.

Brazelton, T. B. *Toddlers and Parents*. New York: Dell, 1974.

Bromwich, R. *Working with Parents and Infants: An Interactional Approach*. Baltimore, Md.: University Park Press, 1980.

Caldwell, B., and Rorex, J. "A Day at the Kramer Baby House." In *Developing Programs for Infants and Toddlers*, ed. M. Cohen. Washington, D.C.: Association for Childhood Education International, 1977.

Caplan, F. *The First Twelve Months of Life*. Princeton, N.J.: Edcom Systems, 1971.

Caplan, F. *The Parenting Advisor*. New York: Macmillan, 1977.

Cataldo, C. "The Parent as Learner: Early Childhood Parent Programs." *Educational Psychologist* 15 (1980): 172–186.

Cataldo, C. *Infant and Toddler Programs: A Guide to Very Early Childhood Education*. Reading, Mass.: Addison-Wesley, 1983.

Church, J. *Understanding Your Child from Birth to Three*. New York: Random House, 1973.

Fowler, W. *Infant and Child Care: A Guide to Education in Group Settings*. Boston: Allyn & Bacon, 1980.

Gonzalez-Mena, J., and Eyer, D. *Infancy and Caregiving*. Palo Alto, Calif.: Mayfield, 1980.

Gordon, I. *Baby Learning Through Baby Play*. New York: St. Martin's Press, 1970.

Harms, T. "Evaluating Settings for Learning." *Young Children* 25 (1970): 304–308.

Herbert-Jackson, E.; O'Brien, M.; Porterfield, J.; and Risley, T. *The Infant Center*. Baltimore, Md.: University Park Press, 1977.

Honig, A., and Lally R. *Infant Caregiving: A Design for Training*. 2nd ed. New York: Syracuse University Press, 1981.

Huntington, D.; Provence, S.; and Parker, R. *Day Care: Serving Infants*. Washington, D.C.: U.S. Department of Health, Education and Welfare, 1971.

Karnes, M. *Small Wonder! Activities for Baby's First 18 Months*. Circle Pines, Minn.: American Guidance Service, 1979.

Keister, M. *The Good Life for Infants and Toddlers*. 2nd ed. Washington, D.C.: National Association for the Education of Young Children, 1977.

Leach, P. *Babyhood*. New York: Knopf, 1976.

Levenstein, P. "The Mother-Child Home Program." In *The Preschool in Action*. 2nd ed., ed. M. Day and R. Parker. Boston: Allyn & Bacon, 1977.

Meier, J. H., and Malone, P. J. *Facilitating Children's Development: A Systematic Guide for Open Learning*. Baltimore, Md.: University Park Press, 1979.

O'Brien, M.; Porterfield, J.; Herbert-Jackson, E.; and Risley, T. *The Toddler Center*. Baltimore, Md.: University Park Press, 1979.

Sparling, J., and Lewis, I. *Infant Learningames: Resources for a Parent-Child Partnership*. New York: Walker, 1979.

Stein, S. *New Parent's Guide to Early Learning*. New York: Plume, 1976.

Willis, A., and Ricciuti, H. *A Good Beginning for Babies*. Washington, D.C.: National Association for the Education of Young Children, 1977.

Harriet A. Alger

# Transitions: Alternatives to Manipulative Management Techniques

From group times to free choice periods, from indoors to outdoors, the beginning of snack or lunch, settling down at naptime, waking up—daily transitions are times that challenge the most experienced teachers and cause nightmares for the beginning teacher.

As beginning teachers in the "survival stage" (Katz 1977) we imitate our more experienced colleagues, but the things which seem to work so well for someone else are often not simple to put in practice without the orientation, judgment, and timing of the model. With more experience, there are still problems as children, families, and society change. Even when things are going well, transitions are always difficult for some children and some days are worse than others for all.

The key to classroom management is to help children develop self-control over their environment in increasingly responsible ways (Stone 1978). "A major task for the parent and teacher is to structure the environment so that the child can begin to direct his own behavior within that environment" (Osborn and Osborn 1981, p. 142).

**Harriet A. Alger,** Ph.D., is Coordinator and Assistant Professor of Early Childhood Education, Cleveland State University, Cleveland, Ohio.

Teachers often use transition strategies that seem manipulative: flicking lights or determining changes by color of clothes or *good* behavior. These teacher-dominated techniques do not build self-control or allow for the gradual transfer of responsibility to the children. Warren states that her "own choice is to eliminate all tricks, including distraction, manipulation, happy face signs, clean plate clubs, and other such gimmicks which, from my point of view, only insult children's intelligence and integrity—and then to establish basic goals for children, from which the how-to will naturally flow" (1977, p. 2).

Stone and the Osborns also emphasize prevention of problems with good programming and good preparation. From arrival to departure every aspect of the program affects individual behavior and group dynamics. Because problems may become more evident in children's behavior at transitions, we need to examine the children's entire day.

## Arrival: A good beginning

One of the most critical times of day for averting trouble is the arrival of children. Good teachers cheerfully greet each child, but it is not easy to do so. When preschool children and parents arrive at about the

Nancy P. Alexander

same time, it is a challenge to give each new arrival genuine attention. A glassy look and artificial smile will be detected and you can miss important communication.

Child care teachers with children's staggered arrival times would seem to have an advantage but child care presents its own problems. The children already in the center may be very active. Some children may be eating breakfast, or morning group time may be in progress when some of the children arrive. Should the teacher leave the group to greet them? Some children arrive before all teachers are in the center. The staff member who receives them may or may not find out what has happened since yesterday, and may not have the opportunity to tell other caregivers if they do.

Despite these difficulties, it is important to check each child's emotional and physical state as they arrive at the center. A disturbed child can suddenly become a disruptive child, and transitions are the most likely times for trouble. It is also important that every parent and child have a few minutes of undivided attention. The respect and rapport established will reinforce your ability to prevent problems and to work together in the future. A good beginning to the day is an investment with substantial dividends.

Preschool teachers should be at the door at arrival time, not working on preparations for the day. Activities available for the children in the classroom should be interesting, easy to monitor, and supervised by capable adults. This often means training parents, volunteers, or students to assist.

Child care centers should have some of their best teachers scheduled in the early morning hours. Sometimes children cling and cry even when separation has not been a problem for months. Sometimes children seem determined to test everyone's affection and temper by refusing to take off coats or running around snatching toys from other children. Parents may be embarrassed, react harshly, or feel badly. Inexperienced caregivers may be unable to cope—it takes a skilled teacher to pick up all the early morning signals.

Good communication is needed between the early morning teachers and others who arrive later. The information gained in those first few minutes of each child's day must be shared with other staff. Some children may need an adult's presence each time a transition nears. A child who feels unhappy or rejected may not only resist changes but trigger a "contagious" reaction from other children (Osborn and Osborn 1981).

If something unavoidable does distract you when children and parents are arriving, excuse yourself rather than talk while your attention is divided. Do, however, make a mental or written note to spend time with that child as soon as possible. When a child is bubbling over with news, you can take her or him by the hand to accompany you while you solve a problem and then resume your conversation if this seems practical in the situation and the child is willing. If children come in, say "Hi," and are off to the blocks or the science table with hardly a glance in your direction, there is no need to go through some forced exchange, but find another opportunity to share a special time together.

When parents want to talk you can ask them if they can stay for a moment. If this is not possible, ask if you can call later or sit down for a few minutes when they return. Sometimes making an appointment is the best option. The important aim is to establish open and honest communication on a regular informal basis. Parent teacher conferences and open houses are not sufficient.

*Transitions work best when there is a good balance of active/quiet play and a gradual increase or decrease of the tempo of activity.*

Jeffrey High

## Sharing time: What's happened?

Sharing time provides another way to ease the transition from home to school and gives teachers information about how children are feeling and what is happening in their lives. Sharing times in which children are encouraged to talk about interests, experiences, and feelings are preferable to show and tell sessions in which children only display their latest toys. It is important that sharing times be short. Long sessions increase the likelihood of discipline problems and lack of respect for each other's contributions. Each child needs enough time to talk, however, not just a routine hurried turn. If many children are eager to share, it may be better to have several short sharing times rather than one long one so the children and the teacher can really listen and enjoy each

Alger

contribution. Let one or two children share before and/or after other activities during the day. A sharing process can be an integral part of the entire program, not pushed into one 10 or 15 minute group time. It should certainly be part of every day. The purpose of sharing time is to establish meaningful relationships and good communication among children and adults. The more teachers and children know each other as real people and the more they care about each other, the more they will be responsive to each other.

Encouraging children to share experiences and feelings may raise the issue of confidentiality. If you stop children who want to tell something personal about their families, they may feel rejected and it may magnify the incident in the other children's minds. It is usually better to accept the information without overemphasis: "That happens sometimes. How did you feel?" Then go on with what others have to share and find a quiet time later to let that child talk further if needed.

John's father had gone out of town on one of his frequent business trips, but this time he had left after a loud argument with the mother which John had overheard. When he expressed some of his frustration and fear in the group sharing time, the teacher said to the children, "John doesn't like what happened and he kicked and screamed about it. What do you do when you are angry?" After each child described going to her or his room, hitting something, or other expressions of anger she asked, "Did that help to make you feel better?" Sometimes the answer was "Yes" and sometimes the child would decide that it had made things worse. The teacher passed no judgments. The children animatedly discussed the pros and cons of various behavior. By the end of this valuable session, no one saw John's situation as something to gossip about.

The things that children share should be respected but cannot always be accepted as truth. Children's level of cognitive understanding and perception may cause them to have distorted views of what they observe. A kindergarten teacher who overheard a young "wife" yelling at her "husband" in the housekeeping corner thought that she was discovering something about family life in the girl's house until a familiar phrase made her realize it was a reenactment of one of the previous night's television shows!

## Transitions from group times: A mad dash?

Transitions from group times to the next activities can be chaotic if group times are uninteresting, too long, or too demanding. When resentment and discomfort grow, the children's desire to escape is focused not only on the situation but also on the domination of the teacher. If children in a group become wiggly and uncomfortable, you can expect a difficult transition.

Even a short, interesting group time may end with a mad exodus, however, if precautions are not taken. At the beginning of the day, the schedule should be shared with the children so that they know what will happen. Any special rules may need to be reviewed. Then as each activity begins and ends, reminders will suffice. "Do you remember what we are going to do after our story today?" "When we get ready for our walk we will need to get our coats. How can we do that without bumping into each other when we leave the circle?" When children help with the plans and participate in setting the limits, they are more apt to understand, to remember, and to be willing to help enforce the rules. Don't forget to give positive reinforcement when things go well, not just reminders when someone fails to manage. However, positive reinforcement should not become so automatic or mechanical that children doubt its sincerity. Some genuine response—a smile, pat, or word—is always more effective than a stock phrase.

A key element in avoiding mad dashes at the beginning of free choice times is the assurance that children will have ample time for their favorite activities. If free choice time is too short or few activities are interesting, some children will run to grab their chosen activity. Others will flit about aimlessly and not bother to start anything because they know they will have to stop soon. It is important to have enough interesting things to do, and to use a system that allows children to select a second activity if the first is not satisfactory. Children who are bored or frustrated during free choice time are rarely cooperative when it is time to clean up. A free choice time that is too long, on the other hand, will result in tired children who are no longer constructively busy. Result—they get into trouble. It takes flexibility and a good eye for the quality of work and play to determine the appropriate amount of time for free play.

## Clean-up: Time to mess around?

Children need at least ten minutes notice of the approach of clean-up time, with reminders at five and one minutes. Teachers can circulate around the room giving quiet notice, which seems more effective than flicking lights or making other peremptory signals.

It may seem reasonable to insist that the children who are involved in an activity are the ones who must clean it up but the result may be an early flight from the block corner by those whose grand building used all 500 blocks. Some clean-up tasks are so time consuming that they may cause children to decide never to play in that area again. These tasks need help from adults and from other children (who will themselves be helped when they play in that area another day). Since blocks take a long time to organize on the shelves, it may take a 15 minute advance warning to get them all put away at the same time that

the rest of clean-up chores are completed. Or you may need to allow some adults and children to finish that task after the next activity has begun, waiting to begin anything particularly fascinating until they are finished. The next activity after free choice should be interesting to the children and anticipated with enthusiasm or you will have lots of dawdling with the clean-up process!

## Transitions to group times: Back together

Moving into a group time is often facilitated by a little advance publicity. It builds interest to have something in a bag and as the children ask about it, say, "I'll show you at group time." Children will look forward to group times in which they have a chance to show their block building or artwork or the book they have drawn and stapled. The morning planning time can give advance notice of exciting things to come and reminders can keep interest alive throughout the day.

From the first arrival at group time, there should be a teacher or classroom assistant there to be with the children. Trying to control behavior at a distance is always hazardous and never more so than during a transition.

Sometimes teachers let children look at books until all are ready for story or music. When the last things are put away at clean-up time, the teacher walks over to the rug and says, "Time to collect the books." Some children have just arrived and have opened the cover of their favorite story. Some children are in the middle of reading their favorite. The children may resist or they may cooperate but be left with the feeling that the teacher does not value books except as a tool to keep them quiet. A Head Start teacher handles this situation much more effectively. When all the children are seated and looking at books, she sits down also. She may share books with some of the children or merely wait for a reasonable period of time. Then she gives a warning that it will soon be time to put their books away. As children finish, she collects their books and allows others to finish while she begins a discussion or finger play to occupy those who are through. When most books have been collected, the group story time begins. This process respects children and their interest in books.

## In and out: Traffic jam or freeway?

Transitions from indoors to outdoors and vice versa have special hazards. Again the deployment of adults is important. When children are asked to get their coats, one adult should already be at the cubbies. As the first group of children are ready, one adult should be available to take them outside instead of making them wait for everyone. Fidgety children usually turn their creative energies to less desirable behaviors.

Lines are to be avoided if at all possible except for fire drills. The amount of energy it takes to keep young children in a line is simply not worth it. We must, of course, stay on sidewalks rather than walk on lawns and negotiate halls without running or bumping into someone but lines are not necessary to achieve these objectives. It is effective for adults to hold the hand of those not quite able to manage these tasks rather than try to keep all the children in a line.

It is also unnecessary for everyone to hold the hand of a buddy on an outing. Some children have two buddies. Some are responsible and independent. Some days are just too hot and sticky to hold hands. Any child who cannot be trusted to stay with the group and obey the rules should be supervised by a capable adult.

Before coming back into the classroom, it is helpful to give advance notice, to review the rules briefly, and to remind the children of what comes next. An adult should precede the group and be in the room as the children come in. If children are taking off their coats, they should know where to go next and an adult should be there.

## Schedule: Keeping up the pace

The rhythm of activities has considerable impact on transition times. If a group time is followed by snack which is followed by a story, children may be restless. Three consecutive group times require too much sitting without enough activity so children will create their own relief by beginning unauthorized creative movement. Too many active periods in a row such as free choice, creative movement, and outdoor play may cause problems too. Transitions work best when there is a good balance of active/quiet play and a gradual increase or decrease of the tempo of activity.

Teachers of young children often schedule outdoor play at the beginning or end of a winter session for practical reasons. This frequently results in too many quiet activities in sequence. Many science activities and other learning opportunities should be pursued outdoors as well as indoors. Young children are learning while dressing and undressing, so it is not wasted time to dress more than once a session. Children will soon become very independent in these skills when they are used frequently.

## Bathrooms are not for groups

Inappropriate routines can cause many management problems. Lining up and mass bathrooming should be avoided if at all possible. Young children simply do not have the control needed to wait. Children should be able to get a drink or go to the bathroom when the need arises. Releasing children a few at a time to wash hands, brush teeth, or go to the bathroom while others are occupied with something interesting to do will make life much easier than trying to herd the whole group in and out before meals or naptime.

If lines and trips to the bathroom en masse cannot be avoided entirely, firm friendly procedures should keep things organized. When we ask the impossible we can at least be kind, not irritated, and expect to give extra help.

## Mealtimes: Keeping the atmosphere pleasant

Teachers use many techniques to prevent the scramble to the table and the fights over who sits where. Most of them are manipulative. There may be a temptation to assign seats but this is authoritarian and does not help the children to behave independently. It also makes it more difficult to encourage a warm, relaxed social atmosphere at mealtimes.

The younger the children the more unrealistic it is to expect them to wait for very long to start eating. With an adult at each table, they should be able to begin when all at that table are seated, without having to wait for the entire class.

A prayer may be appropriate if the program is church-related. Often, it becomes a testing ground: "Kevin didn't close his eyes"; "Lamar started to eat, teacher." Depending on the age of the children, more cooperation and real involvement may be gained by asking the children what they enjoyed during the morning and praying, "Thank you God for fingers and finger paint" or "Thank you God for helping Mark get well so that he could come back to school." If a prayer or a song is used only to quiet children down and start the meal on cue, it is another manipulative gimmick.

A relaxed social atmosphere should include complete freedom to eat what and how much you wish. Pressure on children, even subtle, to eat more than they want or to taste something that looks unappetizing can cause behavior problems. Sometimes children are more active or growing fast and need lots of food. Sometimes they do not need as much. We need to concentrate on providing plenty of exercise, a warm, supportive atmosphere, and good food. If children do not look or act healthy then it is a mistake to try to focus on the eating. The cause needs to be identified.

Lessons in table manners can increase tension and add to problems of management. A continuous stream of reminders to the children such as "Use your fork," "Don't pour too much in your glass," "Be careful, you'll spill" can make anyone lose their appetite! When you set a good model, the children will usually imitate it. A little unobtrusive assistance can be given to avert disaster.

Mealtime is a learning situation as is every time of day for young children. Resist the temptation, however, to ask too many questions intended to nurture cognitive development. "What color is this food?" and "Where does it come from?" are reasonable questions but they can be boring or frustrating if carried on as a predictable routine.

All good things must end and a transition is needed from the table to whatever comes next. One important decision a teacher must make is whether to insist that all children remain seated until everyone is finished. Whether at home or at school, it usually is better to allow children to leave the table soon after they are finished rather than try to keep them captive. Older children can usually wait a little better than the youngest, on some days at least.

As with other transitions, someone needs to be available to assist those who leave the table in finding other appropriate activities. By doing this, slow eaters can be given time to finish. A college student was very impressed with one preschool situa-

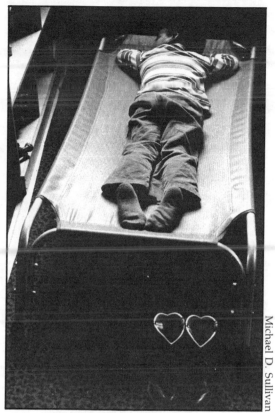

*Low lights, quiet voices, loving people who rub backs and reassure those who need it: these are the ingredients of successful transitions into rest or sleep.*

tion in which he participated. A child who had been talking to him at snack was allowed to stay with him and continue eating and talking after the next activity had begun. It was a special opportunity for social interaction that was respected and facilitated.

## Naptime: Now I lay me down to?

Naptime in a child care center may be anything but restful for some or all of the children and staff. An arbitrary decision that all the children should be sleepy at 12:30 or 1:00 is part of the problem, but most centers have a scheduled time for sleep or at least rest. You can sometimes make a child stay on a cot if most children

are cooperative and/or you have enough adults, but no one can make a child sleep or really rest.

In order to rest or sleep, people usually need to feel comfortable, relaxed, and tired, and not too anxious or tense or over-tired. Most adults have routines at night that help us to shed the worries of the day such as reading or watching television—we too need transitions.

The beginning of naptime needs to be as relaxed and free from stress as we can make it. Something to play with quietly or snuggle with as well as people who are loving and reassuring needs to be made available to children. Reasonable limits on behavior need to be set to allow children to rest or sleep if they wish. Children who cannot or will not be quiet should be removed to another quiet location, not as punishment but as consideration for the others. Children who are still not asleep after some reasonable length of time or who wake up early need a quiet place to play or may be taken outside. Low lights, quiet voices, loving people who rub backs and reassure those who need it: these are the ingredients of successful transitions into rest or sleep.

The practice of using naptime as break time for child care staff is based on several false assumptions: that this is an easy time to monitor, that all the children sleep, that it is safe to have fewer teachers at this time. Naptime is often a difficult time for children and requires individual attention for many. Not all children sleep and they should not be required to stay on cots to accommodate adult needs. A fire at naptime in one center in our community dramatically illustrated the difficulty of coping in an emergency with children who are asleep. Now they not only have full staff on site at naptime but also extra adults in the building who have been trained to assist in case of an emergency. Drills during the year at the end of naptime test their ability to get all the children out.

When children awaken they should be able to get up, have a snack, and have appropriate activities available. Many centers now have juice, fruit, or vegetables and crackers available for children during free choice time rather than at a set time for all. This is homelike and pleasant.

## Departure: Exiting gracefully

If each child has a box or cubby in which to accumulate projects and safeguard belongings, it is easier to locate everything to be taken home. Some paintings that have been hung to dry may have to be added at the last moment but everything else should have been distributed to cubbies earlier. An adult can pin notes on the children or pass them out to parents. A shopping bag or canvas bag for each child is useful and parents should be encouraged to provide them.

Children in a preschool should not have to wait very long in outdoor clothing but be taken outside to wait if parents have not come or be allowed to take off coats until they arrive. A short group time can provide an opportunity to review highlights of the day, to share a little information about what will happen tomorrow, and sometimes to give a quick reminder of safety rules for the trip home. Again, as at the beginning of the day, the teacher should be free to say goodbye and to be available if a parent wants to set a conference time or chat for a few minutes.

Child care departure occurs after a long day for child, parent, and teacher. Tense, preoccupied parents should not have to handle rebellious children who don't want to get their coats or to go home. When parents get to the car and when they are at home, it is their responsibility, but in the center it is a teacher's professional responsibility to help if needed. This is an important opportunity to help parents relax after a stressful day and for teachers and parents to share a few moments as people who like each other, not just professional to parent. One child care center always has coffee and tea available at the end of the day and often has potluck or center prepared suppers.

Sometimes centers penalize parents who are late with extra cost or threats and admonitions. Most parents only need a little assistance in cooperating with the center so that their needs and center needs are compatible. The night when everything has gone wrong and when the family budget is already strained is not the time to be fined for being late.

## Realistic expectations

Transitions between activities in programs for young children are filled with opportunities for learning just as all other aspects of the curriculum are. Therefore, they must be planned in much the same way as other learning experiences are—by taking into consideration the children's interests and abilities.

Unrealistic expectations of children, parents, or ourselves usually cause problems (Hymes 1981; Warren 1977; Stone 1978). When, despite the precautions recommended here and in these books, things do become hectic (or worse), it helps to stop everything, sit down with the children, and say, "Things are not going well. We need to do something about it." Children will help solve the problems, set rules, enforce rules, and get things better organized. Occasions that call for such discussions should be rare if your program is designed to meet the needs of children as you help them develop self-discipline. ▼

**Bibliography**

Hendrick, J. *The Whole Child*. St. Louis, Mo.: Mosby, 1980.
Hildebrand, V. *Guiding Young Children*. New York: Macmillan, 1975.
Hymes, J. L., Jr. *Teaching the Child under Six*. 3rd ed. Columbus, Ohio: Merrill, 1981.
Katz, L. *Talks with Teachers*. Washington, D.C.: National Association for the Education of Young Children, 1977.

Leeper, S. H.; Skipper, D. S.; and Witherspoon, R. L. *Good Schools for Young Children.* New York: Macmillan, 1979.

Lemlech, J. K. *Classroom Management.* New York: Harper & Row, 1979.

Osborn, K., and Osborn, J. D. *Discipline and Classroom Management.* Athens, Ga.: Education Associates, 1981.

Read, K., and Patterson, J. *The Nursery and Kindergarten: Human Relationships and Learning.* 7th ed. New York: Holt, Rinehart & Winston, 1980.

Stone, J. G. *A Guide to Discipline.* Rev. ed. Washington, D.C.: National Association for the Education of Young Children, 1978.

Warren, R. M. *Caring: Supporting Children's Growth.* Washington, D.C.: National Association for the Education of Young Children, 1977.

Wolfgang, C. W. *Helping Aggressive and Passive Preschoolers Through Play.* Columbus, Ohio: Merrill, 1977.

# 3

# Protect Healthy Development

As the number of programs for young children increases and more infants and toddlers are cared for in groups, new concerns may continue to arise for our profession. Physical, social, and emotional health are primary goals for the children and families we work with, as well as for the program's staff.

Even with the best of precautions, children occasionally are injured in group programs. L. Carol Scott reviews legal precedents on teacher liability for classroom injuries. In an effort to help programs reduce the chances for children's injuries, Susan Aronson, M.D., recommends ways to improve program environments.

Allergies can interfere with children's development and learning. They frequently require changes in the environment and the menus in programs for young children. Ruth Voignier and Sharon Bridgewater offer suggestions to reduce children's allergy problems.

One of the most common health problems in young children is middle ear disease. Rita Denk-Glass, Susan Laber, and Kathryn Brewer briefly review why early diagnosis of ear infec-

tions or hearing loss is essential.

Eating habits and proper nutrition are daily considerations in programs for young children. Recommendations are made for infant and preschool children's diets by Phillip Wishon, Robert Bower, and Deri Eller.

Two sensitive issues are also addressed in this section on protecting children's healthy development. Earline Kendall explores possible relationships between child care and the spread of infectious diseases. She suggests ways to reduce the risk of infection based on the limited research that has been conducted. This is one area that directors, especially in programs with children in diapers, will want to be alert for more definitive information as it becomes available.

Although child sexual abuse is a distressing topic, early childhood educators and parents are increasingly aware of the need to work together to protect children. Sally Koblinsky and Nory Behana, who have years of experience in the field, review appropriate prevention and coping strategies and recommend resources for children and adults.

L. Carol Scott

# Injury in the Classroom: *Are Teachers Liable?*

*Accidents and injuries are fairly common in preschools, day care centers, and other early childhood environments. Falls, bumps, bruises, scrapes, and cuts can happen even when teachers exercise all precautions, and more severe injuries, such as concussions and broken bones, are every early childhood educator's nightmare. Are teachers responsible for such injuries and can we be sued for damages? Immediate liability for an injury, or later suit for a condition which may have resulted from the injury are both possibilities for which there are legal precedents.*

As the field of early childhood education continues to expand, the courts have indicated a growing willingness to be involved in problems of the educational process (Ripps 1975). As the number of lawsuits for injury increases (Duvall and Krepel 1972), early childhood educators need to be aware of their potential vulnerability to legal action. Many teachers in public schools assume that, as employees of local school boards, they are not subject to legally imposed responsibility for injuries suffered by their students, but this assumption is false (Vacca 1974). While the judicial cases pertinent to the professional liability of teachers and administrators appear to involve public school personnel, many of the issues are relevant to employees of private programs as well.

## Issues and precedents

Two main liability issues will be discussed here: (1) *whether* teachers and administrators may be held legally responsible, and (2) *when* may they be so judged? Many legal and legislative precedents must be considered in discussing these issues. Some key legal terms are defined in Table 1.

### Whether?

There is little doubt that teachers who serve as substitute parents through the doctrine of *in loco parentis* will be on the firing line if blame is to be laid for injury-causing accidents (Drowartzky 1977). Accidents are a natural part of young children's lives and there is typically close continuous contact between teachers and children in situations where injuries occur (Vacca 1974; Drowartzky 1977). From a situation appearing so inevitable and self-evident, a multitude of legal questions arise in the event of an injury. Is the teacher liable? Is the school liable also? If the school is federally funded, does it have immunity as a governmental agency? If the school has immunity, do the teachers also? If neither has immunity, can they

**L. Carol Scott,** M.A., is Supervisor of the University of Kansas Regents Center Child Development Laboratory, Overland Park, Kansas.

## Table 1. Definitions of legal terms

**Immunity:** Exemption from performing duties which the law generally requires other citizens to perform.

*in loco parentis.* In the place of a parent; instead of a parent; charged, factitiously, with a parent's rights, duties and responsibilities.

**Liability:** The condition of being responsible for a possible or actual loss, penalty, evil, expense or burden.

**Negligence:** The omission to do something which a reasonable man, guided by those ordinary considerations which ordinarily regulate human affairs, would do, or the doing of something which a reasonable and prudent man would not do.

*respondeat superior:* Let the master answer. This doctrine means that a master is liable in certain cases for the wrongful acts of his servants.

Taken from *Black's Law Dictionary*, rev. 4th ed. St. Paul, Minn.: West, 1968.

protect themselves with liability insurance?

*Governmental immunity.* Governmental immunity, as provided by Section 1983 of the Civil Rights Act, is fundamental to any discussion of the liability of any federally funded schools for the acts of their employees. This legal concept, originally applied in the United States in 1812 in *Mower v. The Inhabitants of Leicester*, completely absolves a governmental body from legal responsibility for personal injury, and prevents an injured party from recovering damages (Mancke 1972). Personal injury includes slander and libel, but does not include bodily injury. In *Wood v. Strickland* (1975), the Supreme Court defined the nature and scope of school board member immunity. School districts are quasi-governmental bodies created by states, so in the past they have generally been immune from suit regardless of their acts or those of their employees (Mancke 1972). However, the United States Court of Appeals for the Third, Seventh, and Eighth Circuits have held that school districts were *not* immune (Salowitz 1976). Various federal courts have held that school officials have immunity if they act in good faith, have immunity if they act in their

official capacities, and within the scope of their duties have no immunity in their official capacities, and have no immunity in their individual capacities (Salowitz 1976). These conflicting rulings place in doubt both the existence and the scope of immunity for teachers, school administrators, and school board members.

A Florida court first recognized that the doctrine of governmental immunity was illogical and anachronistic in 1957, and it has now been judicially repealed in varying degrees in 19 jurisdictions (Mancke 1972). For example, courts have often attempted to limit the scope of the rule by creating artificial exceptions, such as unclear distinctions between the governmental and proprietary functions of the school district (*Sewaya v. Tucson School District No. 1* 1955; *Koehn v. Board of Education* 1964; *Dillon v. York City School District* 1966; *Ludwig v. Board of Education* 1962; *Hummer v. City School of Hartford* 1953), and in several cases have permitted recovery against government agencies after it was shown that the government's conduct amounted to a nuisance (*Bush v. City of Norwalk* 1937; *Lehmkulk v. Junction City* 1956; *Popow v. Central School of Hillsdale* 1938).

Where governmental immunity for school districts has been completely abolished, some states (Hawaii, Iowa, Nevada, and Washington) have specifically provided by statute for a direct action against the school district for the acts of its employees under the doctrine of *respondeat superior* (Mancke 1972). *Hoffman* v. *The Board of Education of the City of New York* (1978) is an example of the application of this doctrine where the lack of clarity in a school psychologist's evaluation led to an inappropriate special education placement for one child. The error was determined to be the responsibility of the school board under the rule of *respondeat superior.*

**If immunity is uncertain for public schools, it may not apply at all to federally funded programs such as Head Start.** If the concept were applied, and federally funded programs were deemed to be governmental agencies, that still would not suggest that an employee could not be sued individually.

The Supreme Court has not yet established a standard of immunity from suit for either teachers or administrators. These employees have a narrower range of discretion than school board members, and their actions affect fewer students (Salowitz 1976). In establishing a standard of qualified immunity for teachers and administrators, each of the factors considered in *Wood* v. *Strickland* (1975) should be evaluated: the amount of their responsibility, the extent of their discretion, the potential for the abuse of that discretion, the possibility that total denial of immunity would discourage well-qualified individuals from seeking these positions, and the need for adequate protection of student civil rights.

*Liability insurance.* A corollary issue to governmental immunity revolves around the need of teachers, administrators, and schools for liability insurance. A growing number of states authorize school districts to purchase liability insurance to cover employees' acts, usually at the discretion of the district (Mancke 1972). Statutes in several states provide indemnity protection for employees (Iowa, Connecticut, Idaho, Massachusetts, New York, New Jersey, Oregon, Wyoming, and California). Regardless of the type of statute, many states also limit the amount a claimant can recover (Delaware, Minnesota, Nevada, South Carolina, Wisconsin, Alabama, and Arizona), which serves to reduce the cost of the insurance coverage.

In some cases, the fact that a school district had obtained liability insurance was presented as an indication of its waiver of immunity, with variable results. In *Edmonson* v. *Chicago Board of Education* (1978), the court determined that by obtaining liability insurance, the school board had forfeited its right to an immunity defense. However, a Michigan court determined in *Pichette* v. *Manistique Public Schools* (1977) that a school's purchase of general liability insurance did not constitute a forfeit of the defense of governmental immunity, based on state legislation which provided for this. For teachers and administrators, liability insurance is often available through membership in professional organizations or unions. A group liability plan is generally made available for all members either for a small fee or is included with the annual dues (Duvall and Krepel 1972). The legal ramifications of the insurance issue related to governmental immunity of schools and their employees are still being explored.

### When?

In the past, the intentional injuries of assault and battery resulting from disciplinary actions by administrators or teachers in public schools have been the subject of most litigation (Ripps 1975). Increasingly, injuries by negligence, and occasionally educational negligence, are being heard by courts. The immunity that is provided by the Civil Rights Act does not extend to these types of suits.

*Intentional injury.* The primary scope of suits for intentional injury affecting classroom teachers is the selective interference with the person of the child, usually the result of discipline. In these cases, school rules and regulations lend important authority to the teacher's behavior in acting as substitute parents (Ripps 1975). Two clear lines of authority have been established relating to the acceptable use of corporal punishment. The first, *State v. Pendergrass* (1937), stated that no punishment may be inflicted that might cause lasting injury to body or health. The second, *Sheehan v. Sturges* (1885), stated that the court, not the teacher, should determine the reasonableness of the punishment administered. Cases regarding the appropriateness of disciplinary methods using corporal punishment are still heard frequently by the courts.

Other intentional injuries may also be the foundation for future lawsuits. For example, false imprisonment, generally defined as the restraint of a person of which she or he is aware and which is against the person's will, may be charged against a teacher using the increasingly popular technique of time-out. Another possible intentional injury is that of defamation, in which the teacher states or implies a student's inferior ability in front of peers (Ripps 1975). It remains to be seen whether suits of this nature will be heard by the courts, and if so, how successful the plaintiffs will be.

*Negligence.* When the issue in the suit is not intentional harm, but negligence, no interstate agreement exists on the standard to be applied (Drowartzky 1977). In Illinois, the standard of willful and wanton negligence is used; in California, New York, Oregon, and Utah, mere negligence is the standard; and in Ohio the standards applied in various cases have been contradictory. The Restatement of Torts, Sections 284 and 299A, provides definitions of negligent conduct and the standard of care which is applied to professionals. According to Section 284, negligent conduct may be either "an act which the actor as a reasonable man should recognize as involving an unreasonable risk of causing an invasion of an interest of another, or a failure to do an act which is necessary for the protection or asistance of another and which the actor is under a duty to do" (Drowartzky 1977). According to Section 299A, "one who undertakes to render services in the practice of a profession or trade is required to exercise the skill and knowledge normally possessed by members of that profession or trade in good standing in similar communities" (Drowartzky 1977). Thus, the questions in negligent injury are: what constitutes negligent conduct on the part of teachers and administrators, and should teachers be held to the higher standard of care required of professionals, or to the standard of a reasonable person?

Three components contribute to produce circumstances which lead to teachers' liability: the student's physical development, the classroom or other setting, and the teacher's training (Drowartzky 1977). Vacca (1974) suggests that teacher negligence results from the teacher's failure to carry out a duty owed a student, unreasonable performance of a duty owed a student, and/or dereliction in the safety and upkeep of all supplies and equipment used by children. Various court decisions appear to emphasize the following areas as leading to negligent conduct: (1) failure to give adequate instruction, (2) improper supervision, (3) failure to consider student characteristics, (4) lack of consideration for type of activity involved, and (5) inadequate inspection and storage of equipment or facilities (Drowartzky 1977). Conditions outside the school grounds may increase the element of risk, as children expect more freedom on field trips, yet the need for supervision is greater (Duvall and Krepel 1972).

The duty of instruction implies that students should not be allowed to enter an activity without first receiving proper instruction, especially when the activity is potentially harmful and dangerous (e.g.,

*What can early childhood teachers and administrators do to reduce the risks of injury to children?*

tumbling, even though supervised; any activity based on peer instruction; and the use of equipment in an inappropriate area or with inadequate space). Some court guidelines which have arisen from cases regarding a failure to instruct suggest that teachers consider the degree of difficulty of the activity; consider the age, level of maturity, and past experience of the student; and be certain to give careful instructions and to clarify the dangers before allowing students to attempt tasks (*Damgaard* v. *Oakland* 1931; *Brigham Young University* v. *Lillywhite* 1931; *Keesee* v. *Board of Education* 1962; *Crabbe* v. *County School Board* 1968; Vacca 1974; *Perkins* v. *State Board of Education* 1978). Other individual differences where the teacher's failure to consider will cause a breach of duty are the health, physical, and mental characteristics of the child, including past injuries,

physical disability, and present fear of, or objection to, the activity (Drowartzky 1977).

A failure to meet the duty of supervision can stem from either a lack of supervision or inadequate supervision. What is adequate, necessary, or proper supervision depends on the situation (Vacca 1974). Courts in Wisconsin found that age and other characteristics of students are relevant in determining the nature of supervision required. However, generally supervision has been defined as the use of ordinary care and the ability to foresee the need for additional supervision (Drowartzky 1977). The duty of supervision requires a teacher to be present in the classroom, and liability has been imposed when injury occurred during the teacher's absence (Mancke 1972). In *Cirillo* v. *City of Milwaukee* (1967), a teacher was found negligent through failure to supervise after leaving a class unsupervised for 25 minutes, during which time student rowdiness led to an injury. In *Schnell* v. *Travelers Insurance Company* (1972), a teacher left a first grade classroom under the supervision of an 11-year-old and was found negligent and liable for the injury occurring in her absence.

Failures to fulfill the duty of upkeep generally result from unsafe or defective equipment and facilities or a failure to take proper safety precautions. The failure to reasonably foresee dangers and take precautions or provide reasonable protection is considered a "defective plan of instruction" (Drowartzky 1977). The duty of upkeep also includes storing equipment so that it is harmless. This implies that the teacher has a duty to check the condition of equipment placed in storage by students as well. For protection, it is recommended that teachers finding one or more safety guidelines not met should give immediate verbal notice to the proper authorities, followed by a written note, a copy of which should be retained (Drowartzky 1977). Teachers and administrators have been found liable for an injury

Scott

occurring in an unlit stairwell (*Hovey* v. *State* 1941), injuries caused when a piano fell on a child (*Kidwell* v. *School District* 1959), and injuries caused by the use of faulty playground equipment (*Roman Catholic Church* v. *Keenan* 1952; *Cappel* v. *Board of Education* 1972). In *Everett* v. *Bucky Warren, Inc.* (1978), a school and its hockey coach were found liable in negligence for supplying a defectively designed hockey helmet. According to the court, the school, as a supplier of the helmet, was required to exercise reasonable care not to provide school-owned equipment which it knew or had reason to know was dangerous. This case also provides an illustration of the controversy surrounding the standard of care issue: the court ruled that the coach could be held to a higher standard of care and knowledge than the average person because of his long history of playing and coaching hockey.

In most injury liability cases, the standard of care imposed is that of a reasonable person; that is, protection against unreasonable risk of injury from dangerous or hazardous objects or grounds. According to the definition of the professional standard of care in Section 299A of the Restatement of Torts, one who undertakes to render services in the practice of a profession or trade is required to exercise the skill and knowledge *normally possessed by members of that profession or trade* in good standing in similar communities. Since professionals must exercise care equal to the standard of *customary* conduct, rather than "reasonable conduct for the occupation," and since jurors are not expected to know occupational standards, these cases often require expert testimony (Elson 1978).

The problem in applying a professional standard of care to teachers derives from its inflexibility because such a standard would be inexorably tied to identifying that which is nonexistent—customarily recognized and observed teaching practices. Although a higher standard of care has been imposed in some cases, as in *Ev-*

*erett* v. *Bucky Warren, Inc.*, the standard of care for schoolteachers and administrators has generally been that of a reasonable person in such a position (*Capers* v. *Orleans Parish School Board* 1978; Vacca 1974). However, in addition to a responsibility to help students avoid accidents, as well as a legal obligation to eliminate conditions which are inherently dangerous and hazardous, teachers must foresee possible danger and take the necessary steps to prevent injuries—a slightly higher standard of care than that for a reasonable person (Vacca 1974). It has been determined that teachers are not liable for injuries which result from the sudden and unpredictable acts of children.

*Educational negligence.* A special type of liability suit has been heard recently by courts which may serve to alter the standard of care applied to teachers: the educational negligence suit. The movement in state legislatures, state departments of education, local school boards, and teacher-training institutions for more accountability in education indicates that some form of objective controls must be found for assuring the quality of teacher instruction. The control available through the courts involves suits of educational negligence based on the common law right to redress for purely educational and psychological injuries caused by incompetent or careless teaching practices (Elson 1978). Perhaps the most significant fact about current educational negligence litigation is its paucity. Courts are reluctant to interfere in matters of educational practice in the public schools (Elson 1978). Although court decisions in favor of the plaintiff(s) in such suits may serve the purpose of common law through the amelioration of the court's social role of deterring socially harmful conduct (Elson 1978), the controversy over the appropriateness of such decisions is widespread.

Justice Powell's dissenting opinion in *Goss* v. *Lopez* (1975) covers many of the relevant issues in this controversy. Powell advised against creating an adversary relationship between teachers and children and recommended relying upon the education, experience, good faith, and dedication of teachers (Elson 1978). On the basis of this "teacher knows best" attitude, Powell concluded:

one can only speculate as to the extent to which public education will be disrupted by giving every schoolchild the power to contest *in court* any decision made by his teacher which arguably infringes the state-conferred right to education. (p. 600)

Justice Powell's assumption that frivolous or malicious suits would abound once a precedent is set for educational negligence injury may be false. The cost of negligence suits may make it more likely that high-income potential plaintiffs will seek other alternatives, such as private school placement. Insufficient legal aid resources for low-income clients will also prevent an abundance of frivolous suits. Time investment for the plaintiffs is another deterring factor, along with the reluctance of attorneys to handle educational negligence suits. For them, the cost of preparing a case is rarely offset by a victory in court and the usual percentage of damages awarded which they receive.

*Summary.* The question of when teachers are liable involves many legal issues: intentional injury, standards of negligence and professional care, and, more recently, educational negligence. It is important to note that in all injury liability cases, the plaintiffs must not only prove intent or negligence, but also proximate causation. The universally accepted rule as to proximate cause is that an act, or omission of a duty, or both must be the direct and continuing cause of the injury before legal responsibility can be imposed.

# Implications for liability in early childhood education

**Teachers in nonpublic schools can un-**doubtedly be held liable individually for injurious conduct, in light of the variability of court decisions regarding liability and immunity for public school teachers and officials, and in view of the trend toward repeal of immunity. Where programs are supported by federal funds, immunity from suit for personal injuries may be found by courts viewing such programs (especially Head Start) as federal agencies under Section 1983 of the Civil Rights Act. However, most other early childhood programs would probably not be classified as governmental agencies, because of private funding sources. Administrators would probably only be held liable when there is clear evidence of involvement in the injurious conduct of the teacher or of individual injurious conduct related to the teacher's conduct. If teachers and administrators could not be held individually liable for both intentional and negligent injuries, it is unlikely that preschool programs could survive without strict federal controls on certification, hiring, and classroom procedures. Parents would be unwilling to place their children in a position to be harmed by the negligent conduct of teachers secure in their immunity from liability. Both teachers and administrators would surely be liable for bodily injuries, intentional and negligent.

The primary controversy in determining *when* teachers may be liable revolves around the standard of care applied. Since early childhood education has not yet evolved into what might be considered a true profession, the lay standard of care, that of a reasonable person, seems most appropriate for cases involving the negligence of preschool teachers. Many teachers currently are not required to be certified to teach children younger than kindergarten age, and requirements for levels of education and professional preparation vary widely. Application of a professional standard of care to employees with little training would be unnecessarily stringent. It may be more appropriate to apply the professional standard of care to adminis-

Scott

trators or teachers who hold postbaccalaureate degrees. By virtue of education alone these employees should be expected to adhere to a higher standard of care.

The courts appear to consider the duties of early childhood educators to be instruction, supervision, and upkeep. All people who work with young children must meet those duties to the best of their abilities. Adequate staffing, administrative diligence, and documentation where feasible will do much to reduce the risk of injury in early childhood programs. According to Vacca (1974), when a pupil suffers an injury and the teachers are accused of causing it, the teachers must be able to show that they were performing their duties reasonably and it was not their act or omission to act which was the legal cause of harm.

Programs for young children must build into their procedures safeguards which ensure reasonable care. A well-stocked, easily accessible first aid station (which cannot be reached by children) is a necessary element. Regular maintenance of equipment should include checks for rust or decay in playground equipment, malfunction or breakage in classroom materials, and proper operation of electric appliances. A critical element of reasonable care is the adequate training of teachers in health and safety procedures, including a basic first aid course. Health information on children, such as allergies or other special health needs, should be kept current and visible. It is also wise to maintain records of all injuries to children, no matter how minor. These records should include the date and time of the injury, a description of the injury and how it occurred, and information on how the teacher treated the injury. When possible, each entry should be signed by two witnessing teachers. Such records may be invaluable in proving the reasonable care of the teachers in a courtroom.

It seems likely that, while intentional and negligent injury cases are of concern to preschool educators, educational negligence would not be an issue in early childhood education. Skills which children acquire in preschool programs are generally also readily acquired in a very stimulating home environment. Also, there is as yet no state-conferred right to preschool education except for children with special needs. Unless a preschool teacher were to use inappropriate methods to train skills or to choose skills which were developmentally inappropriate, no grounds would exist for educational negligence at this early level of education.

Injury liability is a real and ever-present concern for early childhood educators, however, and certification programs for preschool teachers should include coursework on the legal parameters of teacher liability. In-service training for teachers is also necessary so that teachers can be more aware of their legal vulnerability. Professional organizations such as the National Association for the Education of Young Children and the National Education Association offer group liability insurance plans to their members. Clearly, the better informed teachers are about what constitutes injurious conduct under the law, and about which ways teachers can reduce the potential for injury to children, the lower the need for using such insurance will be.

## References

Black, H. C. *Black's Law Dictionary*, rev. 4th ed. St. Paul, Minn.: West, 1968.

*Brigham Young University* v. *Lillywhite*, 298 P. 983 (1931).

*Bush* v. *City of Norwalk*, 122 Conn. 426, 189 A. 608 (1937).

*Capers* v. *Orleans Parish School Board*, 365 So. 2d 23 (1978).

*Cappel* v. *Board of Education*, 337 N.Y.S. 2d 836 (1972).

*Cirillo* v. *City of Milwaukee*, 150 N.W. 2d 460 (1967).

*Crabbe* v. *County School Board*, 164 S.E. 2d 639 (1968).

*Damgaard* v. *Oakland*, 298 P. 983 (1931).

*Dillon* v. *York City School District*, 422 Pa. 103, 220 A. 2d 896 (1966).

Drowartzky, J. N. "On the Firing Line: Negligence in Physical Education." *Journal of Law and Education* 6 (1977): 481–90.

Duvall, C. P., and Krepel, W. J. "Teacher Liability During Fieldtrips," *Journal of Law and Education* 1 (1972): 637–48.

*Edmonson* v. *Chicago Board of Education*, 379 N.E. 2d 27 (1978).

Elson, J. "A Common Law Remedy for the Educational Harms Caused by Incompetent or Careless Teaching." *Northwestern University Law Review* 73 (1978): 641–771.

*Everett* v. *Bucky Warren, Inc.*, 380 N.E. 2d 653 (1978).

*Goss* v. *Lopez*, 419 U.S. 565 (1975).

*Hoffman* v. *The Board of Education of the City of New York*, 410 N.Y.S. 2d 99 (1978).

*Hovey* v. *State*, 27 N.Y.S. 2d 195 (1941).

*Hummer* v. *City School of Hartford*, 124 Ind. App. 30, 112 N.E. 2d 891 (1953).

*Keesee* v. *Board of Education*, 235 N.Y.S. 2d 300 (1962).

*Kidwell* v. *School District*, 335 P. 2d 805 (1959).

*Koehn* v. *Board of Education*, 193 Kan. 263, 392 P. 2d 949 (1964).

*Lehmkulk* v. *Junction City*, 179 Kan. 389, 295 P. 2d 621 (1956).

*Ludwig* v. *Board of Education*, 35 Ill. App. 2d 401, 183 N.E. 2d 32 (1962).

Mancke, J. B. "Liability of School Districts for the Negligent Acts of Their Employees." *Journal of Law and Education* 1 (1972): 109–27.

*Mower* v. *The Inhabitants of Leicester*, 9 Mass. Rep. 247 (1812).

*Perkins* v. *State Board of Education*, 364 So. 2d 183 (1978).

*Pichette* v. *Manistique Public Schools*, 269 N.W. 2d 143 (1977).

*Popow* v. *Central School of Hillsdale*, 277 N.Y. 538, 13 N.E. 2d 463 (1938).

Ripps, S. R. "Tort Liability of the Classroom Teacher." *Akron Law Review* 9 (1975): 19–33.

*Roman Catholic Church* v. *Keenan*, 243 P. 2d 455 (1952).

Salowitz, C. B. "Immunity of Teachers, School Administrators, School Board Members, and School Districts from Suit under Section 1983 of the Civil Rights Act." *University of Illinois Law Forum* (1976): 1129–56.

*Schnell* v. *Travelers Insurance Company*, 264 So. 2d 346 (1972).

*Sewaya* v. *Tucson School District No. 1*, 78 Ariz. 389, 281 P. 2d 105 (1955).

*Sheehan* v. *Sturges*, 53 Conn. 481, 2 A. 841 (1885).

*State* v. *Pendergrass*, 19 N.C. 365, 31 Am.Dec. 416 (1837).

Vacca, R. S. "Teacher Malpractice." *University of Richmond Law* 8 (1975): 447–457.

*Wood* v. *Strickland*, 420 U.S. 308 (1975).

---

NAEYC members are now eligible for an Educators Professional Liability Plan through Forrest T. Jones & Co., Inc., 3130 Broadway, Kansas City, MO 64111, 800-821-7303.

---

Susan S. Aronson, M.D.

# Injuries in Child Care

Pediatricians, child care staff, and parents are becoming more involved in the prevention and management of health problems in child care. Child injuries are clearly one of the most significant problem areas for both group and home child care. Although there has been no thorough study of preventive strategies, my study, reported at the American Academy of Pediatrics meeting in April 1983, demonstrates that this topic demands our immediate attention because of the opportunities for preventing injury to children.

I obtained all the claims data for 1981–82 from the Forrest T. Jones Co., Inc., which manages the child care insurance policies through NAEYC's Child Care Center Student Accident Plan. The data are an incomplete view of injury in child care as many centers did not file any claims and others did not provide complete information about the kinds of injuries which occurred. The claims data, however, do indicate areas where preventive action might be taken to avoid the most serious injuries.

From 1981 to 1982, 422 claims were filed. Two-thirds of the injuries occurred on the playground. To assess the data by severity of injury, I used a geometrically progressive scale to rate the injuries.

| Rating | Severity |
|---|---|
| 10 | Outpatient visits, exam only |
| 12 | Outpatient visits, treatment required |
| 31 | Emergency room visits, disability of less than two months |
| 81 | Emergency room visits, disability of more than two months |
| 340 | Permanent disabilities |

By tabulating the severity ratings by the type of product associated with the injury, a total hazard rating was determined based on the *number* and *severity* of injuries. From the tabulation, the 11 products associated with the most frequent or more severe injuries were listed.

| Product | Number of injuries | Sum of injury/ severity rating |
|---|---|---|
| Climbers | 48 | 2,343 |
| Slides | 22 | 944 |
| Hand toys, blocks | 28 | 880 |
| Other playground equipment* | 11 | 700 |
| Doors | 14 | 690 |
| Indoor floor surfaces | 12 | 660 |
| Motor vehicle | 16 | 546 |
| Swings | 12 | 434 |
| Pebbles or rocks | 19 | 432 |
| Pencils | 4 | 403 |

* (Excluding swings, sandboxes, seesaws, and gliders which were listed separately)

According to this rating system, climbers were more than twice as hazardous as the next most hazardous product--slides. There are many correctable hazards represented in the top ten most hazardous products. These data have several important implications for planning early childhood environments, and for the training of staff.

1. Unsafe climbers, slides, and other playground equipment should be modified or eliminated. The U.S. Consumer Product

**Susan S. Aronson**, M.D., F.A.A.P., is Associate Professor, Department of Pediatrics, Hahnemann University; Associate Professor, Department of Community and Preventive Medicine, Medical College of Pennsylvania; and a Pediatrician for the Health Service Plan of Pennsylvania.

Safety Commission suggests these modifications to make safer playgrounds: place climbing structures closer to the ground, mount them over loose fill material such as pea gravel, pine bark, or shredded tires; space all equipment far enough away from other structures and child traffic patterns to prevent collisions; cover sharp edges and exposed bolts; limit the number of children using equipment at one time; and teach children to play safely.

2. Hazardous activities require closer adult supervision than activities with a lower injury rating.

3. Architectural features such as doors and indoor floor surfaces require special attention. Doors should have mechanisms which prevent slamming or rapid closure. Full-length view vision panels will help assure that small children are seen before the door is opened. Changes in floor surfaces and edges which might cause tripping should be modified. Long open spaces should be interrupted to discourage running in areas where running is dangerous.

4. Children must always travel in seat restraints in cars or vans and must follow school bus safety rules in larger vehicles.

5. Training and resources to change hazardous conditions should be made available to all staff. Injury reports should be routinely examined by trained personnel to identify and correct trouble spots. A systematic study of injury in child care centers and in home child care is needed to assist adults in making provision for the safe care of children.

Because child care services are so varied, it is difficult to generalize methods for establishing preventive measures in centers. With the increased involvement of pediatricians helping to keep parents and caregivers informed, there can be greater opportunities for the prevention of injury among children.

\* \* \*

For more information and free brochures about child safety from the U.S. Consumer Product Safety Commission, call 800-638-2772.

The American Academy of Pediatrics has initiated a program/information package which will assist pediatricians in counseling parents on safety. For more information about the program contact a local pediatrician or TIPP (The Injury Prevention Program), AAP, Division of Child and Adolescent Health, P.O. Box 1034, Evanston, IL 60204, or call 800-323-0797.

Ruth R. Voignier and Sharon C. Bridgewater

# Allergies in Young Children

Allergies affect children's development, learning, peer relationships, and behavior. While allergies account for one-third of all chronic conditions in childhood (U.S. Public Health Service 1970), it is estimated that only 35 percent have been diagnosed and adequately treated (Fontana 1969). Several children in your classroom most likely suffer from this problem. What causes allergies? What can you do to help allergic children?

## What causes allergies?

Allergy results from exposure to a substance that is noxious to some individuals but not to most people. The affected person's body reacts abnormally by exhibiting allergy symptoms. Most causes of allergies can be grouped into four broad categories.

*Inhalants* are substances taken into the body through the nose and mouth. Dust, strong odors, pollens, molds, and aerosol sprays are common examples.

*Contactants* are substances that come in contact with the skin, such as cosmetics,

Ruth R. Voignier, M.S.Ed., M.S.N., is an Assistant Professor of Nursing Education and Assistant Dean, Associate Degree Program, University of Louisville, Louisville, Kentucky.

Sharon C. Bridgewater, M.S.Ed., M.S.N., is an Assistant Professor of Nursing Education, Baccalaureate Nursing Program, University of Louisville, Louisville, Kentucky.

fabrics, chemicals, and metals (as in jewelry).

*Ingestants* are substances taken into the gastrointestinal tract. Foods and drugs cause most of the allergies in this category.

*Injectants* are substances that enter the body through the skin, such as mosquito venom, bee stings, and some drugs.

## What are the symptoms?

Teachers play a crucial role in recognizing children who display signs of possible allergies. Watch for signs that are seasonal or seem to be related to weather:

   frequent runny nose, sniffling, colds
   repeated sneezing (four or five times
      in a row)
   cough (usually a dry, hacking type of
      cough)
   red, puffy eyes
   dark circles under eyes (allergic
      shiners)
   skin irritations, rashes
   rubbing the nose (allergic salute)
   rubbing the eyes
   frequent nosebleeds
   wrinkling the nose
   breathing through the mouth

Other signs, harder to identify, are exhibited in ways that may have been labeled as learning or behavior problems:

   fatigue or tiredness, even after
      adequate sleep
   slowed growth and development
   impaired hearing

Photos by Elaine M. Ward

*Which possible sources of allergy in these photographs are also present in your classroom or home?*

restlessness
decreased attention span
pallor
wheezing
irritability
decreased appetite

Children may complain of
  headache
  stomach pains
  sore throat
  earache

Any of these signs may be present in multiple combinations.

## How do I help?

Once you have identified a child who displays possible allergy symptoms talk with the school nurse about the child and your observations. (Written records are best.) If no nurse is available, discuss the frequency of symptoms that indicate possible allergies with the child's parents. Tell them what you have observed and suggest they pursue this concern with their health practitioner. Ask the parents to keep you posted on what they learn. If allergies are found, parents will want to share the list of identified allergies with you, so you can eliminate or reduce the causes in your classroom and the school environment. The following table shows some common sources of allergies at home and school.

### Common Sources of Allergy-Causing Substances

| Source | Allergy-causing substance |
|---|---|
| tennis shoes | mold |
| animals | dander, pollen |
| live plants | molds in soil |
| dried plants | molds, dust |
| carpet, blankets, dress-up clothing, doll clothes | dust, fibers, molds |
| wax, soaps | odor, chemicals |
| paint, glue | odor |
| books, paper | dust, molds in old books |
| furnace blower | dust, molds |
| open window | airborne molds and pollens, insects |
| food, drugs | chemicals |
| pillows, furniture, stuffed animals | feathers, dust, fabric |
| chalk | chalk dust |

In addition to eliminating sources of problems, medical personnel may recommend taking some or all of the following steps to make the allergic child more comfortable:

- frequent scrubbing or vacuuming to reduce dust. (Dusting only redistributes dust.)
- installing a humidifier and/or air cleaner
- adjusting menus to eliminate problem foods
- frequent laundering of blankets, dress-up clothes, paint smocks, draperies, etc.
- selecting dust-free products (oil-based clay that does not harden, marking pens) as substitutes for clay and chalk
- changing furnace/air conditioner filters frequently

### References

Fontana, V. J. *Practical Management of the Allergic Child.* New York: Appleton-Century-Crofts, 1969.
U.S. Public Health Service. *National Health Survey.* Washington, D.C.: U.S. Government Printing Office, 1970.

### Annotated Bibliography

Bergner, M., and Hutelmyer, C. "Teaching Kids How to Live With Their Allergies." *Nursing* 6, no. 8 (1976): 11-12.
  How to cope with the many facets of allergy, food allergens, medications, environmental control, activities of daily living, and emergencies.
Bridgewater, S. C.; Voignier, R. R.; and Smith, C. S. "Allergy in Children: Recognition." *American Journal of Nursing* 78 no. 4 (1978): 614-616.
  Presents the scope of the problem of pediatric allergy and the role of the nurse in recognition and referral. Tools for subjective and objective data assessment are included.

Carty, R. M. "Some Facts About Allergy." *Pediatric Nursing* 3, no. 2 (1977): 7-9.

Broad biopsychosocial aspects of allergy are presented as well as available treatment regime. The parental role is emphasized as having major influence on allergic children.

Marks, M. B. "Recognition of the Allergic Child at School: Visual and Auditory Signs." *The Journal of School Health* 44, no. 5 (1974): 277-284.

Excellent photographs illustrate classical observable signs of allergy. Narrative further describes illustrations.

McGovern, J. P. "Allergy Problems in School-Aged Children." *The Journal of School Health* 44, no. 5 (1974): 260-264.

Outlines the quantitative aspects of allergy with presentation of statistical data on childhood allergies. Qualitative aspects are discussed in terms of the immuno-physiological bases of allergy being influenced by multiple internal and external factors.

McGovern, J. P. "Chronic Respiratory Diseases of School-Age Children." *The Journal of School Health* 46, no. 6 (1976): 344-354.

Broad overview of the presenting forms of respiratory allergies seen at school, such as asthma, rhinitis, conjunctivitis, tension-fatigue syndrome headaches, and cough. The influence of emotions and exertion on allergies is explored.

Rapaport, H. G., and Flint, S. H. "Allergy in the Schools." *The Journal of School Health* 44, no. 5 (1974): 265-270.

Specific activities schools can implement to aid in public recognition of allergy and its crippling effect on the school-age population.

Rapaport, H. G., and Flint, S. H. "Is There a Relationship Between Allergy and Learning Disabilities?" *The Journal of School Health* 46, no. 3 (1976): 139-141.

Allergy as a causal factor of learning disabilities is documented by examples. Nine behavioral manifestations of possible allergy and/or learning disabilities are outlined. Allergy Index profiles classical allergy symptoms.

Rosen, E., and Monnette, V. "Pediatric Allergy Nursing Assessment and History Guide." *Pediatric Nursing* 3, no. 2 (1977): 37-38.

An outline assessment form of five major areas of concern when working with children with suspected allergies—family history, allergic symptoms, systems review, contributing factors, and household environment.

Voignier, R. R., and Bridgewater, S. C. "Allergy in Children: Testing and Treatment." *American Journal of Nursing* 78, no. 4 (1978): 617-619.

Information on major components of allergy testing in children. Major forms of therapy are included with special emphasis on the nurse's role in immunotherapy.

"When Patients Can't Drink Milk." *Nursing Update* 7, no. 8 (1976): 1.

Discusses and differentiates lactose intolerance and milk allergy. Provides an excellent chart of lactose-containing foods and non-lactose-containing foods.

Rita Denk-Glass, Susan S. Laber, and Kathryn Brewer

# Middle Ear Disease in Young Children

Middle ear effusion, or otitis media (fluid in the middle ear space), in young children may adversely affect language and cognitive development, and thus has serious implications for a child's learning (Bluestone 1978; Brooks 1976; Clark 1976; Lamberg 1979; Ruben and Hanson 1979).

Early childhood teachers or parents may notice a child who lowers his head too close to the table as he is drawing. An ophthalmologist confirms the child's need for glasses. Similarly, teachers may note a child who follows verbal directions only after watching her classmates do what is requested. The family, alerted by the teacher, seeks medical assistance for the child, who has a mild hearing loss easily treated with medication. Teachers and families may also observe behavior that might be associated with such a problem. For example, irritability, listlessness, or intermittent inattention may be indicative of treatable mild hearing deficits.

The effects of reduced sound conduction (interruption of sound transmission) resulting from middle ear effusion during the critical learning period from birth to five years may not be apparent until a child begins to experience difficulty in learning, often later in school. The most likely effect is on acquisition of language skills, but the degree to which a child's development is affected depends on a combination of factors in the learning process (Downs 1977; Rapin 1979). Difficulties may occur with as little as a 15 dB (a measure of sound intensity) conductive hearing loss in young children (Rapin 1979; Zinkus, Gottlieb, and Schapiro 1978). Even a temporary fluctuating, mild hearing loss of about 15 dB in a young child, a phenomenon usually associated with middle ear effusion, may have a significant effect on cognitive development (Ruben and Hanson 1979).

## Diagnosis

Middle ear effusion is the disorder most commonly diagnosed in young children during office visits to pediatricians (National Center for Health Statistics 1978). It is second only to the common cold as a disease of childhood, and frequently follows cold symptoms such as a runny or stuffy nose. The prevalence of middle ear effusion in infants and young children has been estimated in some studies to be as

**Rita Denk-Glass**, Ed.D., is a Program Specialist with the Program Services Department of the National Easter Seal Society in Chicago.

**Susan S. Laber**, M.A., is former head of the Communicative Disorders Section in the Department of Pediatrics at the University of Chicago Medical Center, and is currently Supervisor at Flower Hospital in New York City.

**Kathryn Brewer**, M.S., is a clinical audiologist at the Holy Cross Hospital Department of Communicative Disorders in Chicago.

high as 50 percent (Bluestone 1978; Paradise, Smith, and Bluestone 1976). Yet disease of the middle ear has often remained undetected in young children because fever and earache are often absent, and irritability and lethargy are the only observable symptoms.

If middle ear effusion and the resulting hearing loss are detected early in young children, appropriate medical care can be provided, and subsequent language, learning, and cognitive delays might be prevented. The only means of detecting middle ear disease, until recently, was otoscopic examination (visual inspection with a device that illuminates the eardrum). Unfortunately, many cases of middle ear effusion in young children can escape detection when this method is used (Paradise and Smith 1979). Tympanometry, a new, rapid, and objective method for testing the mobility of the eardrum, is more accurate in detecting middle ear disease in patients, including young children, than otoscopic examination of the eardrum (Brooks 1978; Roberts 1976). A plug is placed in the ear canal, and air under a very slight, variable pressure is introduced between the plug and the eardrum. A graph indicating the mobility of the eardrum under this variable pressure is obtained. If presence of fluid behind the eardrum is suspected, the examiner suggests a medical consultation.

Hearing loss in children can be sensorineural, conductive, or both. Sensorineural hearing loss (hearing loss due to abnormality or damage of the eardrum or its nerve) is found in only 4 percent of all children. This condition can be assessed by testing with pure tones. Earphones are placed over the child's ears, and the child listens to beeps at various single frequencies and at different volumes. From the responses, an audiogram (a graph of the child's hearing at different pitches) is obtained. In most hearing screening programs, tests for sensorineural hearing are given, but the far more prevalent conductive hearing loss in children is not

Betsy Danielson

*Regular screening for detection and treatment of middle ear disease is essential in early childhood.*

checked. Brooks (1976) estimates 90 percent of all hearing loss in children is conductive, detecting it in 30 percent of all preschoolers. Therefore, screening tests for young children should include tests for both types of hearing loss.

The Holy Cross Hospital Department of Communicative Disorders in Chicago offers screening tests for conductive and sensorineural hearing for young children as a part of its community outreach program. During 1979–80, 149 preschool and kindergarten children between the ages of three and six years were screened in three school locations. Only children with adequate performance in the preschool program, as judged by classroom teachers, were included; children with gross handicapping disorders were excluded. The children's families were lower-middle socioeconomic status, and approximately 90 percent of the children were White. A

116

questionnaire filled out by the parents prior to testing included questions about familial ear problems and the parents' concerns about their children's development and hearing. The testing technique and criteria used were the *Guidelines for Acoustic Admittance Screening* (American Speech-Language-Hearing Association 1979). The parents of those children whose tympanograms did not conform to normal standards (36 percent) were informed of the results, and the recommendation was made that they seek medical advice.

These results are an indication of the prevalence of loss of hearing in young children due to middle ear disease. Such loss has serious implications for children's development and future school success. Regular screening for detection and treatment of middle ear disease is essential in early childhood (Jaffe 1977). Procedures should include tests for both conductive and sensorineural hearing loss. Parents and teachers are encouraged to be especially observant of young children at risk for middle ear disease. 〽

### References

American Speech-Language-Hearing Association. *Guidelines for Acoustic Admittance Screening of Middle Ear Function* 21 (1979): 283–288.

Bluestone, C. D. "Morbidity Complications and Sequelae to Otitis Media." In *Impedance Screening for Middle Ear Disease in Children*, ed. E. Harford, F. Bess, C. Bluestone, and J. Klein. New York: Grune & Stratton, 1978.

Brooks, D. "Impedance Screening for School Children: State of the Art." In *Impedance Screening for Middle Ear Disease in Children*, ed. E. Harford, F. Bess, C. Bluestone, and J. Klein. New York: Grune & Stratton, 1978.

Brooks, D. "School Screening for Middle Ear Effusions." *Annals of Otology, Rhinology and Laryngology* 85 (1976): 223–228.

Clark, M. "Hearing: A Link to I.Q.?" *Newsweek* 97 (June 14, 1976): 97.

Downs, M. "The Expanding Imperatives of Early Identification." In *Childhood Deafness: Causation, Assessment and Management*, ed. F. Bess. New York: Grune & Stratton, 1977.

Jaffe, B. *Hearing Loss in Children: A Comprehensive Text*. Baltimore: University Park Press, 1977.

Lamberg, L. "The Silent Threat of Middle Ear Infections." *Better Homes and Gardens* 57, no. 11 (November 1979): 132–136.

National Center for Health Statistics. *Office Visits to Pediatricians*. Hyattsville, Md.: National Ambulatory Care Services, 1978.

Paradise, J., and Smith, C. "Impedance Screening for Preschool Children: State of the Art." *Annals of Otology, Rhinology and Laryngology* 88 (1979): 56–65.

Paradise, J.; Smith, C.; and Bluestone, C. "Tympanometric Detection of Middle Ear Effusion in Infants and Young Children." *Pediatrics* 58 (1976): 198–210.

Rapin, I. "Conductive Hearing Loss—Effects on Children's Language and Scholastic Skills." *Annals of Otology, Rhinology and Laryngology* 88 (1979): 3–12.

Roberts, M. "Comparative Study of Pure Tone, Impedance and Otoscopic Hearing Screening Methods." *Archives of Otolaryngology* 102 (1976): 690–694.

Ruben, R., and Hanson, D. "Summary of Discussion and Recommendations Made During the Workshop on Otitis Media and Development." *Annals of Otology, Rhinology and Laryngology* 88 (1979): 107–111.

Zinkus, P.; Gottlieb, M.; and Schapiro, M. "Development and Psychoeducational Sequelae of Chronic Otitis Media." *American Journal of Diseases in Children* 132 (1978): 1100–1104.

Phillip M. Wishon, Robert Bower, and Ben Eller

# Childhood Obesity
## Prevention and Treatment

*Children and adults who are overweight are at great risk for a variety of health and psychological problems. What can parents and teachers do to ensure that they and the children they care for develop good eating and exercise habits to maintain a healthy weight?*

Obesity is as much of a health hazard as any other life-threatening disease. In the United States, obesity has been called our primary health defect. Its relation to diabetes and cardiovascular disease is now acknowledged (Leveille and Romsos 1974). Concern about early childhood obesity and its possible association with later obesity is growing, and although it cannot be said with certainty that early childhood obesity results in adult obesity, children who are obese at seven years seldom change their body build and constitution at later ages (Brasel 1978).

Obesity has been defined as a "clinical presentation characterized by excessive fatness" (Committee on Nutrition of the Mother and Preschool Child 1978, p. 125). There is no consensus, however, as to what constitutes excessive fatness, or how

**Phillip M. Wishon,** Ph.D., is Associate Professor of Early Childhood Education, University of Northern Colorado, Greeley, Colorado.

**Robert Bower,** Ed.D., is Assistant Professor of Education/Psychology, Wayne State College, Wayne, Nebraska.

**Ben Eller,** Ed.D., is Associate Professor of Educational Psychology, East Tennessee State University, Johnson City, Tennessee.

it is to be measured. Most nutritionists and pediatricians agree that an infant above the 85th percentile of weight in relation to length on the growth charts should be considered obese and may be at risk for developing adult obesity. While the measurement of skinfold thickness is not as precise as a careful measurement of height and weight, the routine use of skinfold measurements as a part of well baby care increases the clinician's ability to diagnose early childhood obesity. The routine use of skinfold measurements helps to differentiate large babies with bigger body frames consisting of skeletal and muscular tissues from infants of identical body weight with a high proportion of body fat.

In the first year of life, babies grow faster than during any other time. An infant's birth weight will probably double by 5 months of age, triple by 1 year, and quadruple by the end of the second year. An infant may grow 10 to 11 inches in length between birth and the first birthday, and another 2 to 3 inches by 18 months. The *kind* of tissue a rapidly growing infant is adding is of paramount importance. Baby fat must be taken seriously—fat babies are *not* healthier babies.

In our society, obese older children and adults are invariably subjected to stigmatizing attitudes. Obese individuals are perceived by others to be less likable and less desirable than the nonobese (Richardson et al. 1961; Canning and Mayer 1966; Maddox, Back, and Liederman 1968; Maddox and Liederman 1969; Kalisch 1972). In addition to the adverse mechanical and physiological complications to be dealt with, obese individuals are frequently ridiculed, despised, and often avoided. The worst result of socially derogatory attitudes is that those affected come to accept the negative evaluations of society (Goffman 1963).

## Background Information

### Prevalence

It is estimated that 20 percent of Americans are overweight enough to be at risk for certain diet-related diseases (Winick 1981), and for every 100 children, at least 16 are obese (Mayer 1968). In some population subgroups, such as children in low-income families or children with obese parents and siblings, the rates are considerably higher (Dwyer 1980).

### Pathology

While it is commonly acknowledged that most excess fat tissue is the result of a too sedentary lifestyle and a general lack of nutritional awareness, childhood obesity may involve other factors including heredity, form and structure of fat tissue, energy balance, and central nervous control (Vuille and Mellbin 1979).

*Heredity versus environment.* Until recently, obesity was thought to be caused by problems in the energy balance between eating and physical activity. However, it is now believed that childhood obesity may be to a great extent inherited (Brook, Huntley, and Slack 1975; Biron, Mongeau, and Bertrand 1977). While the genes may have a direct influence on the metabolic rate and on the proliferation of the fat tissue, the environment determines

physical activity and formation of eating habits. Thus both genetic and environmental factors are involved.

*Form and structure of fat tissue.* Overnutrition during infancy is believed to result in an increased risk of a form of obesity characterized by an excessive number of fat cells (Mellbin and Vuille 1973; Charney et al. 1976). The correlation between early childhood nutrition and weight gain with the degree of overweight in later childhood remains the focus of considerable study.

*Energy balance.* The size and number of fat cells at a given time are determined predominantly by the individual's energy balance, which is the product of eating behavior, physical activity, and metabolic rate.

*Central nervous control.* While the autonomic nervous system controls appetite and motor behavior, individual variations might account for some individual differences in energy balance. It is unclear whether the metabolic rate may be modified by stress or other psychological conditions.

Given the devastating mechanical, physiological, and psychological consequences of childhood obesity, parents and teachers should be aware of successful strategies for its prevention, identification, and treatment.

## Infant care

For the infant, the major environmental influences that affect weight gain and the tendency to become obese (energy intake and physical activity) are controlled by the mother. Carefully managed maternal food consumption (especially during the third trimester of pregnancy) will usually result in appropriate weight gain before birth. After birth, feeding practices to maintain an appropriate weight gain should be determined through medical consultation and may include the following.

1. provide only breast milk or commercial formula during the first five to six months and provide it as the major source of nutrients up to one year of age
2. introduce no solids until six months after birth
3. refrain from force-feeding the last milk in the bottle for infants who are not breast-fed
4. select foods low in calories whenever possible
5. offer water between feedings to meet thirst and sucking needs and in an attempt to regulate subsequent milk intake
6. avoid the use of feedings as a response to *all* of a baby's distress signals (a drink of water, a back rub, a snuggle with someone in a rocking chair are noncaloric pacifiers) (Brasel 1978)

Physical activity should be encouraged through play activities and by providing space for crawling, climbing, and rolling. Placing a child in an infant seat or playpen for a long period of time during the waking hours diminishes physical activity. For overweight infants, nutrient intake should be provided at the lower limits of normal requirements. By increasing energy output, the body weight will remain somewhat stable and the infant will grow into body weight. *Weight loss is not the goal of therapy for infants.*

## Eating habits

Eating habits are established when children are very young. A combination of both internal controls (hunger and satiety signals) and external factors (time of day, sight of others eating, visual prominence of food, social factors, cultural habits, and other cues) affect eating habits. Awareness of and resistance to external controls helps to diminish their influence, and contributes to the development of healthful eating habits.

Eating on the run, snacking excessively, and skipping regular meals are just a few of the activities which tend to alter good eating habits. Children should be provided with three well-spaced meals daily—preferably at about the same time every day. Eating should be permitted in one room of the home only, and families should avoid engaging in other activities such as watching television while eating.

A reasonable variety of acceptable food choices should be served at mealtimes. Small to modest quantities of food should be prepared and served as attractively as possible. Food should be chewed slowly and thoroughly after each bite, and children should learn to swallow all of the food in their mouth before continuing to eat or taking a drink. Finger foods or bite-sized pieces are best for infants and toddlers. Children should also be encouraged to use eating utensils as their motor skills develop.

While it is not necessary to always deny a child a favorite non-nutritious food item, the accessibility of foods that can contribute to obesity, tooth decay, or incomplete nutrition such as chips, cake, and candy should be restricted. Bribing children with dessert or other food treats tends to reinforce overeating. Praise, smiles, hugs, and other methods are much more effective and healthy both physically and emotionally for child and adult.

The way children eat can sometimes be as important as what they eat. For example, children should be expected to eat a slice of birthday cake from a prepared setting at a table rather than snacking with their fingers from the pan. The pleasure of human interaction at mealtimes should also be emphasized. When they learn and practice appropriate eating habits, the prospects for children to lead more healthful lives are enhanced. Once mastered, good eating skills become a natural and fundamental element of healthy human experience.

## Nutrition

Proper nutrition is the key to good

Wishon, Bower, and Eller

health. Malnutrition has been associated with deficiencies in visual acuity, intellectual ability, skill development, and motor ability. A causal relationship may exist between nutritional imbalances in children and fatigue, boredom, lack of concentration, and lack of motivation (Goldsmith 1980).

Nutrition refers to the process which begins with eating food, followed by digestion and absorption of the food until its nutrients are distributed throughout the body for growth, development, and overall well-being. The Food and Nutrition Board of the National Academy of Sciences has established Recommended Dietary Allowances (RDAs) which state the amounts of the most important vitamins, minerals, and protein which should be consumed daily. These RDAs are cited in nutrition labels on commercially prepared food. By reading these labels, responsible consumers can select nutritious foods. No one food contains all the nutrients needed for good health and well-being.

The best single rule for good nutrition is to offer a variety of nutritious foods while avoiding empty calorie snack items. Plenty of high protein foods such as meats, eggs, and cheese should be included, while vegetables and fruits should be included as important sources of vitamins, sugar, and starches. Each day a preschool child's diet should include selections from the four basic food groups as listed in Table 1.

We can help children develop an appreciation for healthy eating habits by offering or preparing with them nutritionally well-balanced and appetizing meals (see Wanamaker, Hearn, and Richarz 1979). As children begin to learn about and practice good nutritional skills, they may be less likely to need to lose weight.

### Snacks

When designing a food plan which promotes a good energy balance, we must remember to count snacks as part of the overall eating plan. Many young children seem to need some food between meals— the capacity of their stomachs is small, and they cannot hold as much food at one time. In addition, many children do not seem as likely to become overtired or irritable when food is served more frequently.

Snacks can contribute to a good overall nutrition program if properly selected and thoughtfully planned. Foods chosen from the four basic food groups will help to provide the well-balanced diet that children need. Hard-boiled eggs, raw vegetables, fruits, cheeses, and cold meats are excellent snacks. A glass of water or fruit juice will satisfy thirst which may be mistaken at times for hunger. Snack foods that children or adults have trouble resisting

---

## Table 1. Recommendations for preschool child's diet.

**Meat group**—Two servings daily from this group are recommended. Lean meats, fish, poultry, eggs, and cheese are all good sources of protein, fat, and vitamins.

**Milk group**—Children should have about one quart of milk daily. Other dairy products such as cheese and ice cream may also be considered as milk products. These foods are good sources of protein, fat, calcium, phosphorus, and vitamins.

**Vegetable and fruit group**—Four servings daily from this group will provide an excellent source of vitamins and, to a lesser extent, carbohydrates and minerals. At least one of the recommended four servings should be a food which is high in vitamin C, such as oranges or fruit juices fortified with vitamin C.

**Bread and cereal group**—Four servings daily from this group are suggested as they provide the primary source of carbohydrates. Foods from this group provide some protein, vitamins, and minerals.

## Exercise

Many older preschool and school-age children who are overweight do not eat any more food than children who are not overweight. In many cases, they are heavier because they lead sedentary lives and do not burn up as much energy in their daily activities. Inactivity is as important as food intake in the development of obesity, and many older children who have a weight problem also have a low rate of daily physical activity (Bulen, Reed, and Mayer 1964). Markedly inactive children may be at risk and need special opportunities and stimulation for activity. Children under the age of six who are inactive may be in need of medical attention because most children are naturally attracted to physical activity.

The lack of regular physical activity can contribute to obesity in two ways. Without sufficient exercise, only a small fraction of calories is used and the unused calories are incorporated into fat storage deposits. Also, the normal internal mechanism which regulates appetite and satiety does not operate properly at low levels of physical exercise (National Institutes of Health 1976). To help maintain a positive energy balance, children should engage in any moderate physical activity that they can enjoy and from which they can benefit every day.

Inactive older children should be started slowly on an exercise program in accordance with recommendations from a health specialist. If skipping is too intense, they might begin by taking brisk walks. Other good ways for children to burn calories include jumping rope, jogging, swimming, riding a bicycle, hiking, and playing active games. A good level of energy expenditure requires 15 to 20 minutes per session. Aerobic (with oxygen) activities involving the joints and larger muscles in wide sweeping movements are especially good.

Skill activities may not be as inviting or appropriate because they tend to be diffi-

*Marietta Lynch*

*Children and adults who eat moderate quantities of nutritious foods and who get plenty of exercise will probably be healthier and less likely to have weight control problems.*

should be avoided. Candy, chips, and soda pop only add empty calories. Cookies, cakes, and other sugary items should be offered only rarely and in limited amounts.

Snacks should be served at least one-and-one-half hours before meals and should include foods that will not interfere with the child's appetite. Snacks should be offered at the same times each day, and children should refrain from engaging in any other activities while they are eating.

Aside from preplanned nutritious snacks, children's contact with foods between meals should be minimized. Children who are absorbed in other activities throughout the day will give little thought to food.

122

cult for poorly coordinated or inexperienced children. A variety of activities should be offered. Physical activity might be paired with other things a child enjoys such as listening to music. Physical activity is also stimulated when it is planned ahead of time and when equipment central to activity such as tricycles, balls, roller skates, and dance records is made available. Adults can help children become more physically active by accompanying them to parks, playgrounds, and swimming pools regularly, and by participating with them in a variety of healthy physical pursuits.

Overeating frequently is a reaction to stress or boredom, and exercise is great therapy for dealing with both. Moderate exercise is desirable in the normal routine of any healthy individual. Improving physical fitness and limiting caloric intake are the most effective means of improving and maintaining good health.

## Impact of the family

In many homes, the dinner table is not a site for pleasant mealtime conversation, or the kitchen may be a focal point for many different events. Some parents expect children to clean their plates—eating all the food wins approval. In some homes, certain foods are used as rewards or as punishments. Children learn that food can be a consolation for a lack of love, lack of success, and lack of companionship.

Many children are tempted by well-meaning relatives who offer rich desserts and treats as symbols of affection and insist that they eat them. We must teach children by example that food need not be involved every time we share enjoyable times together. Children need to learn to deal with their needs and feelings in direct and constructive ways with the assistance of caring adults who listen. Anger and boredom are not solved with cake and candy.

Parental encouragement and support can determine the success of nutrition education for young children. According to Bruch (1964), supportive families offer consistent but not rigid cooperation in supporting children with weight problems. In such homes, recommended changes in lifestyle are accepted by family members with a spirit of mutuality and without resentment. Although behavior problems may be present, food is not a focus of the problem and it is not used as a form of discipline.

Families and early childhood education programs for children in which wholesome conventions regarding eating habits, nutrition, and exercise are observed in a consistently supportive climate provide the most positive and realistic opportunities for children to develop healthful lifestyles. Our investment in human potential for future generations depends on our commitment to the advancement of healthier lifestyles both for ourselves and for all young children.

### References

Biron, P.; Mongeau, J. G.; and Bertrand, D. "Familial Resemblance of Body Weight/Height in 374 Homes with Adopted Children." *Journal of Pediatrics* 91, no. 4 (1977): 555–558.

Brasel, J. "Infantile Obesity." *Dialogues in Infant Nutrition* 1, no. 4 (January 1978): 1–4.

Brook, C. G.; Huntley, R. M.; and Slack, J. "Influence of Heredity and Environment in Determination of Skinfold Thickness in Children." *British Medical Journal* 2, no. 5973 (1975): 719–721.

Bruch, H. "Psychological Aspects of Overeating and Obesity." *Psychosomatics* 5, no. 5 (1964): 269–274.

Bulen, B. A.; Reed, R. B.; and Mayer J. "Physical Activity of Obese and Nonobese Adolescent Girls Appraised by Motion Picture Sampling." *American Journal of Clinical Nutrition* 14, no. 4 (1964): 211–223.

Canning, H., and Mayer, J. "Obesity—Its Possible Effects on College Acceptance." *New England Journal of Medicine* 275, no. 21 (1966): 1172–1174.

Charney, M.; Goodman, H. C.; McBride, M.; Lyon, B.; and Pratt, R. "Childhood Antecedents of Adult Obesity: Do Chubby Infants Become Obese Adults?" *New England Journal of Medicine* 295, no. 1 (1976): 6–9.

Committee on Nutrition of the Mother and Preschool Child. "Fetal and Infant Nutrition and Susceptibility to Obesity." *Nutrition Reviews* 36, no. 4 (April 1978): 122–126.

Dwyer, J. "Diets Won't Cure Teenage Obesity." *Community Nutrition Institute* 10, no. 33 (August 14, 1980): 4–5.

Goffman, E. *Stigma: Notes on the Management of Spoiled Identity.* Englewood Cliffs, N.J.: Prentice-Hall, 1963.

Goldsmith, R. H. *Nutrition and Learning.* Bloomington, Ind.: Phi Delta Kappa Educational Foundation, 1980.

Kalisch, B. J. "The Stigma of Obesity." *American Journal of Nursing* 72, no. 6 (June 1972): 1124–1127.

Leveille, G. A., and Romsos, D. R. "Meal Eating and Obesity." *Nutrition Today* 9, no. 6 (November/December 1974): 4–9.

Maddox, G. L.; Back, K. W.; and Liederman, V. "Overweight as Social Deviance and Disability." *Journal of Health and Social Behavior* 9, no. 4 (December 1968): 287–298.

Maddox, G. L.; and Liederman, V. "Overweight as a Social Disability with Medical Implications." *Journal of Medical Education* 44, no. 3 (March 1969): 214–220.

Mayer, J. *Overweight: Causes, Cost, and Control.* Englewood Cliffs, N.J.: Prentice-Hall, 1968.

Mellbin, T., and Vuille, J. C. "Physical Development at 7 Years of Age in Relation to Velocity of Weight Gain in Infancy, with Special Reference to the Incidence of Overweight." *British Journal of Preventative Social Medicine* 27, no. 1 (1973): 225–235.

National Institutes of Health. *Facts about Obesity.* Washington, D.C.: Public Health Service, U.S. Department of Health, Education and Welfare, NIH, DHEW Publication No. 76-974, 1976.

Richardson, S. N.; Goodman, N.; Hastorf, A. H.; and Dornbusch, S. "Cultural Uniformity in Reaction to Physical Disabilities." *American Sociological Review* 26, no. 2 (April 1961): 241–247.

Vuille, J. C., and Mellbin, T. "Obesity in 10-year-olds: An Epidemiologic Study." *Pediatrics* 64, no. 5 (November 1979): 564–572.

Wanamaker, N.; Hearn, K.; and Richarz, S. *More Than Graham Crackers: Nutrition Education and Food Preparation with Young Children.* Washington, D.C.: National Association for the Education of Young Children, 1979.

Winick, M. "Which Diet Would Work Best for You?" *U.S. News and World Report* 91, no. 10 (September 7, 1981): 47–49.

# Research in Review

## Child Care and Disease: What Is the Link?

### *by* Earline D. Kendall

*The issue of disease spread in child care is raising questions for parents, the public, and child care and health care professionals. Is there greater chance of illness for children in child care than for children who are in other groups? What role do parents and caregivers have in providing a safe environment for children? What are some of the diseases linked to child care? Are children the only ones endangered? This article briefly reviews current research in the United States on hepatitis, some diarrheal diseases, and infections caused by H-flu, and makes recommendations for practice.*

A clear trend toward increased use of infant and toddler group care is one result of changes in American family life (Bane 1976). The number of mothers who are in the work force and have children younger than age three increased from 12 percent in 1950 to 42 percent in 1978 (Zigler and Gordon 1982). The child care population has also changed: children are entering group care at younger ages than in the recent past, the number of children younger than three (and therefore in diapers) in group care has increased, and the number of children in full-time care has increased. These factors have an impact on child care and the conditions affecting children who are cared for in child care.

The problem of disease spread through these child care contacts is receiving increasing attention in medical journals (Eichenwald 1982; Pickering and Woodward 1982; Schuman 1983); the lay press (Cohn 1982a; Cohn 1982b; Goodman 1983; Howell 1983); and early childhood literature (Aronson 1983; Highberger and Boynton 1983; Silva 1980). As evidence mounted that outbreaks of bacterial, protozoan, and viral diseases are occurring in child care center environments, the language used became increasingly heated: child care centers were called culprits in disease outbreaks ("Day Care Centers Called Culprits in Disease

Outbreaks in Communities" 1983); child care centers were accused of posing excessive health risks (Hadler 1983); and spread of infections contracted at child care centers was viewed as "reminiscent of the presanitation days of the 17th century" (Schuman 1983, p. 76). These concerns are based on increasing information collected and summarized through the efforts of the Centers for Disease Control (1980; 1981a; 1981b; 1982) and others (Pickering and Woodward 1982).

## Child care health issues

The effects of group care on children's health have been an issue for many years. In the early part of this century, day nurseries provided group care for young children. The day nurseries reflected the health focus of nurses and social workers in such facilities. Day nurseries were seen as a means of giving children of worthy working mothers a sanitary environment. As the years went on, the emphasis on

**Earline D. Kendall**, Ph.D., is Assistant Professor of Education, George Peabody College of Vanderbilt University, Nashville, Tennessee.

cleanliness and nutrition at the day nurseries had to accommodate concern for children's socioemotional needs, which in turn was de-emphasized when cognitive development goals came to the forefront.

Numerous studies constructed according to rigorous scientific criteria have been done, including the work of Loda, Glezen, and Clyde (1972) of the Frank Porter Graham Child Development Center. Aronson and Pizzo (1976) referred to their work as a pioneer effort on a topic where scientific information was scarce and primitive. This study found no difference in the incidence of respiratory illness in child care center children aged one month to five years compared to a similar group of children receiving home care. With the assistance of a variety of health care professionals, the Frank Porter Graham project demonstrated that ill children could be cared for in the child care center without increasing the risk of serious illness if the program met several conditions: stable population; ample child/staff ratios and space; and appropriate attention to careful health practices in feeding, diapering, personal care, immunizations, and prompt treatment of illnesses.

Infant and toddler group care came under particular scrutiny (Caldwell and Smith 1970; Kagan and Whitten 1970) as the number of children younger than three in group care increased. Results indicated that infants in exemplary group care did not contract significantly different diseases nor were they sick more often than similar children in home care (Collier and Ramey 1976; Kearsley et al. 1975; Loda 1980). Doyle (1975) found that center infants had a higher incidence of "flu" but concluded nevertheless that excellent group care was a viable alternative to home care.

Aronson and Pizzo (1976) extensively reviewed health and safety issues for the study of the appropriateness of the Federal Interagency Day Care Requirements (U.S. Department of Health, Education and Welfare 1978). Their study of infectious disease pointed to a relationship between child care and diarrheal diseases, tuberculosis, and infections caused by *Haemophilus influenzae* type B (H-flu). Interestingly, in light of recent findings on the spread of hepatitis A among those in contact with children in diapers who are in group care, Aronson and Pizzo's very thorough review did not disclose indications that the spread of hepatitis and child care were linked. They do cite reports on diseases spread by the fecal-oral route in day nurseries (Gelbach et al. 1973). The Centers for Disease Control's Hepatitis A—Day Care Center study (Schatz 1980) and the work by Hadler and others with the Centers for Disease Control (Black et al. 1981; Hadler et al. 1982; Williams, Huff, and Bryan 1975) were reported after the FIDCR appropriateness study was completed.

Aronson and Pizzo (1976) also analyzed state and local group care licensing code deficiencies. States uniformly viewed licensing requirements as minimal levels of protection for children in group care. Silva (1980) cited hepatitis spread as indicative of the need for adequate standards in federally supported child care. In their 1982 Child Watch survey of state licensing officers, Kendall and Walker (submitted for publication) found licensing standards and enforcement of licensing codes to be weakening due to deregulation and economic restrictions which curtail licensing effectiveness.

Attention to health issues in day care by health professionals has been sporadic, although their interest dates back to 1945 (*Day Care: A Partnership of Three Professions*). A Committee on Day Care was under the Maternal and Child Health Section of the American Public Health Association functioned actively from 1961 to 1969, looking into health standards and

This is one of a regular series of Research in Review columns. The column in this issue was edited by Elizabeth H. Brady, M.A., Professor and Chair, Department of Educational Psychology, California State University, Northridge, Northridge, California.

Kendall

*Small groups of children who are still in diapers, and small centers provide safer environments for very young children.*

health issues (Peters 1962). The American Academy of Pediatrics issued a statement on day care in 1966 outlining the role of the pediatrician (*Pediatricians and Day Care* 1966), and in 1971 published *Standards for Day Care* which included specific health recommendations. However, these were not research based.

In 1973 the American Academy of Pediatrics issued a policy statement endorsing day care (1973), and a Report of the Committee on Infectious Diseases that included a short section on day care (American Academy of Pediatrics 1982). Studies of Head Start (North 1970); the National Day Care Study (Coelen, Glantz, and Calore 1978; Ruopp et al. 1979); and the study of family day care in the United States (Fosburg 1981) report surprisingly little empirical investigation of health issues. Day care was not even listed in the

*Index Medicus* until 1974 (Pickering and Woodward 1982).

Despite the paucity of research in health aspects of child care, these issues remained a concern. Califano (1978) warned teachers that classrooms could be dangerous to their health. Gillis and Sabry (1980) found child care teachers had little knowledge of nutrition. Silver (1980) suggested child health services as a basis for policy reform. Despite these and other indications of concern for and interest in health issues, a "data vacuum surrounding the issue of day care disease" ("Data Vacuum Surrounds Issue of Day Care Diseases, Epidemiologist Says" 1983, p. 5) still existed. Medical microbiological research attention to the link between child care and disease spread is not being conducted, reported, and reviewed by many who are concerned about the implications for children, parents, teachers, and communities.

## Medical evidence of child care disease spread

### Hepatitis

Hepatitis is a viral disease that infects the liver and causes destruction of liver cells. Like many illnesses caused by viruses, individuals can be infected without showing symptoms. Children often show little evidence of infection while adults may be very sick, with jaundice.

In 1975 *The Journal of Infectious Diseases* carried a three-year Centers for Disease Control report: "Hepatitis A and Facilities for Preschool Children" (Williams, Huff, and Bryan 1975). This article reported on hepatitis related to child care centers in ten states; "substandard" hygiene practices were found in four instances. Williams, Huff, and Bryan concluded that "transmission may not depend on substandard facilities" (p. 494), since they estimated that the ratio of asymptomatic to symptomatic children with hepatitis is 30 to 1.

In 1976, 2 outbreaks of hepatitis were reported in New Orleans (Storch et al. 1979). Outbreaks were defined as viral hepatitis in three or more households associated with the same child care center in a three-month period. A total of 11 outbreaks associated with child care was found in New Orleans in a two-year period. Of the 168 cases of viral hepatitis in the New Orleans area, 13 percent were associated with child care center contacts. Two of the diagnosed cases were children; they were diagnosed only after both their parents developed confirmed cases of hepatitis. In 44 percent of the child care related cases of hepatitis, no illness in children in the child care centers was recalled; 56 percent reported that children had gastrointestinal illness and fever. Of the child care related cases, 8 percent were child care children. Parents were at high risk if their children were one to two years old and in child care. Children in this age range were the primary carriers to infected households.

Although the children who became ill exhibited only mild symptoms, the adults to whom they carried hepatitis were often quite ill. The estimated financial cost per household was $1,952. In spite of the assumption that child care contact was a major factor in the spread of hepatitis during the two-year outbreak, and that closing infected child care centers might terminate that outbreak, no centers were closed. It was feared that closing centers would spread hepatitis to children in other child care centers as children were moved to new centers.

In 1979, Patricia Harris, the Secretary of Health, Education and Welfare; Dr. Julius Richmond, Surgeon General of the United States; and Donald Francis of the Centers for Disease Control agreed on a national study to determine the extent of hepatitis spread in child care settings. Twenty locations throughout the United States, where the counties had good hepatitis reporting systems and 40 or more cases per year, were selected for the study. As a result, the Centers for Disease Control unofficially estimated that 20 percent of all serious hepatitis A virus (HAV) cases could be linked to child care centers. Where centers are large (more than 50 children) and children are younger than two years, the percentage of HAV may be as high as 45 percent (Richmond and Janis 1982).

A Phoenix study found 30 percent of HAV related to child care (Hadler et al. 1980). In a two-year study of 279 licensed centers in Phoenix, 85 (30 percent) had three or more families affected. In centers enrolling infants younger than one year of age, 63 percent had outbreaks; in centers with children only aged one year and older, 32 percent had outbreaks; and in centers with children only two years of age and older, 2.5 percent had outbreaks (Hadler et al. 1982). Outbreaks were significantly more frequent (a) in large centers with more than 50 children, (b) in centers open more than 15 hours each day, and (c) in centers operated for profit. The introduction of hepatitis was related to the number of hours a center was open and to the ages of children served, but spread of hepatitis was found to be related solely to the presence of children younger than two years.

Since the Phoenix centers demonstrated such a clear link between child care and the spread of HAV, and had a rate of HAV ten times the national average, the effect of Immunoglobulin on HAV in child care centers was studied as a means of controlling HAV spread (Hadler et al. 1983). After 21 months of use of Immunoglobulin in child care centers that previously had HAV confirmed in one center child or employee, or in parents in at least two families, there was a 75 percent reduction of hepatitis in the community. The Immunoglobulin was administered in 91 child care centers within an average of 17 days of onset of the HAV index case. Child care directors and staff received training in specific hygiene practices and in case reporting as a part of an early detection program.

Another area where hepatitis has been a major problem is Alaska. In 1976 and 1977, Anchorage reported 116 cases of hepatitis during a nine-month period (Benenson et al. 1980). Of the cases linked to child care, 55 percent were related to one center which was modern, well managed, but which enrolled 415 children younger than three years of age. Benenson et al. conclude

> it is possible for youngsters with relatively mild symptoms of disease such as hepatitis to go unrecognized and remain in the facility during the period of infectivity. Despite the most rigid sanitary practices, fecal-oral spread of disease in a group not yet toilet trained is continually possible. It is therefore essential that persons involved in the care of young children be made aware of this potential. (p. 480)

By 1980 the Centers for Disease Control reported that 17 states had found HAV related to child care centers. Usually child care cases were linked to children from one to two years of age who showed minimal symptoms, but communicated HAV to adults at home and in the center.

## Diarrheal diseases

Acute infectious diarrhea in children is usually acquired through person-to-person transmission or ingestion of contaminated food or drink; "food or waterborne outbreaks in day care centers are unusual" (Pickering and Woodward 1982, p. 48). All age groups may be affected, but the highest attack rates occur in children younger than two years. Weissman et al. (1975) found the attack rate for children younger than two years to be 82 percent, compared with 11 to 52 percent in older children. A study of giardiasis found the lowest rate was in infants confined mainly to cribs, in contrast to the highest rate found among one-year-old children who were mobile but not yet toilet trained (Keystone, Krajden, and Warren 1978).

Most diarrheal infections last only 24 to 48 hours, but some caused by different organisms can be much more serious. The major problem with diarrhea is the loss of fluid from the body tissues, which can be much more serious in small children than in adults.

A research project designed with a control group and an experimental group to determine the effects of handwashing to prevent diarrhea in child care centers was instituted for a 35-week period (Black et al. 1981). Four child care centers, all a part of a national chain of child care centers in Atlanta, were monitored: two centers had a handwashing program; two centers did not. In 1976 diarrheal illness in the four centers was monitored. The child care staff recorded daily attendance and occurrence of diarrhea for each child younger than two-and-one-half years. Diarrhea was defined as any stool judged by the child care center staff as watery or looser than usual for that child. No attempt was made to identify diarrhea at home. During the two months of baseline data collection, handwashing and toilet supervision were sporadic. Baseline stool specimens were taken for all children in the program and for all new children entering the program. During the study, stool specimens were taken from each child with diarrhea and from one other child in the group that day. Stools were examined for certain parasites, bacteria, and viruses.

At the end of the baseline period, handwashing procedures were then instituted in the experimental centers. Staff washed hands after arriving at the day care center, before handling food, after diapering children, and when helping a child or self toilet. Children washed hands when they entered the center, used the toilet, were diapered, or were ready to eat. Bar soap and paper towels were used. Supervisors ensured that the handwashing procedure was carried out. A total of 116 children was observed during the equivalent of 2242 child-weeks.

Results reported by Black et al. (1981) indicated that even though children at control centers had less diarrhea than those at handwashing centers during the two-month baseline period, the incidence of diarrhea in the control centers was nearly twice that at handwashing centers for the remainder of the 35-week study. New children entering the control centers had diarrhea within two to four weeks after entering the program. Children not in child care centers usually have one or two diarrheal illnesses per year. Control children in this study had four diarrheal illnesses per year.

## Haemophilus influenzae type B (H-flu)

H-flu is a common infecting organism and is considered responsible for much of the middle-ear infection (otitis media) seen in young children. It is also the leading cause of meningitis in this age group. The organism can be killed by antibiotics and chemotherapeutic agents, but it also can develop resistant strains, a reason some infectious disease experts worry about H-flu infection. In contrast to hepatitis and diarrhea which are spread through the fecal-oral route, infections caused by H-flu are spread by the respiratory route and are highly contagious (Eichenwald 1982).

One case study of a center in Texas with a high level of operating proficiency and cleanliness indicated that one-third of the children in the center carried the H-flu organism and that one staff member did. When various procedures failed to prevent the spread of infections caused by H-flu among the children the center was closed permanently.

The Centers for Disease Control recommend that parents be notified in writing of any case of H-flu infection in a center. The efficacy of treatment (chemoprophylaxis) in child care center related cases is less complete than for household contacts. Unless 75 percent of the contacts receive treatment, it is unlikely to be effective (Centers for Disease Control 1982). As in the case of hepatitis spread, asymptomatic carriers other than the index patient may help spread infections caused by H-flu (Eichenwald 1982). Attempts to immunize children to prevent the disease had not yet proved to be efficacious (Granoff et al. 1980).

"No major epidemic [of meningitis in this country] has occurred in the last 34 years" (Centers for Disease Control 1981a, p. 114). During the first nine weeks of 1981, 893 cases of Meningococcal disease of unspecified cause and for all ages were reported in the United States (Centers for Disease Control 1981a), in contrast to 528 for the same period in 1980 (a 69 percent increase). Only 2 percent occurred in the mid-Atlantic states; 93 percent were reported in the western and south central states. The largest increase was in Texas, Florida, and Connecticut. Clusters appeared in elementary schools, but the high risk group appeared to be those with child care contacts.

## Recommendations

Recommendations from medical sources range from the specific suggestion to ban all nontoilet trained children (Eichenwald 1982) to see a broader view of the child care disease issue. Optimal health programs include preventive health care services such as health education for children, teachers, and parents; training of child care center staff in detection and prompt referral of problems, emergency and safety procedures; and referral and follow-up by health professionals (Richmond and Janis 1982).

A collaboratively designed health care program for child care centers, using the expertise of nursing and child development specialists, is recommended by Pridham and Hurie (1980). Suggestions for handwashing facilities in all diaper-changing areas in addition to those in bathrooms and food preparation areas also come from the nursing literature (Meyer 1980).

An editorial in the *Journal of the American Medical Association* (Schuman 1983) calls for "physicians as a group [to] assist daycare operators as a group in improving health standards" (p. 76). In order to address the issue of child care diseases, Michael Osterholm, Chief of the Acute Disease Epidemiology Section at the Minnesota Department of Health, is coordinating a symposium, Infectious Disease in Day Care: Management and Prevention, to be held in June 1984 in Minneapolis (personal communication, 1983). Only a "renaissance of multidisciplinary concern for new kinds of community services" (Peters 1982, p. 652) can provide the data base of information and ensure the likelihood of implementing change where problems are identified.

This review of the literature addressing the spread of disease through child care contact indicates mounting evidence that group care, especially when not carefully monitored, presents certain risks for very young children, child care providers, families, and the community. Determining the extent of the risks and the procedures necessary to mediate the risks will require the continued attention and expertise of both early childhood and health professionals.

## Recommendations for practice

Conclusions based on the literature related to disease spread in day care settings include the following. As more information on the topic is made clear through additional medical microbiological research other conclusions may be drawn for day care practice.

1. Require careful and consistent attention to handwashing procedures for children and adults (Black et al. 1981). Adults should "wash hands after any toilet/diaper related activity, being careful to use a towel to turn off the water to avoid recontaminating hand surfaces with fecal material left there when turning on the tap" (Aronson 1983, p. 13). Highberger and Boynton (1983) recommended using liquid soap because it is much more sanitary, lathering well, and using friction to remove microorganisms.

2. Post procedures for diapering and feeding in areas where these activities occur (Pickering and Woodward 1982). For example, Aronson (1983) advises cleaning "all surfaces touched during diapering. . . . with a solution of one-half cup household bleach to one gallon tap water kept in a spray bottle in the diaper-changing area, but out of the reach of children" (p. 13). She also recommends using "stepstools and toilet adapters" rather than potty chairs. Additional recommendations are offered in Aronson (1983) and Highberger and Boynton (1983).

3. Separate feeding and diapering activities so that these do not occur in the same areas (Aronson 1983).

4. Place the diaper area adjacent to a sink for immediate handwashing after each dia-

pering (Highberger and Boynton 1983).

5. Be aware that small groups of children who are still in diapers, and small centers (fewer than 50 children) provide safer environments for very young children (Hadler et al. 1982).

6. Continue staff training related to disease spread so that new staff receive information on appropriate procedures for preventing bacterial and viral disease spread and that ongoing staff practice such procedures (Aronson 1983).

7. Separate children who are in diapers from children who are not (Pickering and Woodward 1982).

8. Provide adequate paid sick leave in order for staff to have recovery time when they are ill (Peters 1983).

9. Maintain contact with medical professionals or the infectious disease control personnel in your local public health service for continuing consultation related to health issues of children (Schuman 1983).

### References

American Academy of Pediatrics. "Policy Statement on Day Care." *Pediatrics* 51 (1973): 947.

American Academy of Pediatrics. *The Report of the Committee on Infectious Diseases,* 19th ed. 1982.

Aronson, S. S. "Infection in Day Care." *Child Care Information Exchange* 30 (1983): 10–14.

Aronson, S. S., and Pizzo, P. "Health and Safety Issues in Day Care." Concept paper for the Department of Health, Education and Welfare as a portion of the *Study of the Appropriateness of the Federal Interagency Day Care Requirements.* Washington, D.C.: U.S. Government Printing Office, 1976.

Bane, M. J. *Here to Stay.* New York: Basic Books, 1976.

Benenson, M. W.; Takafuji, E. T.; Bancroft, W. H.; Lemon, S. M; Callahan, M. C.; and Leach, D. A. "A Military Community Outbreak of Hepatitis Type A Related to Transmission in a Child Care Facility." *American Journal of Epidemiology* 112 (1980): 471–481.

Black, R. E.; Dykes, A. C.; Anderson, K. E.; Wells, J. G.; Sinclair S. P.; Gary, G. W., Jr.; Hatch, M. H.; and Gangarosa, E. J. "Handwashing to Prevent Diarrhea in Day Care Centers." *American Journal of Epidemiology* 113 (1981): 445–451.

Caldwell, B. M., and Smith, L. E "Day Care for the Very Young—Prime Opportunity for Primary Prevention." *American Journal of Public Health* 60 (1970): 690–697.

Califano, J. A. "Warning! Your Classroom May Be Dangerous to Your Health." *Teacher* 95, no. 6 (1978): 20–34.

Centers for Disease Control. "Hepatitis A Outbreak in a Day-Care Center—Texas." *Morbidity and Mortality Weekly Report* 29 (1980): 565–567.

Centers for Disease Control. "Meningococcal Disease—United States, 1981." *Morbidity and Mortality Weekly Report* 30, no. 10 (1981a): 113–115.

Centers for Disease Control. "Multiply Resistant Pneumococcus—Colorado." *Morbidity and Mortality Weekly Report* 30, no. 17 (1981b): 197–198.

Centers for Disease Control. "Prevention of Secondary Cases of *Haemophilus influenzae* Type B Disease." *Morbidity and Mortality Weekly Report* 31, no. 50 (1982): 672–674.

Coelen, C.; Glantz, F.; and Calore, D. "Day Care Centers in the U.S.—A National Profile 1976–1977." In *Final Report of National Day Care Study* 3 (1978): 214, Cambridge, Mass: Abt Associates.

Cohn, V. "Day-Care Centers Infection 'Hotbed'." *The Hartford Courant* (December 12, 1982a): A10.

Cohn, V. "Day Care Diseases: A New Children's Health Problem Emerges." *The Washington Post* (November 26, 1982b): A1, A12.

Collier, A. M., and Ramey, C. T. "The Health of Infants in Daycare." *Voice for Children* 9 (1976): 7–22.

"Data Vacuum Surrounds Issue of Day Care Diseases, Epidemiologist Says." *Report on Preschool Education* (January 25, 1983): 5–6.

*Day Care: A Partnership of Three Professions.* Washington, D.C.: Child Welfare League of America, 1945.

"Day Care Centers Called Culprits in Disease Outbreaks in Communities." *Report on Preschool Education* (January 11, 1983): 7.

Doyle, A. B. "Infant Development in Day Care." *Developmental Psychology* 11 (1975): 655–656.

Eichenwald, H. F. "Infections in Day Care Centers." *Pediatric Infectious Disease* 1, no. 3 (1982): s66–s71.

Fosburg, S. "Family Day Care in the U.S.: Summary of Findings," U.S. Department of Health and Human Services Pub. No. (OHDS) 80-30282. Washington, D.C.: U.S. Government Printing Office, 1981.

Gelbach, S. H.; MacCormach, J. N.; Drake, B. M.; and Thompson, W. "Spread of Disease by Fecal-Oral Route in Day Nurseries." *Health Services Report* 88 (1973): 320.

Gillis, D. E. G., and Sabry, J. H. "Daycare Teachers: Nutrition Knowledge, Opinions, and Use of Food." *Journal of Nutrition Education* 12, no. 1 (1900). 200–204.

Goodman, E. "The Story of Day Care Is What's Not Going On." *The Tennessean* (January 14, 1983): 9.

Granoff, D. M.; Gilsdorf, J.; Gessert, C. E.; and Lowe, L. "*Haemophilius influenzae* Type B in a Day Care Center. Relationships of Nasopharyngeal Antibody." *Pediatrics* 65 (1980): 65.

Hadler, S. C. "Do Day-Care Centers Pose Excessive Health Risks to Children?" *Pediatric Alert* 8, no. 2 (1983): 5.

Hadler, S. C.; Webster, H. M.; Erben, J. J.; Swanson, J. E.; and Maynard, J. E. "Hepatitis A in Day-Care Centers: A Community-Wide Assessment." *New England Journal of Medicine* 302 (1980): 1222–1227.

Hadler, S. C.; Erben, J. J.; Francis, D. P.; Webster, H. M.; and Maynard, J. E. "Risk Factors for Hepatitis A in Day-Care Centers." *The Journal of Infectious Diseases* 145, no. 2, (1982): 255–261.

Hadler, S. C.; Erben, J. J.; Matthews, D.; Stanko, K.; Francis, D. P.; and Maynard, J. E. "Effect of Immunoglobulin on Hepatitis A in Day-Care Centers." *Journal of the American Medical Association* 249, no. 1 (1983): 48–53.

Highberger, R., and Boynton, M. "Preventing Illness in Infant/Toddler Day Care." *Young Children* 38, no. 2 (January 1983): 3–8.

Howell, M. "The Healthy Child: How Clean Is Clean Enough?" *Working Mother*, (January 1983): 17–19.

Kagan, V., and Whitten, P. "Day Care Can Be Dangerous." *Psychology Today* 4, no. 7 (1970): 36–39.

Kearsley, R. B.; Zelazo, P. R.; Kagan, J.; and Hartmann, R. "Separation Protest in Day-Care and Home-Reared Infants." *Pediatrics* 52 (1975): 171–175.

Kendall, E. D., and Walker, L. "Day Care Licensing: Eroding Regulations." Submitted to *Child Care Quarterly* for publication.

Keystone, J. S.; Krajden, S.; and Warren, M. R. "Person-to-Person Transmission of *Giardia lamblia* in Day-Care Nurseries." *Canadian Medical Association Journal* 119 (1978): 247.

Loda, F. A. "Daycare." *Pediatric Review* 1 (1980): 277.

Loda, F. A.; Glezen, P.; and Clyde, W. A. "Respiratory Disease in Group Day Care." *Pediatrics* 49 (1972): 428–437.

Meyer, E. H. "Nursing in a Parent Cooperative Child Care Center." *Pediatric Nursing* 5 (1980): 21–25.

North, A. F. "Project Head Start: Its Implications for School Health." *American Journal of Public Health* 60 (1970): 698–703.

Osterholm, M. Personal communication, 1983.

*Pediatricians and Day Care.* Evanston, Ill.: American Academy of Pediatrics, November 1966.

Peters, A. D. "The Committee on Day Care of the American Public Health Association." *The Journal of Nursery Education* 18, no. 1 (1962): 47–48.

Peters, A. D. "Children, Communications, Communities: Enhancing the Environments for Learning." *American Journal of Orthopsychiatry* 52, no. 4 (1982): 646–654.

Peters, A. D. Personal communication, 1983.

Pickering, L. K., and Woodward, W. E. "Diarrhea in Day Care Centers." *Pediatric Infectious Disease* 1, no. 1 (1982): 47–52.

Pridham, K. F., and Hurie, H. R. "A Day Care Health Program: Linking Health Services and Primary Care Nursing Education." *International Journal of Nursing Studies* 17 (1980): 55–62.

Richmond, J. B., and Janis, J. M. "Health Care Services for Children in Day Care Programs." In *Day Care: Scientific and Social Policy Issues,* ed. E. F. Zigler and E. W. Gordon. Boston: Auburn House, 1982.

Ruopp, R.; Travers, J.; Glantz, F.; and Coelen, C. *Children at the Center: Summary Findings and Implications.* In *Final Report of the National Day Care Study* 1 (1979): 251–274, Cambridge, Mass: Abt Associates.

Schatz, G. C. "Hepatitis A—Day Care Center Study Protocol."Personal communication with Day Care Program Specialist Carolyn Deal, Tennessee Department of Human Services, 1980.

Schuman, S. H. "Day-Care Associated Infection: More Than Meets the Eye." *Journal of the American Medical Association* 249, no. 1 (1983): 76.

Silva, R. J. "Hepatitis and the Need for Adequate Standards in Federally Supported Day Care." *Child Welfare* 59, no. 7 (1980): 387–400.

Silver, G. A. "Child Health Services—A Basis for Structural Reform." In *Care and Education of Young Children in America: Policy, Politics, and Social Science,* ed. R. Haskins and J. J. Gallagher. Norwood, N.J.: Ablex, 1980.

*Standards for Day Care.* Evanston, Ill.: American Academy of Pediatrics, 1971.

Storch, G.; McFarland, L. M.; Kelso, K.; Heilman, C. J.; and Caraway, C. T. "Viral Hepatitis Associated with Day-Care Centers." *Journal of the American Medical Association* 242 (1979): 1514–1518.

U.S. Department of Health, Education and Welfare. *The Appropriateness of the Federal In-*

teragency *Day Care Requirements: Report of Findings and Recommendations.* Washington, D.C.: U.S. Government Printing Office, 1978.

Weissman, J. B.; Gangarosa, E. J.; Schmerler, A.; Marier, R. L.; and Lewis, J. N. "Shigellosis in Day Care Centers." *Lancet* 1 (1975):88.

Williams, S. V.; Huff, J. C.; and Bryan, J. A. "Hepatitis A and Facilities for Preschool Children." *Journal of Infectious Diseases* 131 (1975): 491–495.

Zigler, E. F., and Gordon, E. W., eds. *Day Care:* *Scientific and Social Policy Issues.* Boston: Auburn House, 1982.

Sally Koblinsky and Nory Behana

# Child Sexual Abuse

## The Educator's Role in Prevention, Detection, and Intervention

"How can we protect children from sexual abuse without frightening them to death?"

"Preschool kids are too young to understand about molestation—and the subject is much too sensitive for classroom discussion."

"I'm scared that warning my girls will make them feel that all sex is perverted."

"Thank God I have a son and don't have to worry about it."

These responses are typical of those made by early childhood educators and parents in discussions about child sexual abuse. While the topic is highly distressing to most adults, the growing number of media reports on child molestation and the statistics concerning its prevalence emphasize the need for early childhood educators to take an active role in preventing the sexual victimization of children.

According to reported cases alone, girls born in the United States today have a one in four chance of being sexually assaulted before they reach their 18th birthdays (Gagnon 1965; Harborview Medical Center 1980; Kinsey et al. 1953). Cases involving boys are less likely to be reported (Finkelhor 1979), but recent research indicates that boys may be equally at risk (Kent 1979). Young children are among the targets of such abuse, with several studies reporting that children under six are involved in 15 to 25 percent of reported cases (Finkelhor 1979; Harborview Medical Center 1979). There seems little doubt that the secrecy and taboos surrounding this offense prevent the reporting of thousands of additional incidents, with the staggering possibility that almost 1 million children are sexually abused each year (National Committee for the Prevention of Child Abuse 1982).

Despite the growing estimates of sexual abuse cases, most children receive little information to protect themselves from this offense. Warnings about strangers do not alert them to the possibility that an abuser could be a person they know and trust. Children are rarely told that they have the right to control who touches them, and that they should say *no* to an inappropriate touch. Nor do many understand that they don't have to keep a promise of secrecy made to an adult. Children are in great need of realistic information about sexual abuse in order to avoid being tricked or misled into undesirable situations solely out of ignorance.

**Sally Koblinsky,** Ph.D., is Associate Professor of Family Studies and Consumer Sciences, San Diego State University, San Diego, California.

**Nory Behana,** B.A., is an instructor at Grossmont College, El Cajon, California; a master's degree candidate at San Diego State University; and a former children's social worker.

Early childhood educators can play a critical role in protecting young children from sexual abuse. In addition to providing prevention-oriented programs for parents and children, they can identify and report suspected cases that might otherwise go unnoticed. As coordinators of San Diego State University's Early Childhood Sexuality Education Project, we have been making presentations to educators and parents on child sexual abuse. While the topic was originally handled as one component of a general sexuality education program (Koblinsky 1983), the overwhelming concerns of our audience led us to deal exclusively with this topic.

## Comprehensive approach

Because child sexual abuse is a highly emotional topic, it is important for educators to develop a comprehensive staff and parent education program before attempting to work with children. Trained staff can work to increase parents' awareness of the problem, and to supply them with concrete, nonthreatening prevention strategies which they can introduce to young children in their homes. Skills for coping with incidents of sexual assault may also be provided for parents and teachers who might later confront this situation. Finally, educators may elect to organize classroom programs that review ways in which children can avoid potentially abusive situations. The sequence of these initiatives is important in ensuring that both teachers and parents are able to handle children's concerns and to support their acquisition of prevention skills.

## Programs for parents and teachers

Most parents and educators don't discuss sexual abuse with children until *after* it occurs. Their reluctance to present information about this topic stems from their own anxiety and discomfort, as well as their lack of knowledge about the prevalence of this offense (Kent 1979; Sanford 1982). Because they cannot envision young children as victims, many worry that they will frighten children needlessly or make them wary of affection from all adults.

We have found that adults are most comfortable dealing with child sexual abuse as a safety topic. We explain that information about what to do in an abusive situation is just as important to children's welfare as information about what to do when one gets lost, sees a fire, or finds a poisonous snake. The most effective presentations for adults include four components: (1) background information on child sexual abuse; (2) the severity of the problem; (3) effective prevention strategies; and (4) methods for detecting and handling sexual abuse cases (Didi Hirsch Community Mental Health Center 1982; Koblinsky 1983). Presentation of local statistics and cases involving sexual abuse, together with nationally published data, may emphasize the need for parents and teachers to become informed about this topic.

### Definition of sexual abuse

The terms *child sexual abuse, child sexual assault*, and *child molestation* refer to the exploitation of a child for the sexual gratification of an adult. Such abuse should not be confused with the warm, affectionate, physical exchanges between an adult and a child which show respect for the child's feelings. Rather, sexual abuse involves coercing a child to engage in sexual activity through subtle deceit, bribes, or outright threats and force (Adams and Fay 1981; Summit and Kryso 1978). Incest refers to sexual contact between nonmarried family members, such as a father and daughter or a boy and his uncle (Justice and Justice 1979).

Most child sexual abuse involves genital handling, oral-genital contact, or sexual abuse of the breasts or anus, rather than sexual intercourse (Finkelhor 1979; Peters 1976). Some abuse situations involve no physical contact, but require the child to undress and/or look at the genitals of adults (May 1982). While violent acts may include injury and even murder, the sexual abuse of children typically involves less physical force and violence than adult rape (Peters 1976). Since children are small and often compliant, the authority and persuasive powers of abusers are generally sufficient to establish sexual contact.

## Characteristics of offenders

One of the common myths is that abusers are likely to be strangers to the child. In fact, 70 to 90 percent of sexual abuse cases involve someone the child knows, such as a family member, a neighbor, or a babysitter (DeFrancis 1969; Finkelhor 1979). More than 40 percent of offenders in these cases are related in some way to the victim. Thus, it is not surprising to discover that child molestation most often occurs in the home of the victim or offender, rather than in automobiles, parks, or local school yards (DeFrancis 1969; Geiser 1979; Peters 1976).

Sexual offenders are not easily identified by their appearances. More than 97 percent are male, but contrary to the stereotype of the dirty old man, their age range spans from the early teen through elderly years (Groth 1978). In some cases, the offensive behavior is a continuation of the offender's own childhood abuse. Sexual offenders are unlikely to have prior criminal convictions (DeFrancis 1969), but this does not mean that they typically offend only one child. Indeed, the most extensive investigation to date indicates that the average molester of girls abuses 62 victims in his life, while the average molester of boys offends 31 victims (Sanford 1982).

Child sexual abusers typically exhibit low self-esteem, poor impulse control, and child-like emotional needs (Groth 1978; Summit and Kryso 1978). Many are married or have another sexual outlet, but continue to use children in an exploitive manner (DeFrancis 1969). Men who molest boys are rarely homosexual; they are men whose preference stems from the greater accessibility of boys or the fact that they were victimized as boys (Gebhard et al. 1965). The discovery that a significant proportion of convicted offenders report sexual abuse in their own families (Groth 1978) emphasizes the need to accelerate prevention efforts in order to halt this destructive cycle.

## Characteristics of victims

Angela, age 5, is a typical victim of sexual abuse. When her mother needed to handle business downtown, she sometimes left Angela with her uncle. Angela enjoyed playing hide-and-seek and other games with Uncle Jim; but one day he asked her to play a *secret* game in which they both undressed and touched each other's bodies. Angela felt funny about this request, but she liked Uncle Jim and her parents had taught her to "do as adults tell you." She continued to comply with his requests for more than a year before the abuse was discovered.

Angela is similar to thousands of children from all ethnic backgrounds, religions, and social classes who are vulnerable to sexual victimization. Her lack of information about the problem and the steps she might take to prevent sexual abuse place her at greater risk than children who have been prepared to protect themselves. There are other factors which also appear to increase children's vulnerability. Specifically, children with low self-esteem or who are lonely or hungry for affection are often sought out by offenders (DeFrancis 1969; Weiss et al. 1955). Abusers may similarly gravitate toward children who have been taught to blindly obey adults (Sanford 1982). Parents who leave their children poorly supervised (DeFrancis 1969), or entrust their children to individuals who drink heavily also increase the risk of victimization. At least one-third of assaults involve the use of alcohol by the offender (Browning and Boatman 1977; Gebhard et al. 1965).

## Severity of the offense

Child sexual abuse is a serious crime, regardless of the amount of coercion involved. Professionals agree that this offense is always the responsibility and fault of the adult. Children do not seduce adults; it is always the case of an adult taking advantage of a frightened or dependent child. Most sexual assaults of children follow a gradually escalating pattern in which the offender attempts to gain the child's trust before attempting sexual contact (DeFrancis 1969). Children may then be repeatedly victimized over a period of months or even years (Geiser 1979).

The impact of such incidents can be traumatic for both the child and the family involved. The degree of harm depends upon a variety of factors, including the relationship between the victim and offender, the age of the child, the nature and duration of the offense, and the manner in which it is handled by others (Sgroi 1978). While there are few studies involving the long-term effects of sexual abuse, researchers have found that some victims experience shame, guilt, depression, low self-esteem, and difficulty in establishing intimate, trusting relationships with others (Finkelhor 1979; Steele and Alexander 1981). Daughters involved in incestuous relationships may suffer anxiety, masochism, and a need for punishment, especially if the situation resulted in the break-up of the family (Kaufman, Peck, and Tagiuri 1954). Yet despite these pessimistic findings, there is evidence to suggest that detrimental effects can be modified or overcome by sensitive intervention efforts (Steele and Alexander 1981). Significant adults may help to reduce the probability of adverse reactions, and to prevent future occurrence of the abuse.

## Prevention strategies

There are many ways in which parents and educators can prepare children to avoid potential abuse situations, and to prevent an initial approach from becoming a sexual assault. These prevention strategies can be presented in a realistic, non-threatening manner, just as one might give children other safety advice. While adults may worry that children will be frightened by discussions of sexual abuse, it appears that children who know what to look for and who to tell will be less fearful than those with sketchy or exaggerated information. For example, one child whose parents had not discussed this issue believed "sex maniacs take off your clothes, murder you, and cut you up into about a hundred pieces."

*Teach children that some parts of their bodies are private.* It is important to provide children with correct terms for their genitals and the private areas of their bodies, just as they are given correct terms for other body parts. Such terms not only give them a vocabulary for discussing body functions, but also help them to recognize and report sexual abuse. Children should be informed that their breasts, buttocks, anus, and genitals (penis, vulva/vagina) are *private parts*. They may be helped to remember these areas by noting that they are parts of the body covered by their bathing suits. Point out that no one has the right to touch these private areas—even when one is wearing clothing—with the possible exception of a parent or teacher dressing a child or a health professional conducting an examination in a medical office. Children should also know that no one has the right to ask them to touch another person's private parts.

*Help children identify different types of touching.* Rather than teaching children to be wary of certain individuals, adults should help children to discriminate between different types of touching. Parents and teachers can provide examples of *good, confusing*, and *bad* touches (Kent 1979). *Good touches* make children feel positive about themselves and include the welcome hugs, kisses, and handshakes from relatives and friends. *Confusing touches* make the child feel a little uncomfortable, such as when a parent requests that a child kiss an unfamiliar relative or friend. *Bad touches* include hitting, prolonged or excessive tickling, or touches involving the private areas of the body.

Children should be given concrete examples of bad touches to ensure that they understand the concept. For example, adults might explain that, "It would be very bad for an adult to put her or his hand on a child's breasts, anus, vulva, or penis, or to ask the child to touch the adult's own vulva or penis. It would also be wrong for someone to take pictures of you without clothes on or to ask you to lie down in bed with her or him." Emphasize that adults may try to bribe, trick, or force children into *bad* types of touching.

***Teach children to say no to unwanted touches.*** Children should be told of their right to control who touches them. Teaching them when and how to say *no* is important in preventing the onset of abuse. *No* should be used whenever the child encounters unwanted touches or is offered special treats in exchange for certain behaviors. Children can be coached to respond to these situations with statements such as "No, don't touch me there! That part of my body is private!" or "No, I'm not allowed to do that." Practicing such phrases may help children to respond assertively when approached by a potential offender.

***Explain that bad touches could come from someone the child knows.*** Children often believe that an abuser is *weird, ugly, monster-looking,* or *wearing a dark coat* (Kent 1979). Therefore, it is important to point out that bad touches may not only come from unattractive strangers, but from friendly, attractive relatives or people the

child knows. Children may be told that, "Although most teenagers and adults are nice, there are some who have a hard time making friends. They may ask you to do things that aren't right, such as getting undressed or putting your hands in their pants" (Sanford 1982). If children ask why an adult would do this, try to avoid saying "because she or he is mean or sick." These words have concrete meaning to the child and may not fit the situation the child encounters. For example, when one boy was told that abusers were "sick in the head," he looked for men with bandages on their heads (Sanford 1982). Adults can admit that they don't know why some people do these things, but they want to warn children about individuals who might try to touch them in uncomfortable ways.

***Encourage open communication and discourage secrets.*** Sexual offenders often instruct children to keep abusive behaviors secret, and may frighten children by threatening that telling will bring harm to the child, the child's parents, or the offender ("If you tell, I'll go to jail"). Offenders may also attempt to convince children that their behavior is normal or a reflection of the offender's love for the victim (Adams and Fay 1981). Therefore, children should be encouraged to share all incidents that make them feel frightened or uncomfortable with a parent or a trusted adult. Children should be told that they never have to keep secrets from these significant adults, even if the abuser made them promise or threatened to hurt them in some way.

Adults should also inform children that they will not be angry or blame them if an abusive event occurs—even though they were warned about bad touching—but want children to come to them with the information. They can explain that everyone makes mistakes, and that the inappropriate touching was not the child's fault. Children should be helped to understand that reporting an assaultive attempt or actual incident involving themselves or one of their friends will protect others and make it possible for the offender to receive help.

Although most adults believe children's accounts of abusive incidents, children may be prepared for the possibility that someone (for example, a grandparent or caregiver) may doubt the truth of their story. After acknowledging how hurt or sad a child might feel if this occurred, adults should emphasize the importance of telling another person so that the problem can be eliminated. Children may be asked to name several adults they could tell if they were to encounter bad or confusing touches.

*Teach children how to tell.* Children may have difficulty informing adults about unwanted touches, especially if they involve a relative or family friend. Therefore, adults may help them to practice ways of reporting sexual abuse until they feel comfortable with the words. For example, if a child encountered unwanted touching, he might say, "Mr. Smith is touching my penis and the private parts of my body. I want him to stop."

*Use games and stories to reinforce prevention concepts.* Games such as "What if . . . " are effective in helping children to think for themselves and to formulate a plan for responding to possible abuse. Adults might ask a child, "What would you do if a neighbor asked you to look at some kittens in his bedroom?" or "What would you do if a cousin put his hand on a private part of your body at a family picnic?" Parents and teachers may also tell stories about other children who have successfully avoided difficult situations, providing children with positive role models. For example:

Timmy, age 4, was being cared for by his favorite babysitter, 16-year-old John. When John put Timmy in the bath, he tried to rub his penis over and over—even though it wasn't dirty. Timmy remembered what his mother had told him about bad touching and firmly told John not to touch his penis or private parts. The next morning Timmy told his parents about his "touching problem."

Opportunities to talk about sexual assault and play prevention games arise frequently. For example, parents may initiate "what if" games on general safety during dinner, interspersing questions about sexual assault with other safety predicaments. Discussions may also be motivated by news articles or televised reports of sexual assault. Currently, most of the curriculum materials which address the problem of sexual abuse in children are in coloring book or workbook format. Parents and teachers can use these materials for background information, and adapt them for use with children in more creative ways. (See the Resources section at the end of the article for a listing of recommended resources for children, parents, and teachers.)

*Continue to discuss safety rules concerning strangers.* Although the majority of sexual assault cases involve adults familiar to the child, a significant number of offenses are perpetrated by strangers (DeFrancis 1969). Offers of candy, a ride in a car, or the chance to play with some puppies or kittens are common inducements used to obtain a child's company (Macdonald 1981). While most parents do warn their children about the dangers of accompanying strangers, our own research indicates that many children do not understand the definition of *stranger*. Adults might explain that, "A stranger is a person you don't know, even if the person says she or he knows your mom and dad. Strangers often look and act very nice, so you can't spot them by the way they look."

Children should be warned to say, "No, I'm not allowed to do (the stranger's request)," even if they feel that there is no harm intended. Permission should first be obtained from a parent or responsible caregiver. Parents, teachers, and crime prevention specialists may also convey spe-

*The most effective classroom presentations on sexual abuse prevention for preschool and elementary children employ high interest, non-threatening materials such as puppets.*

Nory Behana

municate that sexuality is not bad or wrong. Rather it is the trickery, bribery, coercion, and taking advantage of another person that is harmful. To balance the information provided about exploitive touch, adults should make special efforts to point out the positive, nurturing, and joyful aspects of sexual interactions between loving persons. Adults who demonstrate warmth, affection, and support for others provide children with positive role models for later intimate relationships.

## Prevention programs for children

Teachers may complement their staff and parent education efforts with classroom presentations on sexual abuse prevention and stranger awareness for young children. It is important, however, that parents be supportive of and informed about these classroom activities. Parent meetings on sexual abuse prevention provide an excellent opportunity for review of curriculum materials intended for classroom use.

The most effective curriculum units for preschoolers and elementary school children employ high interest, nonthreatening materials such as puppets, skits, and stories (see Resources). These units ensure that children learn: (1) the private areas of their bodies; (2) the difference between good and bad touches; (3) children's right to say *no* to touches they don't like; (4) the importance of telling a trusted adult about unwanted touch; and (5) that sexual assault is never the child's fault. Curriculum materials should include many examples of nonstranger sexual abuse.

The Coalition for Child Advocacy has developed one of the few week-long prevention programs designed specifically for preschool children (McFaddin 1982). Early sessions focus on helping children to identify different feelings. A general safety film, "Who Do You Tell?" (see Resources)

cific safety tips about what a child should do and where a child should go (for example, to a neighbor's house or crime watch house) if bothered by a stranger.

*Encourage children to trust their own instincts.* Children cannot be protected from sexual assault by safety rules alone since specific rules may not apply to all potential abuse situations. Consequently, they should be encouraged to trust their own feelings and intuitions about people and places in order to protect themselves from possible harm. Adults can encourage children to rely on their *inner voice* which tells them that some requests from adults are unreasonable or inappropriate (Sanford 1982).

*Teach children about the positive aspects of sexuality.* In teaching children about sexual abuse, it is important to com-

gives children the chance to consider who they could inform if they had uncomfortable feelings about being touched by a specific adult. Later sessions ensure that children understand the private parts of their bodies, and allow them to rehearse ways of avoiding potential sexual abuse.

Programs for the kindergarten and elementary school children emphasize similar prevention concepts, with activities appropriate for the child's developmental level (Kent 1979). Role play activities are one means of helping elementary age children to think about how they might handle approaches from abusers. Incomplete stories, as exemplified below, are another technique which may familiarize teachers with children's understanding of the problem and may spark discussion about prevention strategies.

> One hot day Sara was invited to run through the sprinklers of the man who lived next door. After a little while the neighbor asked her to sit on his lap. As he began to tell Sara a story, he rubbed his hand between her legs. Sara didn't like it and wiggled free. She ran home without saying goodbye. Should Sara tell someone? Who?
> Had Sara done anything wrong? Why or why not?
> Had her neighbor done anything wrong? Why or why not?
> How do you think Sara felt?

Because adults rarely discuss child sexual abuse, it is important to help children feel comfortable with the topic. Should children begin to act silly, embarrassed, or restless in classroom activities, teachers may acknowledge their discomfort with a new topic, and encourage discussion about why they feel this way. A few children may appear especially agitated by a prevention program, avoiding eye contact with the teacher, withdrawing from the discussion, and/or asking to be excused. In such cases, teachers need to seriously evaluate the child's behavior for any sign of victimization. It is also possible that a child may display considerable interest in the topic, and relate incidents of current or past sexual assault. Should this occur during the program, teachers should calmly thank the child for bringing it up and explain that they will talk about it privately after the presentation.

## Detecting child sexual abuse

Because educators are in close personal contact with young children, they are in a strategic position to detect sexual abuse. Any report suggesting its occurrence should be addressed immediately, since research indicates that it is extremely rare for a child to invent a story about being sexually molested (Kent 1979). Educators should be especially alert to behaviors that go beyond the normal sex play and curiosity of a young child. For example, one five-year-old boy demonstrated a game involving oral-genital contact to other little boys on the preschool playground. Another four-year-old girl told her friends that she liked to tickle her stepfather's "peepee." Any unusually precocious or seductive behavior, such as a child attempting to fondle an adult's breasts or genitals should be treated as highly suspect. Teachers may also be wary of artwork with a dominant sexual theme, such as paintings of men with very large penises or pictures of sexual encounters between children and adults.

A variety of physical symptoms are similarly indicative of victimization. These include unexplainable pain or injury in the genital area, sexually-transmitted disease, discomfort in walking or sitting, and unusual odors around the genitals.

Other indicators of sexual abuse may be more subtle. Although one symptom may not be positive evidence of an assault, it does suggest the need to explore further. Virtually any change in the child's normal behavior may stem from sexual victimization, including abnormal sleep patterns or nightmares, bedwetting, loss of appetite, sudden dependency, unusual shyness, running away, behavior problems, or difficulties in school. Personality changes may be accompanied by changes in social skills, with some abused children exhibiting low self-esteem and withdrawal from friends. Sudden fear of being alone with male teachers and reluctance to accompany a babysitter, parent, or stepparent home may also be considered as possible signs of a problem (Schultz 1973).

Although sexually abused children come from a variety of different family situations, certain family characteristics are more strongly associated with the offense. Some victimized children come from families in which there is a marked role reversal between the mother and daughter, with the father responding to the daughter in a flirtatious manner that is usually reserved for a spouse or girlfriend (Forward and Buck 1982). It is not uncommon for fathers or stepfathers who sexually abuse children to exhibit extreme dominance and overprotectiveness of the child, and to personally handle school transportation, parent conferences, and notes for illness (Justice and Justice 1979).

Family loyalty, fear, and confusion about how to tell prevent many children from reporting sexual abuse or make it likely that they will be misunderstood by others. Teachers, therefore, must be alert to statements suggestive of sexual relations between children and teenagers or adults. Examples of such comments include, "My father does things to me when mom's not there," "The babysitter fooled around with me yesterday," "He checked me inside my privates," and "Will you help me to live with my aunt?" (Adams and Fay 1981; National Committee for the Prevention of Child Abuse 1982).

## Coping with child sexual abuse

Teachers who suspect sexual abuse of children should immediately discuss their suspicions with their administrator or head teacher. Dates and observations pertinent to the situation should be carefully noted for future use. If the decision is made to ask a child about a specific problem (for example, injury to the genital area), adults should remember that young children generally lack the cognitive maturity to remember exact details, such as times and places. Indeed, younger children may appear less traumatized by sexual abuse than their older peers who have a more sophisticated understanding of the offense (Summit and Kryso 1978). A child should never be asked to confront the accused offender because her or his denial will only make the event more upsetting.

The discovery of a sexually abusive situation can be a traumatic experience for both the teachers and parents involved. Anger, guilt, and the desire for swift revenge are normal reactions, especially if the offender is a relative or trusted adult. It is essential, however, that adults stay calm, sympathetic, and supportive for the child's sake. Professionals agree that handling the incident in a sensitive and direct manner may considerably lessen the likelihood that a child will suffer permanently from the offense (Summit and Kryso 1978).

A teacher who has learned of a sexual assault might say to the child: "I know how scared and hurt you must feel. I feel that way too. But I'm so proud of you for telling me. I'm sorry you had such a bad experience, but it wasn't your fault. Come to me, your parents, or another adult you trust if he or anyone else ever bothers you again."

### Reporting offenses

Educators have both a moral and legal obligation to report any reasonable suspicion or known case of child sexual assault to the police, child protective services, or the appropriate social service agency. All states include sexual abuse in their criminal codes (National Committee for the Prevention of Child Abuse 1982). The laws state that teachers do not have to prove the existence of such abuse, nor do they have to know who did it. If further investigation indicates that there was no offense, teachers who reported in good faith are protected from any possible prosecution. On the other hand, teachers who had reasonable knowledge of an incident and did not report it can be prosecuted.

Reports are generally followed up by a visit from a child protective services worker or a representative of the reporting agency, often in the home or at the school site. Teachers should make efforts to prepare the child and the nonoffending parents for the visit, informing them that the child will be asked to discuss the situation in a sensitive manner. Teachers may volunteer to attend the interview for moral support, especially in cases where the suspected offender is a member of the child's family.

Teachers or parents should consult with the child protective services worker about the need for the child to receive a medical examination. If so, adults should carefully select medical personnel trained in handling sexual abuse cases. Such individuals can explain the reasons for the examination and can reassure children that their bodies haven't been changed by this experience. Some children may also benefit from the opportunity to discuss the event with a psychologist, psychiatrist, or family counselor. Parents may also need professional help, since they often bottle up a great deal of rage and emotion.

### Continuing support for the victim

Teachers should show respect for the privacy of the child and family by only sharing the incident with others who must know (for example, parents whose children may be in contact with the suspected offender). Care should be taken to avoid projecting judgmental attitudes toward the family since this may only hinder the recovery process. The abused child should be helped to follow regular routines, rather than being treated in a special, overprotective manner.

Sexually abused children often have questions for a long time after the incident was discovered. Allowing them to talk about the experience with a trusted adult may be an important therapeutic step. It is especially important to reassure children that the abusive incidents were not their fault. The continuing support of nonoffending fathers and other male caregivers is especially important in reassuring children that most men are not like the offender.

If parents elect to pursue prosecution of the offender, it is the district attorney who has the major responsibility for deciding whether to go to trial (Adams and Fay 1981). Teachers may assist parents of victims by helping them to investigate local procedures that are followed in court cases involving sexual abuse. In many cities the district attorney allows children to use anatomically correct dolls to explain what happened, which increases the chance that children will be understood and that offenders will be convicted. In some areas, a rape crisis worker can assist the child during the proceedings, and an advocate can testify on behalf of the child.

Unfortunately, the majority of child sexual abuse cases are never reported. Many of the sexual offenders brought to trial are not convicted because these cases are difficult to prove (National Committee for the Prevention of Child Abuse 1982). However, failure to press charges increases the likelihood that sexual assault will continue. Most offenders go on victimizing children as long as there is no outside intervention from authorities (Finkelhor 1979).

## Conclusion

Early childhood educators can play a critical role in prevention, detection, and intervention efforts related to child sexual

Koblinsky and Behana

abuse. To take effective action against this problem, they must be knowledgeable about sexual abuse, alert to its symptoms, and prepared to report and follow up on suspected cases. Staff and parent education programs should be organized to assist adults in communicating with young children about this sensitive issue. Teachers may cooperate with parents in planning classroom activities that attempt to protect children from sexual exploitation. Finally, support can be provided for legislative, treatment, and law enforcement programs aimed at combating this problem. Although there is currently no panacea for child sexual abuse, the efforts and skills of informed educators can make children's lives more safe and secure. 🐦

## Recommended Resources for Children, Parents, and Teachers

### Books for children

Suggested age levels are designated with overlapping age ranges as follows:

N—nursery, up to age 5
K—kindergarten, ages 4–6
P—primary, ages 5–9

*Red Flag, Green Flag People* (1980). Joy Williams. Rape and Abuse Crisis Center, P.O. Box 1655, Fargo, ND 58107. KP
Designed to be used with adult direction, this coloring book describes good, *green flag* touches and bad, *red flag* touches involving strangers or relatives. Includes suggestions about what children can do if they encounter bad touches.

*Annie: Once I Was a Little Bit Frightened* (1983). Becky Montgomery, Carol Grimm, and Peg Schwandt. Rape and Abuse Crisis Center, P.O. Box 1655, Fargo, ND 58107. NKP
A brief story about a young girl who is touched in a hurtful way by a familiar person. Annie learns that children can get help for a touching problem from a trusted adult.

*My Very Own Book About Me!* (1983). Jo Stowell and Mary Dietzel. Lutheran Social Services of Washington, 1226 N. Howard St., Spokane, WA 99201. KP
Emphasizing children's rights, this informative workbook helps children to respond assertively to avoid touches they don't like. Includes multicultural illustrations and comes with a guide for parents. Guides for teachers and therapists are also available.

*Private Zones* (1982). Frances Dayee. The Charles Franklin Press, 18409 90th Ave., W., Edmonds, WA 98020. NKP
A short, nonthreatening book that helps children understand the private areas of their bodies, who can touch their private zones, and what to do if they are threatened by sexual abuse. Includes guidelines for adults on prevention and coping with the problem.

*What If I Say No!* (1982). Jill Haddad and Lloyd Martin. M. H. Cap and Co., P.O. Box 3584, Bakersfield, CA 93385. KP
A clever workbook that defines strangers, friends, and relatives, and explains that any of these individuals could try to touch the private parts of children's bodies. Presents *what if* situations that allow children to practice saying *no*.

*Something Happened to Me* (1981). Phyllis Sweet. Mother Courage Press, 224 State St., Racine, WI 53403. NKP
Designed for victimized children to read with the loving guidance of a parent and/or therapist. A girl tells of her fear and confusion after an incident involving sexual abuse, but does not describe the incident. Her self-worth and confidence are restored after discussing her feelings with trusted adults.

### Resources for parents and teachers

*Come Tell Me Right Away* (1982). Linda Sanford. Ed-U Press, P.O. Box 583, Fayetteville, NY 13066.
A concise, easy-to-read pamphlet presenting the most important strategies adults can use to prevent and cope with child sexual abuse.

*He Told Me Not to Tell* (1979). Jennifer Fay. King County Rape Relief, 305 S. 43rd, Renton, WA 98055.
Nonthreatening games and storytelling ideas in this pamphlet prepare children to say *no* to a potential abuser. Includes information for reporting child molestation.

*The Silent Children: A Parent's Guide to the Pre-*

*vention of Child Sexual Abuse* (1982). Linda Sanford. New York: McGraw-Hill.

In addition to providing background on the problem of child sexual abuse, this straight-forward book helps parents teach children to act assertively and confidently in trouble-some situations. Includes advice on building children's self-esteem and chapters which address the special needs of single and minority parents.

*No More Secrets: Protecting Your Child from Sexual Assault* (1981). Caren Adams and Jennifer Fay. Impact Publishers, P.O. Box 1094, San Luis Obispo, CA 93406.

A practical, thorough book that defines sexual abuse, carefully describes preventive techniques, and discusses what parents should do if their child is assaulted.

*The Touching Problem* (1982). MTI Teleprograms, 3710 Commercial Ave., Northbrook, IL 60062.

An 18 minute film/docudrama that increases awareness of the emotional trauma experienced by a victimized child, while presenting techniques for teaching prevention skills to children. Suitable for staff and parent education programs.

## Resources for curriculum development

*Feelings and Your Body: A Prevention Curriculum for Preschoolers* (1982). Shelly McFaddin. Coalition for Child Advocacy, P.O. Box 159, Bellingham, WA 98227.

*Sexual Abuse Prevention: A Lesson Plan* (1982). Sandra Kleven. Coalition for Child Advocacy, P.O. Box 159, Bellingham, WA 98227. Simple, direct lesson plans for classroom presentations in the preschool or grades K–6. Units review different types of touching, private body zones, and what children should do if they encounter a touching problem.

*Child Abuse Research and Education Kit* (1982). Jan Sippel and Catharine Smailes. Harold Bishop Public School, 15670 104th Ave., Surrey, British Columbia, Canada Z3R 1P3.

A comprehensive teaching kit for use in the elementary grades which includes a puppet, child's book, visual aids, and parent and teacher's manual.

*Child Sexual Abuse Prevention Project: An Educational Program for Children* (1979). Cordelia Kent. Hennepin County Attorney's Office, C-2000 Government Center, Minneapolis, MN 55487.

A carefully developed and field-tested curriculum for elementary and secondary teachers on sexual abuse prevention. The touch continuum shown in the book is a major component of most recent prevention work.

*Talking about Touching—A Personal Safety Curriculum* (1981). Ruth Harms and Donna James. Committee for Children, P.O. Box 15190, Seattle, WA 98115.

A three to six week curriculum for K–6 students focusing upon decision making, assertiveness, touching, and available community support systems.

*Who Do You Tell?* (1978). MTI Teleprograms, 3710 Commercial Ave., Northbrook, IL 60062.

Aimed at children 5–11, this 11 minute film uses both animation and live action to show children who they should tell if there is a fire in their house, they are lost, or they encounter an uncomfortable touch. A good discussion starter.

## References

Adams, C., and Fay, J. *No More Secrets.* San Luis Obispo, Calif.: Impact Publishers, 1981.

Browning, D., and Boatman, B. "Incest: Children at Risk." *American Journal of Psychiatry* 134 (1977): 69–72.

DeFrancis, V. *Protecting the Child Victim of Sex Crimes Committed by Adults.* Denver, Colo.: American Humane Association, 1969.

Didi Hirsh Community Mental Health Center. *Primary Prevention of Sexual Assault.* Culver City, Calif.: Southern California Rape Prevention Study Center, 1982.

Finkelhor, D. *Sexually Victimized Children.* New York: Free Press, 1979.

Forward, S., and Buck, C. *Betrayal of Innocence: Incest and Its Devastation.* Los Angeles: J. P. Tarcher, 1978.

Gagnon, J. "Female Child Victims of Sex Offenses." *Social Problems* 13 (1965): 176–192.

Gebhard, P.; Gagnon, J.; Pomeroy, W.; and Christenson, V. *Sex Offenders.* New York: Harper & Row, 1965.

Geiser, R. *Hidden Victims: Sexual Abuse of Children.* Boston: Beacon, 1979.

Groth, A. "Patterns of Sexual Assault Against Children and Adolescents." In *Sexual Assault of Children and Adolescents,* ed. A. Groth, L. Holstrom, and S. M. Sgroi. Lexington, Mass.: Lexington Books, 1978.

Harborview Medical Center. *Sexual Assault Center Client Characteristics, 1979.* Seattle, Wash.: Harborview Medical Center, 1980.

Justice, B., and Justice, J. *The Broken Taboo: Sex in the Family.* New York: Human Sciences Press, 1979.

Kaufman, I.; Peck, A. L.; and Tagiuri, C. K. "The Family Constellation and Overt Incestuous Relations Between Father and Daughter." *American Journal of Orthopsychiatry* 24 (1954): 266–277.

Kent, C. *Child Sexual Abuse Prevention Project: An Educational Program for Children.* Hennepin County, Minn.: Hennepin County Attorney's Office, 1979.

Kinsey, A.; Pomeroy, W.; Martin, C.; and Gebhard, P. *Sexual Behavior in the Human Female.* Philadelphia: Saunders, 1953.

Koblinsky, S. *Sexuality Education for Parents of Young Children*. Fayetteville, N. Y.: Ed-U Press, 1983.

May, G. *Understanding Sexual Child Abuse*. Chicago: National Committee for the Prevention of Child Abuse, 1982.

Macdonald, J. M. "Sexual Deviance: The Adult Offender." In *Sexually Abused Children and Their Families*, ed. P. Mrazek and C. Kempe. New York: Pergamon, 1981.

McFaddin, S. *Feelings and Your Body: A Prevention Curriculum for Preschoolers*. Bellingham, Wash.: Coalition for Child Advocacy, 1982.

National Committee for the Prevention of Child Abuse. *Basic Facts About Sexual Child Abuse*. Chicago: National Committee for the Prevention of Child Abuse, 1982.

Peters, J. "Children Who Are Victims of Sexual Assault and the Psychology of Offenders." *American Journal of Psychotherapy* 30, no. 3 (1976): 398–421.

Sanford, L. *The Silent Children*. New York: McGraw Hill, 1982.

Schultz, L. "The Child Sex Victim: Social, Psychological and Legal Perspectives." *Child Welfare* 52, no. 3 (1973): 146–157.

Sgroi, S. M. "Child Sexual Assault: Some Guidelines for Intervention and Assessment." In *Sexual Assault of Children and Adolescents*, ed. A. Groth, L. Hol-strom, and S. M. Sgroi. Lexington, Mass.: Lexington Books, 1978.

Steele, B. F., and Alexander, H. A. "Long-Term Effects of Sexual Abuse in Childhood." In *Sexually Abused Children and Their Families*, ed. P. Mrazek and C. Kempe. New York: Pergamon, 1981.

Summit, R., and Kryso, J. "Sexual Abuse of Children: A Clinical Spectrum." *American Journal of Orthopsychiatry* 48, no. 2 (1978): 237–251.

Weiss, J.; Rogers, E.; Darwin, M.; and Dutton, C. "A Study of Girl Sex Victims." *Psychiatric Quarterly* 29 (1955): 1–27.

# 4

# Strengthen Families

One of the major differences between early childhood and other phases of education is the necessity of developing strong personal relationships with the families of the children served. This enables the director, teachers, and parents to work closely together to determine the best kinds of experiences for infants, toddlers, and preschool children. Mutual support between program and family is vital if children are to achieve a sense of self, family, and community.

Parents are welcome contributors and visitors in good early childhood programs. Every teacher and director is challenged to find ways to involve tightly-scheduled parents.

Daily arrivals and departures offer excellent opportunities for parents, teachers, and directors to share insights. Alger suggests ways to encourage parent involvement at these times in her discussion of transitions which begins on page 88.

A unique method for building communication between child, parent, and teacher is proposed by Christine Readdick, Susan Golbeck, Elisa Klein, and Carol Cartwright. You may want to encourage your staff to implement this model with older children.

Groups of parents have typically gathered to discuss common concerns. As program director you may be called upon to lead the discussion. Francis Kelly shares his experiences for guiding groups of parents.

Christine A. Readdick, Susan L. Golbeck, Elisa L. Klein, and Carol A. Cartwright

# The Child-Parent-Teacher Conference

## *A Setting for Child Development*

*Young children are usually excluded from parent-teacher conferences. If we believe that teachers should seek more opportunities for furthering development, perhaps children should not only attend but also actively participate in conferences where goals and objectives for their development and education are being determined.*

The concept of child inclusion in conferences with parents and teachers has been advocated by a number of educators. Tanner (1978) notes that it is important to let children play an active role in evaluating and setting goals for learning. Indeed, if permitted an early and continued role in the conference process, young children will likely become increasingly skillful in self-evaluation and decision making (Kunz 1972).

Certainly in the conference setting children can provide information no one else can (Foundation for Exceptional Children 1978). Both parents and teachers are more apt to be positive in their discussions if children are present (Mathias 1967). Further, children's presence assures there will be no loss of valuable information through any secondhand reports about the conference (Tanner 1978).

Several educators report the successful incorporation of children in conferences with parents and teachers within a variety of preschool and elementary school settings (Mathias 1967; Saeli 1973; Readdick 1980). Saeli (1973) demonstrated that young children can become contributing conference participants. Thirty-six children from grades one through six, 36 parents, and 12 teachers participated in two task-setting conferences. Saeli reported progressive child and parent involvement and diminished teacher dominance. The conference gradually became a relaxed session where parents, teachers, and children could jointly diagnose the child's educational status and set realistic tasks to remedy weak areas and complement strong areas of the child's educational program. A majority of participants favored continued inclusion of the child as a conference participant.

A concrete framework for systematically

**Christine A. Readdick,** M.S., has taught young children in a variety of settings.

**Susan L. Golbeck,** Ph.D., is Assistant Professor of Early Childhood Education at the Graduate School of Education, Rutgers University, New Brunswick, New Jersey.

**Elisa L. Klein,** Ph.D., is Assistant Professor of Education, The Ohio State University, Columbus, Ohio.

**Carol A. Cartwright,** Ph.D., is Professor of Education and Associate Dean for Academic Affairs, The Pennsylvania State University, University Park, Pennsylvania.

Readdick, Golbeck, Klein, and Cartwright

incorporating young children as active participants in constructive information-sharing, task-setting, and/or problem-solving sessions with parents and teachers could stimulate further success by other educators. This article presents a child-centered, developmental model as an alternative to the traditional parent-teacher conference for mildly handicapped, normal, and gifted children in preschools and elementary schools.

# A conference model

All children can become progressively active decision makers regarding issues in their own lives. The child-parent-teacher conference can be used as a vehicle for facilitating development toward that goal. However, simply allowing children to sit in on the conference during the traditional parent-teacher interaction is not sufficient. Rather, we propose an approach that calls for careful consideration of different modes of involving children in the conference, recognizing that children function at different developmental levels. The conference process can be broken into four steps (Figure 1).

## Three modes of child involvement

Child involvement in the conference is of primary importance to the proposed approach. Ideally, children are active contributors to decisions throughout the conference. However, not all children are developmentally capable of such active participation. For some children, *reactive* involvement in the conference is more appropriate. Using this mode, the child is integrated into the conference process through reactions to questions and proposals generated by the teacher and parents. Reactive involvement allows the parents and teacher to incorporate the child into important decisions and encourages more active involvement later. Finally, for some children, during certain phases of the conference, *passive* involvement is the

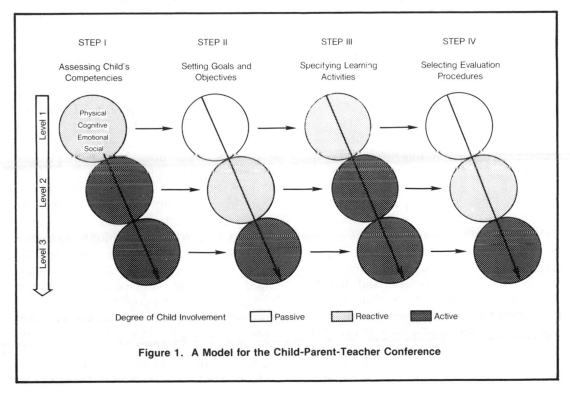

Figure 1. A Model for the Child-Parent-Teacher Conference

most appropriate mode of child involvement. The passively involved child is an onlooker or observer. However, passive involvement may serve as a first step toward later reactive and active involvement.

In this model, all children *can* be involved at least reactively during some phase of the conference. There should be no situation in which the child is involved only passively throughout the entire conference. The appropriate level of child involvement in the conference is determined by the child's development (general intellectual, social, and emotional competencies) and prior experience in dealing with the specific tasks of the conference.

## Conference steps

The three modes of child involvement become clearer when considered in the context of the conference process. In any conference between parents and teacher a variety of interactions occurs. Issues and problems may be identified, clarified, and discussed, or conference participants may focus upon the identification and development of an educational program such as the development of an Individualized Education Plan (IEP). In all conference situations, parents, teachers, and children have access to and contribute different information, skills, and expertise. We have identified four steps that contribute to the conference process in this model.

The child's level of functioning is assessed in Step I. Information is gathered concerning the child's capabilities and accomplishments. Step II of the conference includes establishing appropriate learning goals and objectives for the child. Step III concerns identification of learning activities to meet those objectives and Step IV addresses evaluation of the child's progress toward meeting the goals and objectives. Ideally, the child is actively involved in each of these four conference steps. However, because each of the four steps involves different tasks, not all children initially possess the knowledge and skills that would enable them to be actively involved in all conference steps. Nevertheless, all children should be given the opportunity to participate and to become, over time, progressively active members of the child-parent-teacher conference.

## Preparing for the conference

Clearly, the parents, the child, and the teacher need to be prepared for the group conference. All participants need to be introduced to the idea that the child can and should be progressively involved as an active decision maker in the conference as well as to the process of the conference itself. A number of techniques help the teacher convey this information to the other participants.

Parents can be introduced to the idea of and rationale for permitting children to participate in decisions about their education at the first parent meeting, through newsletters, or on home visits. An excellent beginning is to suggest ways to observe and record children's accomplishments at home since this permits parents to become more accurate observers and contribute more valuable information at the conference. Meanwhile, the teacher keeps parents informed of children's learning and progress with brief personal notes, regular newsletters, or logs of children's work.

Parents can be prepared for the process of the conference informally. For example, at the first home visit the teacher might say that "in our school, we traditionally hold a conference with the child and parents twice a year to let us evaluate together what your child has accomplished and set an agenda for further learning." To ensure child and parent participation the teacher should send home a note requesting a specific time and date for a conference. This same note might include statements for the parents and child to consider, complete, and return to the teacher.

Saeli (1973) recommends three state-

Readdick, Golbeck, Klein, and Cartwright

ments be completed and returned by the elementary-age child and parents:

1. My child and I have determined that the following seem to be areas of strength: _____

   _____

2. My child and I have determined that the following seem to be areas of weakness: _____

   _____

3. My child and I would like to discuss the following points at the conference: _____

   _____ (p. 142)

The teacher then incorporates these items into the agenda, and confirms a date, location, and time.

Despite this preparation some parents may be hesitant and ask if there are times when children should not be included. Parents can be reassured that there may be occasions when problems or topics are more appropriately discussed between parents and teachers. Usually, it is still desirable, after information has been shared and emotions aired, to include children in a discussion of a problem and in the determination of a solution.

Children also need to be prepared for the idea and the process of the conference. The teacher can acquaint the children with the idea of the conference while talking with them at group or circle time, by using puppets to act out the roles of participants in a pretend conference, or by conversing individually with children at snack or mealtimes, for example.

As the date of the conference approaches, the teacher helps children prepare for their role in the conference. First, the teacher should remind the child that this is her or his conference, and that the child, parents, and teacher will be talking about helping the child grow and learn in school. The purpose of the conference must also be shared with the children—whether a problem is to be solved,

learning tasks set, or information simply exchanged. Older children should be asked what they would like to talk about at the conference, and can be guided to gather samples of their work to discuss. Children should be encouraged to select items from all areas of the curriculum. Keeping a box where children can place favorite projects, artwork, and handwriting samples will facilitate their preparation.

Teacher preparation is also important. First, the teacher needs to determine the conference agenda, including assessment of the child's present status, establishment of goals, definition of learning tasks, and clarification of evaluation procedures as well as plans for beginning and ending the conference.

After preparing the conference agenda and setting a day, time, and place, the teacher should gather support material such as personal observations of the child, anecdotal records, interpretations of any test results, and in the case of an IEP meeting, a rough draft of that document. The class photo album may be useful for generating discussion. Any other equipment and props that the teacher will use for demonstration or that will be available for the child to use should be assembled as well.

Finally, the teacher selects a room and seating arrangement that is conducive to communication. The room may be a special conference or meeting room, the classroom, or the family's home. A small table with comfortable chairs enables the child and teacher to present necessary materials and provides younger children an activity spot within the conference setting.

### Conducting the conference

When the child and parents arrive, greetings are exchanged. If the child is very young, the teacher may ask the child to select an activity such as a puzzle or crayons and paper "to work with as we talk." Next it is useful to reiterate the importance of the child's participation in the conference and to give an overview of the conference agenda.

Teachers should keep some general guidelines in mind while conducting the conference.

1. Keep the discussion positive. Remember the ultimate goal of the conference is to enhance the child's development and learning.

2. Be a good listener. This conveys to the child and parents that they are important and have valuable contributions to make.

3. Be a good moderator. Defer to the child and the parents. Be prepared to incorporate their suggestions when possible as well as to clarify or summarize comments.

*Facilitating child participation.* Specific techniques for facilitating children's participation are related to each step in the conference. The teacher's role in facilitating child participation at the appropriate developmental level through each step of the conference is summarized in Table 1. In Step I, assessment of the child's level of functioning, the teacher, child, and parents convey information in order to construct a total picture of the child as a growing and learning person. Strategies useful in helping children participate during this phase include *simple ques-*

## Table 1. Teacher's role in facilitating appropriate child participation.

### Conference sequence

| | | Step I | Step II | Step III | Step IV |
|---|---|---|---|---|---|
| | | Assessing child's competencies | Setting goals and objectives | Specifying learning activities | Selecting evaluation procedures |
| Developmental level of child | Level 1 | Teacher uses direct or indirect cuing to elicit responses from child and parents, then gives own additional assessment. | Teacher suggests goals for child based on previous assessment. | Teacher informs child and parents of feasible learning activity alternatives. Child and parents express preferences and select with teacher. | Teacher identifies how child's accomplishments will be evaluated by child, parents, and teacher. |
| | | *Reactive* | *Passive* | *Reactive* | *Passive* |
| | Level 2 | Teacher uses simple questioning to elicit child and parent assessment of child's abilities. Teacher adds own assessment. | Teacher presents goals and objectives with reasonable alternatives. Child and parents express preferences and select with teacher. | Child, parents, and teacher brainstorm list of activities. Child selects. | Teacher stipulates available modes of evaluation. Child and parents select with teacher. |
| | | *Active* | *Reactive* | *Active* | *Reactive* |
| | Level 3 | Same as for Level 2. | Teacher invites child's formulation of goals and objectives for future learning. | Same as for Level 2. | Teacher asks child to state how learning will be evaluated. |
| | | *Active* | *Active* | *Active* | *Active* |

Readdick, Golbeck, Klein, and Cartwright

*tioning, indirect cuing*, and *direct cuing*. Imagine for a moment that you are talking with Jessica, a precocious four-year-old, and her parents. Using simple questioning, you might ask, "Jessica, can you tell us what you like to do with blocks in nursery school?" If Jessica replies "play" or hesitates to respond at all, providing an indirect cue may help her to elaborate. For instance, referring to an earlier anecdotal record you might say, "Jessica, I remember the day you and Robby built a castle out of blocks, and you liked it so much we wrote a sign saying, 'Please leave.' " If such a verbal and indirect cue is insufficient for eliciting a response, direct cuing may be called for. Turning through the class photo album you might say, "Oh, look, Jessica, here is the picture of the castle you and Robby built. What can you tell your mother and father about it?"

Older children, who have selected some representative work, can play a more active role in this phase. For instance, in showing a writing sample, a third grader might declare, "I really have pretty handwriting," or thumbing through some arithmetic papers, "I still can't multiply." It is the role of the parents and teacher to corroborate, supplement, or refine the child's view in light of their own observations and interactions.

Having constructed a picture of the child's competencies, the teacher moves to Step II, the formulation of goals and objectives. Prior to the conference, the teacher will have written some goals and objectives for the child, but it is important to be prepared to add to, delete, or modify these based on any new information shared in Step I. Suggestions from the child and parent should be accepted only if they are developmentally appropriate.

In Step III the child, parents, and teacher determine specific learning tasks. To promote child decision making it is important for the teacher to present reasonable alternatives. Thinking ahead, the teacher can let the child make legitimate choices since there are usually a number of ways to achieve any one goal. For example, a child can easily choose the next reading book from among several selected by the teacher. A similar technique permits the child to make decisions actively. When confronted with a series of cards or photos of possible learning tasks, the child may express interest by putting a sticker beside the most preferred activity. Another strategy is the use of the sociometric technique. Using simple questioning or direct cuing with a class photo, the child can make decisions relative to peer tutoring, group work, or peer relations. Here the teacher might ask, "Who would you like to work with on your science project?" or "Who would you like to help you with your leg exercises?"

In Step IV the conference participants come to agreement on how they are going to know when the child has accomplished the learning tasks and achieved the goals and objectives. The teacher can guide the selection of the most appropriate evaluation procedures for the child.

In completing the conference, it is appropriate for the teacher to summarize briefly all mutual decisions. If another conference is necessary an appointment may be made. Goodbyes are exchanged as the conference comes to an end.

## Conclusion

Just as teachers design the classroom to foster self-reliance and decision making in all children, they can design the conference setting to integrate the child as an active participant. All participants can contribute their special insights in order to enhance the child's development and learning.

Adler (1957) speaks of the child being at once the picture and the artist. He says that by focusing on the whole child, we "avoid the problem of trying to understand the significance of a few individual notes torn from the context of an entire melody" (p. 25). The child-parent-teacher conference as presented here is an appropriate environment for the consideration of the whole child. ◪

## References

Adler, A. *The Education of Children*. London: George Allen & Unwin, Ltd., 1957.

The Foundation for Exceptional Children. *A Primer on Individualized Programs for Handicapped Children*. Reston, Va.: FEC, 1978. Film.

Kunz, J. Personal communication, May 1972.

Mathias, D. "Parent-Teacher Conferences: There *Is* a Better Way." *Grade Teacher* 85 (October 1967): 86–87.

Readdick, C. A. "The Child-Parent-Teacher Conference: A Setting for Optimizing Child Developmental Potential." Paper presented at the Annual Conference of the National Association for the Education of Young Children, San Francisco, California, November 1980.

Saeli, J. A. "Parent-Teacher-Child Task-Setting Conferences in the Elementary Grades." Ed.D. dissertation, University of Pittsburgh, 1973.

Tanner, L. N. *Classroom Discipline for Effective Teaching and Learning*. New York: Holt, Rinehart & Winston, 1978.

Readdick, Golbeck, Klein, and Cartwright

Francis J. Kelly

# Guiding Groups of Parents of Young Children

The intimate relationship between teachers and parents of young children makes involving parents imperative for the success of early childhood education programs. Teachers often are responsible for initiating, organizing, and leading regular parent group meetings as one of many ways in which parents can participate in their child's education. Such parent discussion groups have often been scheduled during school hours for the convenience of staff with limited attendance by parents. If the primary purpose of the discussion groups is to involve parents in the educational process and to assist them to better understand their children and facilitate children's growth, then teachers will want to attempt to adapt to the needs of families with varying life styles and work schedules.

## Need for parent groups

Most parents want to learn more about childhood. How parents embark on the responsibility of their child's upbringing in a manner not harmful to the child depends to a great extent upon their personalities and emotional responses together with their knowledge of child development.

Within the parameters of consistent physical care, love, acceptance, and sup-

Francis J. Kelly, Ed.D., is Professor of Education, and Director, Division of Counseling Psychology, Boston College, Chestnut Hill, Massachusetts.

port, there is much variability in child-rearing across cultures, socioeconomic levels, and geography. Nevertheless, most parents want to learn more about how to facilitate their child's development. One way in which early childhood professionals can impart information and help parents share their experiences is small discussion groups. Auerbach (1968) reports that parent discussion groups help parents to understand and accept their own feelings and concerns and provide a sense of fellowship with others going through the same experience. Dinkmeyer (1968) maintains that teachers, within the context of the school program, can have their most profound effect upon children through parent discussion groups. He feels these sessions help parents relate more effectively to their children by increasing their general knowledge of children and specific knowledge regarding effective parent-child relationships.

Personal contact with parents is easily established in early childhood programs because parents are usually in daily contact with the staff.

## Characteristics of parent guidance groups

Parent guidance groups differ from psychotherapy and teaching, two other forms of group interaction. In group psychotherapy the shared goal is to achieve insight into the motivations for personal behaviors, so that each group member can function more effectively and more efficiently (Slavson 1974; Dinkmeyer and Muro 1971; Yalom 1970). In parent guidance groups the aims are to clarify misconceptions of what the function of parenthood is and what the parents' role is in the development of the child, and to increase the parents' knowledge and understanding of the needs of young children (Slavson 1974). Auerbach (1968) sharpens this distinction, stating that educational groups deal with the parents' present sources of concern and anxiety. Group psychotherapy, however, is a process of emotional re-education designed to remove pathological blocks. This is not to imply that parent discussion groups do not have a therapeutic effect, but this effect is secondary. The primary purposes of parent discussion groups are to sensitize parents to their children and to assist them to understand their children's needs.

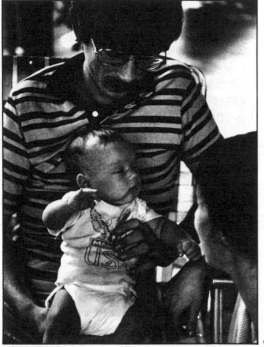

*The primary purpose of parent discussion groups is to sensitize parents to their children and to assist them to understand their children's needs.*

Parent guidance groups are not intended to teach. Lewin (1947) demonstrated that more mothers changed behavior and attitudes following group discussion than following lectures on the subject area. No matter how experienced the teacher and how careful the preparation and presentation of the selected subject matter, if the parents are not personally involved with the subject or are preoccupied with other overriding concerns, the experience will be a mere academic exercise. Therefore, parents should define their curriculum through an initial needs assessment in which the leader solicits topics for the meetings. During the remaining meet-

ings, however, the group leader must be flexible enough to capitalize upon teachable moments, always allowing parents to bring to the discussion topics of momentary concern. Directing the discussion away from theoretical abstraction and pedantry, the leader must focus on situations in the parents' daily lives such as bedwetting, sibling rivalry, and temper tantrums. Once parents understand the process, the leader's responsibility is to encourage them to seek their own solutions to problems and methods of dealing with them. The findings of Alpert and Smith (1949) suggest that group discussion is the most effective method for dealing with topics that have an emotional as well as an intellectual aspect. Scovern (1980) suggests that the critical components of parent counseling may be the mere presentation of relevant information.

Group discussions may need to be supplemented or substituted on some occasions with individual conferences designed to achieve the same objectives as the group sessions.

## Instituting the group process

*Announce the service.* In pamphlets or program descriptions prominent mention is made of the formation of parent discussion groups, parent coffee hours, or some other function which connotes a nonthreatening atmosphere. Scheduling the meetings to insure the highest attendance by working parents is critical. Once a convenient time and place for the first meeting is determined, announcements are given to all parents and posted in places such as newspapers, churches, and shopping centers, if the groups are open to the public.

*Set the tone.* At the first meeting, the group leader introduces herself or himself and defines the parameters and purpose of the group. This introductory statement should stress these points:

Kelly

1. Participation is voluntary.

2. The group is open-ended, and while regular attendance is encouraged, attendance is not mandatory. Many parents will not be able to attend every session and need to know they are always welcome.

3. Due to the nature and openness of the group, confidentiality of communication, while desired, cannot be assured. Consequently, the leader should make it clear at the outset that she or he will intervene if a member is revealing personal problems that would be better dealt with in an individual conference. Group discussions can sometimes encourage people to disclose information that should be addressed in a more private setting.

4. Discussion topics will emanate from the group and group solutions will be encouraged. The leader's role is primarily to facilitate the search for these solutions. There will be occasions, of course, when the leader will share professional information with the group or recommend selected readings dealing with the topic.

5. Discussions will concern themselves with common situations in the lives of the parents and will be limited to those that affect their children.

6. The meetings are not psychotherapy sessions for parent or child.

### Role of leader

The principal role of the group leader is to encourage group growth toward a better understanding of the children by their parents. The leader must avoid being placed in the role of teacher, information giver, or psychotherapist. The leader shares knowledge and experience with the group and permits the group to accept or reject it. All discussions must be focused on the child. Each presentation or topic must be translated into actual situations without resorting to theoretical or abstract formulations. Information must be provided in clear, unambiguous language, avoiding professional jargon. A sense of mutual trust is developed through estab-lishing warm relationships with empathy; personal regard and congruence are essential.

*Attributes of the group leader.* The leader of a parent discussion group need not be a professionally trained child psychologist or group dynamics specialist. The minimal qualifications for this responsible role should include a thorough knowledge of early childhood development obtained through professional training, study, and supervised experience. Group leaders must be caring, sensitive people with capacities for understanding, sensitivity to others, and above all, an awareness of themselves. They must be friendly but objective; they must be sympathetic yet not over-involved; they must be empathic but understanding and firm. They must be certain that their advice does not reflect their own needs, biases, values, or perceptions, but is genuinely aimed at assisting parents. Leaders must assume they are dealing with parents who love their children dearly but who occasionally need information, guidance, and advice in order to become a better parent.

### Some recurring themes

Concerns expressed by group members appear to arise in the group in the following sequence:

1. *Issues relating to the child's entrance into the school.* Most often these will be direct inquiries about teachers' qualifications, curriculum, program goals, bus schedules, and health and safety concerns. Parents are attempting to deal with their anxiety for their child. Parents need to be reassured that they are doing what is best for their child.

2. *Separation issues.* Following soon after the initial issues will be expression of concerns centered around separation problems for both parent and child. The child who is unwilling to leave home or a parent unwilling to allow the child to leave are topics frequently introduced.

3. *Changes in behavior.* Usually a few weeks after the children's enrollment, the parent will introduce concern over changing behaviors in their children. The child's behavior change may take the form of increased rivalry with younger siblings who remain at home, or a child's independent behavior due to feeling grown up. Many parents will also express frustration because their child will not provide a detailed account of the school day after returning home.

4. *Chronic problems.* As these initial concerns are resolved, and members feel more trust and confidence in the group, the parents move to more general concerns depending on their child's level of development. Among the more frequent topics introduced are toilet training, enuresis, temper outbursts, aggressive behavior, sibling rivalry, activity levels, stubbornness and resistance to parental demands, shyness, withdrawal, and the need for social skills.

5. *Program issues reappear.* Approximately three to four months after children begin the program, parents may express concern over the school's programs. They may question the effectiveness of the curriculum and activities and their goals, and occasionally complain about the teachers, the teacher aides, or the cost. Some parents feel their child is not progressing rapidly enough, while others express concern that the program is demanding too much of their child.

6. *Seasonal issues.* There will be subjects introduced by the group that reflect temporal or seasonal concerns. Among these are questions about what to tell a child about Santa Claus or concerns over vacation periods.

7. *Termination.* As the school year closes or the child leaves the program, issues related to termination frequently surface. Concern over children's progress, preparations for further enrollment, and continuation of the group informally will need to be addressed.

Other issues do not appear in any predictable sequence but are of equal, if not greater, importance.

1. *Current concerns.* These may include a response to some trauma in the child's or family's life, a sudden illness, behavioral changes, or other issues that may affect the child or family.

2. *Parents' expectations for their children.* Parents often have expectations for a child that are not age-appropriate. Group discussions focusing on normal expectations can be helpful.

3. *Additional themes interwoven throughout the school year reflecting familial concerns.* Issues such as single-parent families, working parents, separation, divorce, and death are introduced. Occasionally a related issue, such as the intrusion of grandparents, is introduced. The leader must judge whether these topics serve the purpose of the group or if they reflect a need for individual counseling.

Discussion groups may be helpful in all these areas because group leaders can share information on child growth and normal expectancies as well as clarify the program, curriculum, and goals. Members can share experiences in similar areas and resolve their own problems. Parents who discover that a problem they believed unique to them is a fairly common one experience a sense of relief and are enabled to explore solutions with other parents.

**Bibliography**

Alpert, B., and Smith, P.A. "How Participation Works." *Journal of Social Issues* 5, no. 1 (1949): 3–13.

Auerbach, A. *Parents Learn Through Discussion: Principles and Practices of Parent Group Education.* New York: Wiley, 1968.

Diament, C., and Colletti, G. "Evaluation of Behavioral Group Counseling for Parents of Learning Disabled Children." *Journal of Abnormal Child Psychology* 6, no. 3 (1978): 385–400.

Dinkmeyer, D. *Guidance and Counseling in the Elementary School.* New York: Holt, Rinehart & Winston, 1968.

Dinkmeyer, D., and Muro, J. *Group Counseling: Theory and Practice*. Itasca, Ill.: Peacock, 1971.

Lewin, K. "Frontiers in Group Dynamics." *Human Behavior* 1 (1947): 5–42.

Plenk, A. "Activity Group Therapy for Emotionally Disturbed Children." *Behavior Disorders* 3, no. 1 (1978): 210–218.

Ruben, M. *Parent Guidance in the Nursery School*. New York: International Universities Press, 1960.

Scovern, A. W. "Effects of Parent Counseling on the Family System." *Journal of Counseling Psychology* 27, no. 3 (1980): 268–275.

Slavson, S. R. *Child Centered Group-Guidance of Parents*. New York: International Universities Press, 1974.

Yalom, I. D. *Theory and Practice of Group Psychotherapy*. New York: Basic Books, 1970.

Single reprints are available for $1 from Dr. Francis J. Kelly, McGuinn Hall, Rm. 314, Boston College, Chestnut Hill, MA 02167.

# 5

# Manage Resources Wisely

**D**irectors of early childhood programs who were teachers already have some experience in working with other staff, program planning, instituting health measures, and meeting the needs of families. Financial management for programs, however, is less likely to have been part of formal education or on-the-job learning. Graduate programs, workshops, and consultation with experienced directors are the best sources for improving skills in this area. This final section of the book includes tips from several administrators who address the specific needs of directors of programs for young children.

Robert Halpern introduces the basic economic principles for setting fee schedules, enrollment levels, monitoring finances, and budget analysis.

Stretching tight budgets to cover equipment, materials, and supplies is common practice for nearly every early childhood program. A step-by-step approach for making purchases and getting the most value is outlined by John Miller and Kathryn Miller.

One major expenditure that early childhood educators never dreamed of a decade ago is now a possibility—a computer. Without question, a computer can ease administrative tasks. The value of computers for young children is not quite so clear. Alan Ziajka introduces you to computer terminology and offers some basic guidelines for purchasing both hardware and software.

Many early childhood programs are renovating their facilities to improve access for handicapped children, adults, or teachers. The checklist devised by Kenneth Brooks and Carol Deen makes concrete suggestions for designing or changing facilities for young children.

With the growing demand for child care, new resources must be found to offset the high costs of good programs. Businesses who realize the value of reliable child care for employees' children are supporting programs in a variety of ways. Marce Verzaro-O'Brien, Denise LeBlanc, and Charles Hennon explore some of the options and trends in industry-related child care.

Wasted time is expensive—program quality suffers and money is wasted. Practical solutions to this common problem are offered by Karen Zimmerman and Judith Herr.

Robert Halpern

# Surviving the Competition: Economic Skills and Arguments for Program Directors

*Economic analysis can be useful for early childhood program directors, both as a management tool, and as a lever that can be used to secure scarce public and private resources. This article is intended to introduce program directors to the basic vocabulary and concepts they will need to use economic analysis effectively—and thus to stay competitive with other human services.*

With the trend toward reduction in federal, state, and local human service budgets, those of us involved with social and educational programs are under increasing pressure to demonstrate that we are using our share of public and private funds effectively and efficiently. Government, corporations, foundations, individual consumers, and consumer groups are increasingly using the language and ideas of economics to evaluate the worth of various social programs: all want the most results for dollars spent, and they want to spend money on those activities that will increase our society's economic productivity.

Early childhood program directors must be aware of and act upon these trends if we are to justify and acquire funds at a time when less money is available to meet dozens of legitimate and pressing human needs. Directors need to demonstrate to funders that they are managing funds efficiently and effectively, and need to de-

**Robert Halpern**, Ph.D., is Research Associate at the High/Scope Educational Research Foundation in Ypsilanti, Michigan.

velop their skills to use these limited resources wisely.

## How will economic analysis result in a better-managed early childhood program?

Economic analysis can help program directors answer many management questions. What is the best number of children to enroll? What should the fee policy be? What salaries can be afforded for program staff? What program improvements can be made this year? Where can program costs be cut? Where might expenditures increase? Are expenditures appropriate for our program goals and priorities? How much non-fee income will it be necessary to raise? What will it be used for? Where might that income come from? Are expenditures running ahead of income during the year?

None of these questions require the assistance of an accountant or economist to answer, although periodic use of such professionals can be more than worth the one- or two-day consulting fee. Rather, they require basic economic and budgeting information, much of which will be covered in the rest of this article. Most important management decisions are ultimately not economic or budgetary decisions; they are philosophical ones. Economic information is most useful in *contributing* to an informed decision.

The centerpiece of economic analysis in early childhood programs is budget formulation. Directors make educated projections of income and expenditures for a fixed future period of time, usually a year. To make these projections the director needs certain kinds of information, and should use a certain standard format. Projected expenditures, or costs, should be broken down into *fixed* and *variable* costs. Fixed costs do not change with the number of children enrolled; variable costs do. Fixed costs include initial and projected investments in the physical facility, start-up and program preparation expenses, mortgage or rent, real estate taxes, utilities, certain salaries, and certain supplies. Variable costs include most staff wages, food, curriculum supplies, costs for in-service training, and so forth.

Some variable costs do not change *steadily* with increases or decreases in enrollment, but only at certain points. The most obvious of these is staff wages, which jump dramatically when enrollment increases beyond a certain number, since a new staff member must be hired, or decline dramatically when enrollment shrinks to a certain size. Between those two extremes, wages are fixed costs. In calculating projected program expenditures, the director should also include *shared costs,* those incurred with other programs or agencies, and *hidden costs,* those stemming from free use of goods and services. Including these factors gives a truer picture of program cost.

To project the program's income the director must calculate as realistically as possible the likely amount of fees to be collected, and other sources of income sure to be generated through donation, subsidy, grant, etc. To project income realistically

the director will need historical data on enrollment, actual attendance, losses due to failure to pay, and sliding fees, if applicable, and information on current external factors—the local economy, new competition, etc. Other income besides fees should be included only if there is 90 percent certainty it is coming in. Staley (1978) outlines in detail one method for calculating income from fees and other sources.

What is a budget useful for? Its most obvious use is to assure at the beginning of a budget year that plans made can be afforded, or to point out where monies must be raised. The most basic rule of budget formulation is that planned expenditures *cannot* exceed projected income. As the year proceeds, the director projects which expenses and income are ahead of or behind schedule, discovers why, and acts to make appropriate modifications. Budget projections can also help the director address a number of the questions outlined at the beginning of this section. These projections bring the key economic data on the program together in one place, and provide the conceptual framework—expenditures cannot exceed income—for decision making on key questions.

## Setting fee schedules and fee policy

Fees are one category of income that can be changed to assure a certain level of income, and, vice versa, fee decisions have implications for the amount of income which may be generated. For example, raising fees may lower income, if enrollment decreases as a result. If a director expects fees to provide a given percentage of total income, then the fee policy and schedule must bring in that amount of income. Decisions as to whether to charge no fees or reduced fees when a child is out sick, or when a family is on vacation, and decisions about whether to have a sliding scale fee, have crucial implications for income raised. Those policies must be reflected in income projections.

Neugebauer (1979) discusses whether and how to implement sliding scale fees, based on family ability to pay, and suggests two ways to administer such a fee policy: (1) calculate actual cost per child, given expected enrollment, then charge wealthier families a set amount more than that cost, and less wealthy families the same amount less; and (2) charge no family more than a set amount, and make up the difference through outside subsidies. In his article Neugebauer presents a formula for calculating the size of the sliding fee, given the second approach noted above.

In thinking about sliding fees, the director should take into account (1) the number of families who might benefit (in other words, is the result worth the effort?), (2) the security of non-fee subsidies (Title XX funds, slots bought by companies, local government funds, etc.) on a year-to-year basis, and (3) the difficulty and loss of privacy in determining families' income. The fee system should be perceived as fair by the families using the program.

## Determining optimal enrollment

There are enrollment levels (or points) at which any early childhood program is optimally using its resources (costs per child are at a minimum). Beyond that optimal number of children, costs per child jump, because a new teacher must be hired, new space rented, or new equipment bought. As enrollment moves toward an optimum point, costs per child may decline gradually. The reason for that decline is the operation of *economies of scale*—as enrollment expands, fixed costs, for example, physical facilities and salaries, are spread out over a greater number of children. All other things being equal, decisions to expand or constrict enrollment, necessitating hiring or firing of staff, should be based on the likelihood of reaching the next point of maximum economy up or down on the scale at some time in the near future. For example, with a desired staff-child ratio of 1 to 12, most directors do not add a new teacher until the waiting list has close to 12 children.

By knowing the possible costs of expanding, a program director can plan growth more carefully. Basically, she or he must simply pay attention to the points at which significant new expenses are acquired as a result of deciding to expand. Aside from enrollment, licensing regulations and availability of space or staff may determine these points, as does sensitivity to the need to maintain quality. Nontangibles are important also: some programs seem to function more effectively at a certain size.

## Monitoring spending

Budget projections can help directors decide where savings can and should come from if costs are running ahead of income. For example, a program director may determine that halfway through a budget year she or he has spent two-thirds of the planned salary budget. This fact requires a reduction of expenses or an increase in income. One way to use budget projections to monitor costs is to translate projected expenditures into functional categories and determine the percentage of total costs each category represents. For example, salary expenditures of $40,000 can be broken down into care and teaching, $25,000; administration, $10,000; and health screening, $5,000. Cutting costs in the *larger* categories, "care and teaching" or "administration," are more likely to contribute to solving over-spending problems.

Morgan, Morgan, and Neugebauer (1976), in a study of day care in Worcester, Massachusetts, found the following functional breakdown of costs: care and teaching, 49 percent; administration, 18 percent; nutrition, 12 percent; occupancy, 9 percent; social services, 5 percent; training, 3 percent; transportation, 3 percent; and health, 1 percent. They note that to reduce the total budget of the average day care program in Worcester by 1 percent would require reducing care and teaching costs by 2 percent, and would require reducing transportation costs by 33 percent. Efforts to reduce costs most usefully focus on large expenditure items.

Budget preparation generally gives the program director a sense of the expenses over which she or he has some control. There is generally much more control over variable costs than over fixed costs. Regulations and labor laws reduce control over some costs (such as minimum wage requirements). Also, certain program elements, because of the percentage of total costs they take up, or because of their nature (e.g., number of children enrolled) are easier to manipulate to influence costs.

## Determining appropriateness of expenditures and income

The way income is spent influences the outcomes of an early childhood program. For example, spending more social service funds on a mental health consultant and less on a medical consultant implies certain priorities and will have certain effects on participating families. Thus, program directors should identify their goals and priorities, and then examine whether their pattern of spending reflects those priorities. If a director chooses staff development as a goal for one year, then funds must be budgeted to pay for that expense. A director should annually compare the structure of her or his expenditures with that of similar programs in the community to get a sense of whether expenses appear to be appropriate.

Program directors should also examine sources of income annually, to see if they correspond to the kind of program desired, and if they are likely to remain secure in coming months and years. Setting fees at realistic and yet affordable levels is a difficult task. Yet decisions about the size of fees, and the percentage of total

income to be generated through fees, will have direct implications for the kinds of families the program serves, and the amount of separate fundraising activity that will be necessary.

Early childhood program directors should, in most cases, plan to acquire income from a mixture of sources—government, business, fees from families, and other fundraising activities. Relying on public funding is not wise, because such funding will become scarcer and more competitive to acquire. Thousands of families will be pushed out of public assistance, and yet will not have resources to pay for child care and other needs. The amount of corporate and private foundation money will grow slightly, but competition for that money will increase dramatically.

Planning future sources of non-fee income will be a special challenge. To do this planning, the program director will have to analyze the local market, including corporations, foundations, and other private sources; keep track of coming changes in public funding patterns at the federal and state levels; and identify the selling points in her or his program. Directors should also know the strategies for fundraising. One that relates to budgeting, for example, is to identify specific program elements for which external assistance is clearly needed, based on budget projections. It is easier to raise private funds when one can identify such elements, and demonstrate that she or he has done the analytic work to back up the request (see Halpern 1981 and Finn 1982 for details on fundraising strategies).

## Who might help do an economic analysis?

Much of the day-to-day work of budgeting, accounting, and analyzing budget information to answer management questions should be done by the program director. An accountant, or management

*Early childhood program directors need to be familiar with the logic and language of the economic arguments which support the value of the services they provide.*

consultant with accounting skills would probably be helpful when setting up a bookkeeping system, in examining the books at least once a year (nonprofit programs may be required to do this), and when considering a basic program change with financial implications. Directors (and their boards or advisory groups) who monitor expenditures and income themselves on a regular basis will have a much better feel for the financial status and needs of the program.

To gain the skills needed to do budgeting and other kinds of economic analysis, most program directors can probably refer to a basic accounting book (a concise, useful list was published in the November 1980 *Child Care Information Exchange*). A

local business college or university with a business administration program will often be glad to have a student, or whole class, work with a center to develop a financial management system. Parents of children enrolled may have accounting and/or other financial management skills, and might be glad to help. Investment of time and resources in this area will almost always prove to be an economically sound investment.

## How can directors use economic arguments to solicit funds?

Early childhood program directors— whether in Head Start, other public early intervention programs, day care centers, family day care, or private preschools—are facing more competition for public and private funds than ever before. One of the central criteria almost certain to be used by most prospective funders, especially private funders, to evaluate the worth of a program will be economic: whether that program is increasing individuals' and society's productivity, whether the program is using its current funds efficiently, whether that program is demonstrating benefits that exceed its costs. There *is* evidence that early childhood programs are good economic (as well as social) investments, and directors should be able both to cite this evidence, and to use it as a model when arguing the case for their own programs.

## Use economic terms and definitions

Early childhood program directors can use three basic kinds of economic arguments to justify funding of their programs. They can argue that their program is *cost-beneficial:* that is, the monetary benefits of the program exceed the monetary costs of that program. They can argue that their program is *cost-efficient:* that is, their management of funds and personnel is yielding optimal outcomes for children, optimal services, and so forth. (They are getting the most out of funds available.) They can argue that their program is *cost-effective:* that is, the program offers a low-cost approach (relative to other approaches) to achieving certain societal goals (e.g., increasing worker productivity).

Each of these arguments is useful in different circumstances, and they can be used together. For example, corporate funders certainly like to see a good return on any investment they make (cost-beneficial); they like to see well-managed financial operations (cost-efficient); and they like to see low-cost approaches to solving particular problems (cost-effective). The most difficult argument to make, and probably the most important, is that early

childhood programs are cost-beneficial. Many benefits from early childhood programs are difficult to convert to monetary terms, and appear only in the future. For example, attitudes toward reading fostered during early childhood years, often in early childhood programs, provide a basis for a lifetime of pleasure and learning through reading—a fact extremely difficult to translate into monetary terms. Nonetheless, cost-benefit analysis is an important tool used by legislatures, local government, bureaucrats, and private businesses or foundations in deciding whether to consider funding early childhood programs as a way to solve social problems and meet social needs.

## Cite evidence that early childhood programs are cost-beneficial

Evidence from two kinds of early childhood programs can be discussed as appropriate: from preschool intervention programs, and from day care programs. Evidence supporting each can and should be used, albeit carefully, to support the other.

The most powerful evidence that preschool intervention—programs that are designed to enhance the social, cognitive, and physical development of children from low-income families—is cost-beneficial comes from the findings of 14 longitudinal studies of the effects of intervention programs started in the 1960s (Consortium for Longitudinal Studies 1978). These findings demonstrate that in comparison to control groups, children from low-income families who participated in carefully supervised and implemented programs in the 1960s have required over the succeeding years less special education, have been held back in grade less often, and in a few of the studies have demonstrated generally more successful adaptation to the demands of schooling. Researchers from one of the studies, the Perry Preschool Project, have actually converted emerging benefits into economic terms, and found the ratio of partial benefits (just through the elementary years) to costs to be 2.4 to 1 (Weber, Foster, and Weikart 1978). In late winter 1982 the next major report on the cost beneficiality of the Perry Preschool Project is due, analyzing benefits through the high school years for participating children. Tentative findings suggest that over the lifetime of the participants the estimated total economic return will be over four times the initial investment (High/Scope Foundation 1982).

Early childhood program directors can use this evidence to argue that whenever programs focus on services to low-income children of preschool age, there is a long chain of benefits to the child and to society:

1. Immediate physical welfare (health and nutrition status) may be improved.
2. The child's potential ability to succeed in school is generally enhanced.
3. Ultimately, as a result of better health and greater ability to take advantage of schooling, employment opportunities are increased, the child's future earnings are increased, and she or he is likely to become a more economically productive member of society.
4. Less remediation for participating children during their years of schooling saves society money, and makes public investment in the educational system more efficient and productive.
5. Emerging findings from the Perry Preschool Study also suggest savings to society in the form of lower rates of juvenile deliquency among participating children.

Evidence that day care is cost-beneficial centers around the argument that it helps families become more economically productive. A recent study in California (Freis and Miller 1981) examines the costs and benefits of state subsidy of child care for a diverse group of families. The findings indicated that the families involved became significantly more productive as a result of being better able to afford and use child care services. Their increased productivity (family income increased by a total of $250,000 for 30 of the participating families over a two-and-one-half year period) led to 63 percent more taxes assessed, 50 percent less public assistance costs, and an increasing ability of the families over time to pay for their own child care. These benefits, in the form of savings to and income generated for the state, far more than offset costs of the program. The subsidies provided a strong incentive for many participating families, especially those on public assistance, to find work.

Another recent study in central Florida produced similar findings (Hosni 1979). The study team interviewed hundreds of families who had received financial and other child care assistance from 4-C in the mid- and late seventies. The study team found that child care assistance had freed large numbers of parents to more actively seek employment. As a result, half of those families who had been on welfare (50 percent of the families in the study) went off public assistance. Income generated by participating families increased more than 100 percent, as did rates of employment. The authors found that total savings to federal, state, and local government, each of which contributed a percentage of the total assistance for participating families, more than compensated for costs.

Early childhood program directors can use the evidence from studies such as these to argue that making day care more accessible to families, especially low-income families, makes it easier for them to seek and acquire productive employment. *That* employment generates tax revenues, discretionary income spent in the local economy, and an increasing ability of families to pay for their own child care. It also decreases families' dependence on public assistance. This chain of effects is not just relevant to a small percentage of families. Half the families with young children in the United States cannot afford to pay for child care within the limits of their own resources (Horner, et al. 1980; Winget 1982).

## Stress related arguments that support early childhood programs

Advocates of early childhood programs should also frame their arguments in the context of the interests, needs, and goals of the potential funder. In working with corporations, for example, they should stress program effects such as productivity of employees, and decreased absenteeism, turnover, and tardiness (Horner et al. 1980). Availability of day care can also be an incentive to attract workers to communities and industries where there is a scarcity of labor, such as high technology, and certain allied health professions. In approaching corporate officers, the program director should be able to demonstrate that she or he is running a beneficial, cost-efficient operation, and that the specific kind of support requested will have a high rate of return; this is the language spoken by the business community. For an in-depth discussion of the issues inherent in seeking corporate support, see Friedman (1980, 1981) and Verzaro-Lawrence, LeBlanc, and Hennon (1982).

Businesses and state government both have a strong interest in the need for a regular stream of adequately educated young people who do not require a great deal of further training in literacy and computational skills. Preschool intervention, with its stream of previously described benefits, helps assure the development of the pool of potential human resources. Adequate day care and preschool services improve the quality of life in a state or community, another incentive for businesses to relocate.

In general, state and local government will be concerned about the costs of remediation, whether in mental health, physical health, criminal justice, or education. Early childhood programs are cost-beneficial because of their preventive nature vis-a-vis these problems. Most early childhood programs, especially day care, generate income through a variety of sources, and are not overly dependent on government for support. State and local governments will feel most positive about contributing to efforts that meet public needs and yet charge a fee for service provided. Such practice demonstrates fiscal responsibility on the part of the program.

The key for program directors in using economic arguments to seek public and private support for their programs will be to tailor the general argument to their own program's strengths, services, and particular value to the community, and to the potential funders' priorities and interests. For example, knowing the employers of parents whose children participate in one's program is often useful, since services provided for the family indirectly benefit the employer. The program director should define the services being provided to the community, and have an economist from a local bank or university estimate the value of those services as a basis for an effective local corporate, foundation, or government fundraising effort. Effective internal financial management, discussed earlier, will help the program director to pinpoint clear, specific funding assistance needs.

A number of local day care programs around the country have begun to collect economic data—usually with technical assistance from local universities, public interest groups, or other agencies. This activity is not too costly (indeed is sometimes free), and it can be valuable for securing funds. (See, for example, Urban League Child Care Department 1979.) Some group with a national constituency might begin organizing this data to make it more accessible. Meanwhile, individual program directors can easily acquire the understanding necessary to use at least the *language* of economics in seeking funds, if not all the tools.

## Making the transition

Until the last 20 years, early childhood services and programs were generally viewed as marginal to the central social and economic issues facing our country. Hints of a more fundamental role have appeared during times of crisis and rapid social change, as in the late nineteenth and early twentieth centuries when society dealt with the social effects of rapid urbanization, industrialization, and immigration, and during World War II to induce women into the labor force. But only in the last 20 years has the general importance of early childhood experience to later functioning in school, in the work place, and in society been more widely recognized. Only during this time have women been recognized as significant in the out-of-home work force. Largely because of these two factors, early childhood programs have begun to be seen not just as activities that consume society's resources, but as one investment option among many in attempts to meet economic and social needs.

Yet, just as the potential returns of investing public and private funds in early childhood programs have begun to be appreciated, a social climate has emerged that dictates an end to the era of social program growth. Thus, the transition to the economic perspective by early childhood programs discussed in this article will be crucial to the acquisition of a fair share of public and private resources. Those working in early childhood should encourage the incorporation of the investment perspective, as cold-hearted and limited as it might seem, to complement other perspectives on the value of early childhood programs.

How will early childhood programs stand up as an investment relative to other social programs? Is it risky to stake the

justification for their support on benefits difficult to quantify? Many early childhood professionals argue that the real value of their programs is best expressed in social, not economic terms. This in fact may be true of most programs for children. Certainly, economic return to individuals and society should be only one of many criteria used in evaluating investment in early childhood programs. Nonetheless, given the likely funding climate and sources for early childhood programs in the 1980s, economic arguments used to acquire funds will be among the most persuasive. Program directors who use the economic concepts discussed here may well have a competitive edge.

## Bibliography

Center for Educational Research and Innovation. *The Economics of Early Childhood Services.* Paris: Organization for Economic Cooperation and Development, 1980.

*Child Care Information Exchange.* "Director's Bookshelf: Financial Management Resources," 16 (November 1980): 17.

Consortium for Longitudinal Studies. *Lasting Effects after Preschool.* Denver: Educational Commission of the States, 1978.

Finn, M. *Fundraising for Early Childhood Programs.* Washington, D.C.: National Association for the Education of Young Children, 1982.

Friedman, D. "Child Care in the 80's—Reaching Out to Business and Labor." *Child Care Information Exchange,* two-part article: 15 (September 1980): 7–12; 16 (November 1980): 7–12.

Friedman, D. "Employers and Child Care Update—A Solution in Search of a Problem." *Child Care Information Exchange* 20 (July/August 1981): 10–14.

Freis, R., and Miller, M. "The Economic Impact of Subsidized Child Care." *Day Care and Early Education* 9 (Fall 1981): 39–44.

Halpern, R. *Assuring Quality Early Childhood Services: The Challenge Ahead. A Report on the Conference: State Commitments to Young Children.* Ypsilanti, Mich.: Center for the Study of Public Policy for Young Children, High/Scope Foundation, 1981.

High/Scope Foundation. *Report on Longitudinal Findings of the Perry Preschool Project Through the High School Years.* Ypsilanti, Mich.: Center for the Study of Public Policy for Young Children, 1982.

Horner, M.; Benson, R.; Brooks, G.; Cooney, J.; Edelman, M.; Marty, M.; and Schacht, H. *The Quality of American Life in the Eighties: Report of the President's Commission for a National Agenda for the Eighties.* Washington, D.C.: U.S. Government Printing Office, 1980.

Hosni, D. A. *An Economic Analysis of Child Care Support to Low Income Mothers.* Orlando, Fla.: Community Coordinated Child Care for Central Florida, 1979.

Lohman, R. *Breaking Even: Financial Management in Human Services Organization.* Boulder, Colo.: National Center for Citizen Involvement, 1980.

Morgan, G.; Morgan, H.; and Neugebauer, R. *Caring about Children in Worcester.* Worcester, Mass.: United Way of Central Massachusetts, 1976.

Neugebauer, R. "Money Management Tools: Sliding Fee Scales." *Child Care Information Exchange* 8 (June 1979): 27–32.

Rowe, M., and Husby, R. "Economics of Child Care: Costs, Needs, and Issues." In *Child Care: Who Cares?* ed. P. Roby. New York: Basic Books, 1973.

Staley, C. "Budgeting: When Fees Control Expenditures." *Child Care Information Exchange* 1 (Spring 1978): 21–28.

Urban League Child Care Department. *Cost Effectiveness of Day Care.* Mimeographed. Colorado Springs, Colo., 1979.

Verzaro-Lawrence, M.; LeBlanc, D.; and Hennon, C. "Industry-Related Day Care: Trends and Options." *Young Children* 37, no. 2 (January 1982): 4–10.

Weber, C.; Foster, P.; and Weikart, D. *An Economic Analysis of the Ypsilanti-Perry Preschool Project.* Ypsilanti, Mich.: High/Scope Educational Research Foundation, 1978.

Winget, W. "The Dilemma of Affordable Child Care." In *Day Care: Scientific and Social Policy Issues,* ed. E. Zigler and E. Gordon. Boston: Auburn House Publishers, 1982.

John B. Miller and Kathryn Madera Miller

# Informed purchasing can stretch short dollars

Do you have plenty of money in your program budget for everything you want to do? Is your program income greater than expenses? Read no further here, but share your fundraising secrets with us. If, on the other hand, you work in and for a program like most of us, drawing up the annual budget is a task exceeded in difficulty only by the task of living within that budget. We look for sources of increased income. We fret over ever-increasing costs. We worry because our programs do not meet the needs we see. And sometimes we make mistakes and learn too late that we have not used our funds wisely.

Most of us in programs for young children and their families have worked at understanding children, learning about families, planning curricula, developing facilities, organizing schedules, and even balancing budgets. Sadly, when many of us try to wisely spend our funds we encounter roadblocks. Many enthusiastic members of the selling profession want to convince us their products are just what we need. We may be unable to find the products we think we need. We encounter "hidden costs" like shipping and installation charges. Somehow everything seems to cost too much, wear out too soon, or not do the job we had hoped.

Understanding some procedures and terminology of the selling-purchasing world can help us meet our goals in that arena just as increased understanding of developmental principles can help us meet our goals in working with children and families. If you work in a large agency that has specialized personnel, you may have a purchasing agent on your staff. If you do not need to do the actual purchasing yourself, understanding the purchasing procedures can help to better understand and accept or improve purchasing procedures in your agency. If one of your many roles *is* that of purchasing agent, it is especially important to know terms to help you understand the legal documents involved in purchasing. In all situations, an informed customer is in a better position to get the best value for money spent.

## Goals and programs

Establishing goals for your program and determining how to work at serving the needs of children and families is your job as a professional. You cannot expect, nor do you want, salespeople to take on those tasks. Program is your responsibility. The task we address here is how to work better in the selling-purchasing world so we can

**John B. Miller,** B.A., is Assistant Purchasing Agent for Iowa State University, Ames, Iowa.

**Kathryn Madera Miller,** M.S., is Associate Professor, Department of Child Development, College of Home Economics, Iowa State University, Ames.

better meet our goals. You can develop several purchasing tools to aid you in meeting these goals.

## Purchasing tools

The purchasing task involves working with legal documents; terminology is important. For those of us in the helping professions it may be difficult but necessary to assume a new role since the selling-purchasing relationship is basically an adversary one. You must work to develop purchasing tools to use in every transaction, ranging from a shopping trip in a local store to a formal public bid opening. Among these purchasing tools and skills are:

1. writing specifications
2. finding and developing sources (vendors)
3. receiving quotations (bids)
4. analyzing bids
5. writing purchase orders
6. receiving merchandise

### 1. Writing specifications

Whether you are buying at the retail price or obtaining bids to save money, you must determine specifications. Specifications are statements containing the details of construction of a piece of merchandise.

Carefully stating specifications is vital for effective purchasing through bidding. Specifications that are too vague may bring in bids for items totally unsatisfactory for your needs. On the other hand, a very detailed set of specifications may result in the expensive process of making a custom item for you. Many of us tend to be too vague rather than too specific as we begin to learn to write specifications. We want something durable, versatile, and well-suited for the developmental level of the child. Do you know any manufacturer or sales representative who will

tell you the merchandise is something that will wear out too quickly, is of too limited use for your purposes, and is probably not safe for use with children as young as those in your group? That is not the way to make the sale! Help the seller make the sale and please the purchaser by learning to clearly *specify* your needs.

For example, in planning for climbing equipment you might define durable as wood construction with nut and bolt fastened joints and a varnished finish. You might define versatile as portable enough to move from room to room, suitable for indoor or outdoor use, and coming in sections that can be combined in different ways. You might define the developmental level of the climbing equipment as no higher than six feet tall, ladder rungs no farther apart than eight inches, and the lowest level no more than six inches from the ground. The task in writing good specifications is to not be so vague that virtually any item in the category will fit and yet not be so specific that no manufacturer or supplier can meet your demands. Your specifications establish a standard of quality so that you receive a good value in your purchase. Good value is here defined as a quality item at a competitive price.

One way to establish a standard of quality is to give a manufacturer a model or item number. If this is done, it is also helpful to list acceptable alternates. That is, if you specify that a particular model of a General Electric refrigerator is your standard of quality, you might add that a specific model of a Sears refrigerator would be an acceptable alternate.

For a refrigerator:

#### Too vague

A big refrigerator to hold milk for 40 children with a freezer for making Popsicles.

#### Better

A white, self-defrosting refrigerator with freezer section on top.

Miller and Miller

No less than 20 cu. ft. capacity nor more than 35 inches wide, outside dimension.
To run on house current.
General Electric Model GE 100 standard of quality.
Sears Model SR 100 acceptable alternate.

Make your list specific enough to tell potential bidders what is important to you but not so detailed that they either cannot hope to meet your specifications or the checking of your specifications is so time-consuming the effort required to get your business in not worthwhile. Since most business concerns are familiar with their line and the usual competitors, giving examples of acceptable models will help you receive more desirable bids.

## 2. Finding and developing sources (vendors)

You need to know what is on the market to meet your needs so you can write reasonable specifications. You also need to find vendors who are likely to want your business. Your library, Chamber of Commerce, or local telephone company will have the yellow pages for the major cities in your area. Call or write companies asking them to send you catalogs or other information. Refer to your current file of catalogs. Pick up catalogs and information at commercial exhibits during conferences. Contact the local public school purchasing office or other agencies similar to yours to locate vendors that have provided satisfactory services.

The resources listed at the end of the article may help you determine quality of a product or locate a specific supplier. They provide information on what is available and some consumer information or ratings, but the decision on *what* to buy remains with the purchaser. That is, what do you need to store in the refrigerator? Juice and milk and snacks for a nursery school program? Or do you need refrigerator *and* freezer space for a large program preparing and serving two or three meals every day? Will you be making homemade paste and fingerpaint that needs refrigerator space? Will employees want refrigerator space for their meals and snacks?

## 3. Receiving quotations (bids)

Once you are clear on what you are trying to buy and have written specifications, you are ready to get quotations from possible suppliers for the item or items you need. This can be done by making telephone calls or visits to vendors and writing down the quotations. If personal contacts of these kinds are made, you will want written confirmation of the quotations received to avoid later misunderstanding. You may prefer to send a letter for major purchases and ask for detailed written quotations as a first step.

There are several elements of a quotation, and you will want to be sure you receive them all. Incomplete information often leads to unwise decisions. In addition to *getting* information, the process of getting bids or quotations requires that you *give* information.

### Information Provided to Vendors

1. specifications
2. who you are
3. requested delivery date
4. method of payment
5. qualifiers
6. bid due date

### Information Received in Quotation

1. product or service offered
2. price
3. cash terms
4. shipping terms
5. promised delivery date
6. length of time bid is valid

Complete information is required for analysis of bids. It is necessary to put your best foot forward in the information you give and to understand the information received.

*Providing information*: We have already examined at some length the more informative and helpful ways to give *specifications* when asking for a quote. Clarifying *who you are* can help you in the purchasing process but is a little less tangible than the writing of specifications. If you want a firm to do business with you, it is important to let them know you are a reasonable, reliable, intelligent representative of an established organization. In other words, you will handle business in a businesslike way. Working with those who already know you and your organization may reduce the identification task but personal friends may not always be those who are best equipped to do business with you, and expecting friends to come up with low prices puts a strain on any relationship. An organized and informative visit, telephone call, or letter speaks well for you and your organization.

Be clear about when you want *delivery*. If your old refrigerator has just stopped and you need the replacement immediately, prospective suppliers need to know that. Maybe they have just what you need on the floor or in the warehouse. On the other hand, maybe you are depending on volunteer help to take the aging but still operating refrigerator to the Salvation Army and simply have *no place* to put a refrigerator until the thirtieth of next month. Immediate delivery is not needed and not acceptable.

Any business wants to know *your method of payment*. If you are an unknown organization to the business providing quotations, you might need to establish a credit rating before the vendor can offer you the most favorable terms.

Circumstances may require that you attach *special requirements* such as compliance with affirmative action statutes and OSHA standards, protection from patent infringement suits, insurance coverage for installers, or desired warranty.

These special requirements are called qualifiers and are needed to strengthen the buyer part of the contract.

*Information received*: The quotation must state whether the *product or service* offered exactly meets your specifications or is an alternate. If an alternate is offered the quotation should state clearly how the alternate differs from your specifications.

In checking *prices* on quotations you will want to know what additions might be made when you pay the bill. Does that price include sales tax (if your organization pays sales tax)? What might be an installation charge?

What *terms* does this business offer? Do they offer a discount for cash? How soon must the bill be paid to receive the cash discount? When is net payment due?

*Shipping terms* are a matter of prime concern. Freight costs or shipping damages can easily wipe out that good price you received. *FOB* is the term used to designate when ownership of merchandise transfers from seller to buyer. *FOB Destination* means the company still owns the merchandise until it is delivered to you in apparent good condition. This is the most desirable situation for the buyer because shipping losses or damages are the responsibility of the seller and dealing with the trucking firms or other transporters can be *very* difficult.

*FOB Company Dock* means you own the merchandise as soon as it leaves the seller's hands—you pay the shipping costs *and* deal with the problems. *FFA* means full freight allowed or that the seller will pay for the shipping of your merchandise (and charge you) but you take ownership when it leaves the seller so any losses or damage claims will be yours to settle with the transportation company. While FFA is not as desirable as FOB Destination, it is frequently more convenient to pay one bill to the seller rather than one bill to the seller and an additional bill to the shipper. Some freight companies demand payment on delivery and most others give you only seven days to pay.

*Delivery date* is important. A bid with a low price is not a good price if the delivery date offered cannot match your needed delivery date. Buying last year's model now instead of waiting for the new models to come out may be a good buy, or you might find paying extra for faster service is a good buy for your special needs.

Quotations submitted to you are *valid prices* for only a limited time and you need to know the length of that time. Plan purchasing procedures to match time demands of your organization. For example, you may need quotes valid long enough to allow for analysis, board approval of purchase, and processing of the order.

### 4. Analyzing bids

Once quotations are received, you are ready to analyze the bids. Look for the lowest bid that meets your specifications. However, your practices are bound by ethics and procedures outlined in the UCC (Uniform Commercial Code) which has become law in all states but Louisiana. It is unethical to engage in a "dutch auction" approach by going in turn to each vendor with the intimation that a lower bid will be rewarded with an order. If bids are indeed higher than the purchaser can accept, the only ethical way to manage the situation is to contact all bidders at once and ask how to change the specifications or conditions to lower the price. Under the UCC, the legal price is the unit price and no errors in addition or multiplication can be exploited by the buyer.

Prepurchase judging of quality is not always easy, especially if you are purchasing an item that is new to you. If you do not know from experience whether the particular product and/or supplier have been satisfactory, ask others who have purchased the item, and ask others who have done business with the companies you are considering. You must make the final judgment for your particular situa-

tion, but individuals with experience you lack may be helpful in providing information. You might also ask the company to provide you with a sample item to check that the bid has indeed met your specifications.

### 5. Writing purchase orders

Once you are ready to buy on the basis of bids received, it is time to write a purchase order. The quote is the vendor's offer to sell—the purchase order is your offer to buy. Together, they constitute a legal contract. You will want to include in your written purchase order all the elements of the quotation once again in order to make a contract acceptable to you. It is advantageous to have a specific acceptance of your purchase order. Good business practice requires that the purchase must be mutually beneficial to the buyer and to the seller and that the purchase order must be clearly understood by both parties to the contract.

### 6. Receiving merchandise

Receipt of goods from the shipper is another point where you can lose money—be sure someone is on hand to inspect a shipment as it arrives. The receiver should count boxes and be sure that the number agrees with the number of boxes shipped as given on the freight bill. If it is impossible to unpack and check the shipment for damage while the shipper is still unloading, at least be sure that *all* sides of the boxes are checked for external damage. That one box might be placed against the wall to hide the large gash in the side! If damage of the package is detected, unpack that carton immediately and write the extent of the damage, if any, on the freight bill before signing it. Make sure that the extent of the damage and the driver's signature are on the copy of the freight bill left with you!

If any damage (apparent at time of delivery or concealed) is found, the receiver must ask in writing for an inspection. Although one legally has up to fifteen days to request an inspection, faster action on your part increases the probability of your receiving a favorable adjustment. In addition, it is important to keep the shipment in the receiving area and to keep the original carton and all packing material until after the inspection is made. Since all damage claim payments will be based on the written inspection report, insist that your position is clearly and accurately stated just as you would insist on clarity and accuracy in a written report of an automobile accident.

Writing specifications, finding and developing sources, receiving quotations, analyzing bids, writing purchase orders, and receiving merchandise as outlined here are procedures that can improve your purchasing capabilities. Informed purchasing can stretch your program's dollars. ▣

## Resources

### Monthly magazines:

**Consumer Reports.** Consumers Union of United States, Inc., 256 Washington St., Mount Vernon, NY 10550.

Rates common consumer products. Especially helpful.

**Consumers' Research Magazine.** Consumers' Research, Inc., Bowerstown Rd., Washington, NJ 07882.

Rates common consumer products.

**School Products News.** Penton/IPC, Inc., 1111 Chester Ave., Cleveland, OH 44114.

Mostly advertisements of new products.

**American School and University.** North American Publishing Company, Educational Division, 401 North Broad St., Philadelphia, PA 19108.

Articles on a wide variety of administrative topics plus many advertisements.

**Office Products News.** Cox Broadcasting Corporation, United Technical Publications, Inc., 645 Stewart Ave., Garden City, NY 11530.

Many advertisements of new office products.

**The Office Magazine of Management ● Equipment ● Automation.** Office Publications, Inc., 1200 Summer St., Stamford, CT 06905.

General articles, advertisements, plus a regular special feature giving information on a specific product classification.

### Annual directories:

**Thomas Register of American Manufacturers and Thomas Register Catalog File.** Thomas Publishing Company, One Penn Plaza, New York, NY 10001.

Fourteen volume work: seven volumes products and services; one volume company names, addresses, and some telephone numbers; six volumes of catalogs. Especially helpful.

**Industrial Product Directory** (formerly Conover-Mast). Cahners Publishing Company, 1200 Summer St., Stamford, CT 06905.

Two volumes; dual lists: (1) manufacturers with products, (2) products and manufacturers.

**Macrae's Blue Book.** Macrae's Blue Book Company, 100 Shore Dr., Hinsdale, IL 60520.

Five volumes; dual lists: (1) manufacturers with products, (2) products and manufacturers.

### Special resources:

**Sweet's Catalog Files.** McGraw Hill Information Systems Company, Sweet's Division, 1221 Avenue of the Americas, New York, NY 10020.

Vendors' catalogs selected for use by architects and interior designers.

**Buyers Laboratory Test Reports.** Buyers Laboratory, Inc., 20 Railroad Ave., Hackensack, NJ 07601.

Bimonthly test reports of office equipment and office furniture.

**EPIE Report.** EPIE Institute, 475 Riverside Dr., New York, NY 10027.

Educational Products Information Exchange Institute publishes special analyses of materials and laboratory-test findings on educational products.

Miller and Miller

Alan Ziajka

# Microcomputers in Early Childhood Education? *A First Look*

*Have you been asked when your early childhood program will install a computer? Are the record-keeping tasks in administering your program consuming a great deal of your time? As professionals, we must begin to explore the possible uses and abuses of microcomputers in our field. Ziajka's article introduces the basic terminology and capabilities of computers so that we can become better informed about this new technology.*

Microcomputers are increasingly common features in America's schools and homes. The number of public school microcomputers more than tripled between 1980 and 1982, increasing to nearly 100,000 by the spring of 1982 (Magarrell 1982). As many as 35 percent of all elementary schools have microcomputers in their buildings (Titus 1982). The growth in the number of microcomputers and educational software (sets of instructions to run the computer) in America's homes is even more dramatic (Future Computing 1982). Between 1980 and 1982 the number of home computers in use increased more than sevenfold, and the number of educational programs increased nearly tenfold. Educational software is also being developed for children younger than five years of age, and microcomputers are beginning to be incorporated into the teaching and management of a growing number of early childhood programs around the country.

Given the potential impact of microcomputers on the education and development of children, it is essential that all educational professionals have at least some basic information about microcomputers so they can raise questions and make decisions about their use, both with young children and as an administrative tool. This article will provide that first look at microcomputers.

## Computer history

The history of the computer goes back at least to 1833, when an English mathematician, Charles Babbage, designed an "analytical engine." This was a steam-driven device, programmed by machine cards, and was intended for various mathematical calculations. Although Babbage's machine was never completed (his government funding ran out), his ideas were used more than a century later in the development of the world's first computers. One of these electronic giants, called ENIAC, went into service in 1946. It weighed 30 tons, filled 1500 square feet of space, used more than 19,000 vacuum tubes, and required a special air-conditioned room because of the heat it produced. It was not

**Alan Ziajka,** Ph.D., is Director of Special Programs at the University of San Francisco.

until the late 1950s, when vacuum tubes were replaced by smaller devices called transistors, that computers became refrigerator-sized instead of room-sized. The "brains" of this new generation of computers consisted of about a dozen circuit boards composed of hundreds of transistors through which electric current passed. The invention of the microprocessor chip in 1971 heralded still another generation of computers: the desktop microcomputer. The chip, the heart of the microcomputer, is made of silicon coated with crystal and is no larger than an infant's fingernail. Silicon chips are produced by a process analogous to the printing of a photograph from a negative: large numbers of physical components such as wires and transistors are etched in miniature onto the coating of a chip through a photographic or laser process. This microprocessor gives today's microcomputers the power of the giants of 30 years ago.

## Parts of a computer

The parts of a computer and the functions they perform are similar to those first described in Babbage's work in the 1830s. Like his analytic engine, today's microcomputer has four major components: input, central processing unit, memory, and output.

### Input

Input is the process of entering information into the computer. The most common input device for the typical microcomputer is a *keyboard*. Many microcomputers have a full-sized, standard typewriter keyboard, with perhaps a few additional keys for special functions. On other microcomputers, the keyboard is smaller, and some keys appear in nonstandard positions. Some microcomputers have touch panels rather than full-stroke typewriter keys. Appropriately, many individuals use a microcomputer as a word

processor—a superintelligent typewriter that can delete and rearrange words, sentences, paragraphs, and whole pages with the touch of a key or two; can save and print memos, letters, and manuscripts; and can perform myriad other functions useful to a writer. Early childhood teachers and administrators can, for instance, use a microcomputer to write and edit newsletters, curriculum guides, or letters to parents and legislators, automatically individualizing each letter.

Using the microcomputer as an aid to writing, or for a host of other functions, may call for another input device: a *disk drive*. Although some microcomputers have built-in disk drives in most computers they must be added. A disk drive permits information to be entered into the computer from a *software* program stored on a disk. A software program is simply a list of instructions that tell a computer to perform certain jobs, such as word processing. The disk is a thin piece of coated magnetic material, either rigid or flexible (floppy), on which prewritten programs are stored and on which new programs or other information, such as a letter to parents, can be recorded for future printing and mailing.

There are other input devices for a microcomputer, none of which is essential for the early childhood educator. One is a *cassette tape recorder* designed specifically for microcomputers. This device performs the same function as a disk drive, but not as well. It is less efficient than a disk drive because it takes much longer to find information on a cassette tape than on a floppy disk, just as a specific song is less rapidly found on a tape than on a record. Other nonessential input devices include *joysticks* and *paddle controllers*. These are used primarily for games, though they also are useful in certain educational programs to be discussed later in this article.

### Central processing unit

The central processing unit (CPU) is the brain of the computer. It contains the circuits that interpret and execute instructions, perform all of the computer's logical operations, and conduct the flow of information to and from the other three components of the computer. These circuits are etched on the tiny silicon chip discussed previously.

### Memory

A computer's memory is where information and programs are stored. Generally, the larger the memory, the more powerful the computer. Memory capacity is expressed in *bits, bytes,* and *kilobytes.* A bit is the computer's smallest unit of digital information (mathematically represented by a 0 or 1). Essentially, computers are binary-based machines composed of thousands of on/off switches miniaturized on that silicon chip. It is the combination of these switches grouped in particular sequences that permits the computer to perform mathematical operations, process words, and control its own operations. In the majority of microcomputers, bits are organized into groups of 8 (though 16- and 32-bit machines are starting to appear on the market). Eight such bits comprise a byte, and 1 kilobyte (1K) equals 1,024 bytes. Therefore, a 16-kilobyte machine (16K) has space to store slightly more than 16,000 characters of information at any one time. Generally, computers with less than 64K have very limited capabilities.

### Output

As the name suggests, output is the information—completed tasks, solved problems, requests for information, and other communications—that comes from the computer to the user. Output devices for displaying computer-generated information include a standard television set connected to the computer, a monitor designed for a specific microcomputer, and various types of printers.

# Choosing your hardware

The microcomputer and its accompanying keyboard, disk drives, monitors, printers, and other equipment are collectively referred to as *hardware.* Choosing the right hardware at an affordable price can be a challenge. Scores of nearly identical machines, each with their own peripheral hardware devices, are now on the market. Prices can range from just less than $100 to more than $2,000, and that usually buys just the microcomputer—a complete system that includes disk drives, a monitor, and a printer can be double or triple the price of the microcomputer itself. For the teacher, administrator, or parent who has never owned a microcomputer system before, here are several factors to consider.

*Is the computer "friendly"?* A friendly computer is one that is easy for staff, parents, and children (with adult guidance) to use; it does not call for complicated steps every time the user wants to do something, and the instructions in the user's guide are clear. The keyboard on a friendly computer is also easy to use. For most purposes, a full-stroke keyboard with keys that go up and down is vastly superior to a membrane keyboard that has no keys but relies on a slight touch to a flat board. Errors are less frequent on a full-stroke than on a membrane keyboard. It is also important for children to have the full sensory and fine-motor feedback and control produced by pushing a key completely down and feeling it come back up. Other friendly factors include the simplicity of overall design and the ease with which devices such as monitors, disk drives, printers, and paddle controllers can be connected to the microcomputer when they are needed.

*Is the microcomputer part of a system that can be expanded?* An expandable system is one that can accommodate additional disk drives, a printer, and a monitor or television set that functions as a monitor. The potential for memory expansion is also important. Even the beginner should start with a system of no less than 32K that is expandable to at least 64K.

*What kind of software is available for the computer?* This question is crucial because the availability of software for educational uses, word processing, or whatever purpose you will be using the computer for, should determine the model of computer to be purchased. A program written for one computer usually is not compatible (cannot be used) on another brand of computer and may not even be usable on a different model made by the same manufacturer.

## Software for children

Software denotes the programs, or lists of instructions, that tell the computer what to do. The most important rule for the newcomer is not to buy software you have not used and evaluated yourself. To run a program, all you need to know is how to turn on a computer and how to load a program. This is easily learned in a few minutes from a person who already knows how. All else should simply involve following the instructions that appear on the monitor and pushing the appropriate keys.

Educational software currently is being used by elementary and secondary teachers for drill and practice in basic skill areas such as reading and math, for tutoring in specific areas of knowledge such as the scientific concept of density, for demonstrating phenomena in the natural world such as planetary motion or geographical processes, for simulating the economic principles involved in running a lemonade stand, and for playing instructional games involving logic or mathematical concepts (Coburn et al. 1982).

In the last year or so, several programs have been developed for use by children younger than five years of age. One such program uses music and color graphics to promote the concepts of above/below and left/right. When the child presses various keys, colored bars, jugglers, and butterflies appear; boxes fill with color; and rainbows arch across the screen. In another program, children can move an animated playing piece into a "shape room," where they can shape that piece any way they want. Muppets are used in another program involving the creation of a face by using game paddles to select from a variety of eyes, noses, and other facial features. A recently developed program also allows children to create drawings on a screen by moving a joystick. This program potentially can generate 150 shades of color, checkerboard patterns, and different widths of "brush" stroke. In this same program, circles and rectangles can also be created by pressing specified keys, and then those shapes can be filled with color.

Teachers, administrators, and parents should seek out reliable computer stores with knowledgeable staffs, computer centers, and schools that already use computers in order to evaluate educational software for young children. Professional educators can use the growing number of computer-related publications and organizations such as those listed at the end of this article for further information about the rapidly changing field of educational software.

## Computer languages

A computer language is a code employed by a user to organize a computer's internal circuits so that the machine will perform certain tasks. Computer programs such as those described in the previous section are written in a computer language by the manufacturer, and it is unnecessary for a person to know a computer language to use them. There may come a day, however, when teachers or children tire of using "canned" programs and may want to write their own programs. That is when

Ziajka

knowledge of a computer language will be necessary. The most common microcomputer languages are

1. *BASIC* (Beginner's All-Purpose Symbolic Instruction Code). Developed at Dartmouth College by John Kemeny and Thomas Kurtz, BASIC is the most frequently used microcomputer language. BASIC has a vocabulary of about 400 English words and a fairly elaborate syntax. It is useful for the beginner as well as the more sophisticated programmer.

2. *LOGO.* Developed by Seymour Papert at MIT, this language is intended specifically for helping children use computers in creative ways, beginning with the manipulation of a triangular turtle to draw geometric shapes. The best description of LOGO and its Piagetian underpinnings can be found in Papert's book *Mindstorms* (1980).

3. *Pascal.* Named for the French scientist Blaise Pascal, this language uses standard English commands, called key commands, and in that sense it is similar to BASIC. It differs from BASIC, however, in that it has fewer variations and is more structured, intricate, and difficult to learn.

Some other languages that professional educators may hear about in their quest for computer literacy are *PILOT* (another relatively simple language for introducing adults and children to programming), *COBOL* (a language commonly used in the business world), and *FORTRAN* (a language primarily for scientists and mathematicians).

## A few questions

Until recently I felt that computers were inappropriate for the education of young children. I granted that computers were valuable for science and math students at the secondary level and that they perhaps even had a place in the upper elementary grades. I could see no practical application nor educational rationale, however, for their use with primary-grade children, and certainly not with preschoolers. My view began to change, however, when I started to observe children as young as four years of age using microcomputers in various school settings, including the Bing Nursery School at Stanford University. I began to discuss the pros and cons of microcomputers with preschool teachers, administrators, parents, and computer specialists; to attend conferences that dealt with microcomputers and young children; and to read widely in books and journals. As often happens in quests for new knowledge, more questions than answers surfaced. Let me share just a few of those questions, along with some tentative conclusions I have reached.

*What can preschool children do with microcomputers?* A surprising amount. Four-year-old children can push keys on a microcomputer keyboard to move objects right and left and up and down on a screen; generate various patterns, colors, letters, and numbers; compare and match objects; discriminate between items; create and recreate shapes; and figure out the intricacies of some fairly complex puzzles. Coleta Lewis, a preschool teacher in Dallas, has developed programs for young children using LOGO. Her programs allow three- and four-year-old children to assemble animated people on the microcomputer monitor and manipulate color and direction. Another of Lewis's programs permits children to paint a car on the screen, place a garage in various locations, and drive the car anywhere they want before parking it in the garage (Swigger 1982; Nelson 1981).

The developers of educational software are just beginning to explore the potential for the young child's use of microcomputers, and the next few months and years should see an increasing range of possibilities for professional educators to choose from. **The question, however, of whether or not these various microcomputer programs can more effectively promote concept formation than other more traditional** (and certainly less expensive) methods and materials remains to be answered. A great deal of research needs to be done.

*Is there a rationale for preschoolers to use microcomputers?* Perhaps. The fostering of fine-motor skills and eye-hand coordination certainly appears to be a benefit derived by children who use microcomputers. Computers may also provide children with another avenue—along with play, drawing, imagery, imitation, and language—to engage in what Piaget (1962; 1969) called symbolic representation. Someday we may want to add computer-generated images on a screen as a new form of representation that the child evokes and manipulates.

Microcomputers may also have some value for the child's emotional and social development. The observer of young children using microcomputers is immediately struck by the children's long attention span, high level of motivation, and obvious enjoyment in actively engaging a powerful machine. Although close adult supervision is needed when young children are first introduced to computers, children can soon be given considerable independence. The sense of control and competence young children seem to have as they use a microcomputer may serve as another option for the development of autonomy, an important psychosocial need of children so cogently described in the work of Erikson (1963).

Contrary to some of my initial fears, the young children I observed working with microcomputers were neither passive nor socially isolated from other children. Although a microcomputer's monitor looks like a television screen and many microcomputers are indeed connected to televisions, a microcomputer does not function like a television set. In contrast to passive children watching television, the children I observed working with a microcomputer were actively manipulating what appeared on the screen, pushing keys, and commanding the machine to perform tasks. What also came as a surprise to me was the amount of social interaction generated by the microcomputer in the classroom. The children usually worked in pairs, or even small groups, with the microcomputer at an interest center, and they shared ideas about what to do next, made extensive use of oral language in the process, and occasionally astounded the observer with a little computer jargon.

*Is a good microcomputer system worth the expense, given the other economic demands on an early childhood program's budget?* It depends. What may be an affordable curriculum addition for one school may be economically prohibitive for another. Prices continue to drop, but a good and expandable microcomputer system still costs from $1,000 to $2,000. Before you despair at the price, however, consider involving parents in a fundraiser for the purchase of a microcomputer, or contact major microcomputer firms for possible hardware and software donations. Some schools have been successful in both of these endeavors. Remember also that a good microcomputer is multifunctional: it has educational uses for children, but it can also help preschool administrators balance the books, develop newsletters, maintain children's records, and write anything that a typewriter would usually be used for, only faster.

In the final analysis, a microcomputer should perhaps be viewed as simply another curriculum material whose value is dependent on how it is used by sensitive and knowledgeable teachers. Computers will never replace teachers, nor will they ever take the place of those activities and materials that are already effectively used for music, language arts, cooking, art, science, and the rest. A microcomputer is merely another potential addition to the early childhood classroom, another opportunity for young children to experience the surrounding world.

## References

Coburn, P.; Kelman, P.; Roberts, N.; Snyder, T.; Watt, D.; and Weiner, C. *Practical Guide to Computers in Education*. Reading, Mass.: Addison-Wesley, 1982.

Erikson, E. *Childhood and Society*. New York: Norton, 1963.

Future Computing Incorporated. "Home Computer Market Forum." Research monograph presented at Home Computer Market Conference, Dallas, Texas, December, 1982.

Magarrell, J. "Notes on Computers." *The Chronicle of Higher Education*, 25, no. 8 (October 20, 1982): 3.

Nelson, H. "Learning with Logo." *onComputing* 3, no. 1 (Summer 1981): 14–16.

Papert, S. *Mindstorms*. New York: Basic Books, 1980.

Piaget, J. *Play, Dreams and Imitation in Childhood*. New York: Norton, 1962.

Piaget, J., and Inhelder, B. *The Psychology of the Child*. New York: Basic Books, 1969.

Swigger, K. "Computer-Based Materials for Kids." *Educational Computer Magazine* (September/October 1982): 48–50.

Titus, R. "Local School Support for Micros Is Alive and Growing." *InfoWorld* 4, no. 46 (November 22, 1982): 36.

## Sources for further information

Capital Children's Museum
800 3rd St., N.E.
Washington, DC 20002
202-543-8600
Contact: Bob Evans

Computer Science Press
11 Taft Court
Rockville, MD 20850
301-251-9050

ERIC Clearinghouse on Elementary and Early Childhood Education
College of Education
University of Illinois
1310 S. Sixth St.
Champaign, IL 61820
217-333-1386

Microcomputer Center
San Mateo County Office of Education
333 Main St.
Redwood City, CA 94063
415-363-5400 ext. 469

Misco Market Examiner (newsletter)
P.O. Box 411
Eureka Springs, AR 72632
501-253-8053

*Teaching and Computers*
Scholastic Inc.
730 Broadway
New York, NY 10003
212-505-3000

Kenneth W. Brooks and Carol Deen

# Improving Accessibility of Preschool Facilities for the Handicapped

Early childhood programs and facilities are subject to several types of legislation designed to secure and protect the rights of the disabled. This article focuses on the implications of this legislation for preschool facilities.

## Programs affected

Early childhood programs typically come under the requirements of current legislation for the handicapped in two ways. Federal mandates requiring both program and facility accessibility explicitly state that any agency receiving direct or indirect federal assistance must comply. These requirements include public and private programs serving children of all ages and involve not only handicapped children but disabled employees as well (U.S. Department of Health, Education and Welfare 1978).

In addition, zoning laws in many localities require that all facilities—both newly constructed and those undergoing major renovation—be planned to accommodate the handicapped. While requirements vary from one location to another, federal standards are generally taken into consideration in all building projects.

Many preschool programs already function within federal guidelines. The vast majority of early childhood programs—

possibly all—eventually will be touched by some type of local or federal legislation. Even without a requirement forcing compliance, it would seem that early childhood educators have a moral obligation to provide the handicapped with services fully integrated with those intended for the nonhandicapped population.

## Legislation

Today's concern for accessibility is the result of a continuing escalation of attention (Nigent 1978). The first milestone in the movement to remove barriers came in 1948 when the University of Illinois decided to make its programs and facilities accessible. By 1950, the cities of Champaign and Urbana agreed to make their communities accessible and usable by the handicapped. Through the Fifties other cities and states enacted similar legislation.

**Kenneth W. Brooks,** Ph.D., is Director, Center for Professional Development, and Assistant Professor, Administration and Supervision, College of Education, University of Kentucky, Lexington.
**Carol Deen,** M.S., is a graduate student in Educational Administration at the University of Kentucky, Lexington.

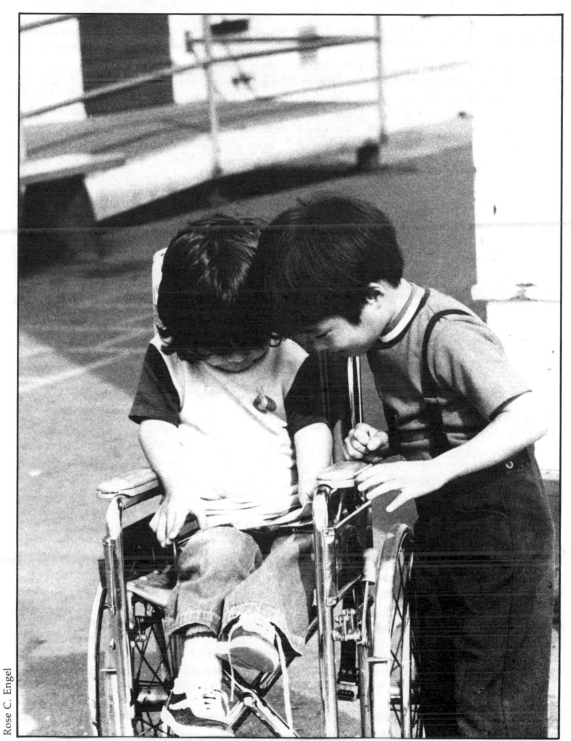

*What modifications are necessary for your early childhood facility to become accessible to handicapped children and adults?*

*Facilities for the Handicapped*

An initial accomplishment on the national level was the publication of the American National Standards Institute (ANSI) document *Specifications for Making Buildings and Facilities Accessible To, and Usable By, the Physically Handicapped* (1961). These specifications were adopted by federal agencies and several states. The ANSI reviewed and reaffirmed the standards in 1971; since that time they have been reviewed and expanded to include additional requirements related to residential environments.

The ANSI standards have been supported by several federal laws, the most important of which is the 1973 Rehabilitation Act (National Association of State Directors of Special Education 1977) that provides that handicapped persons cannot be discriminated against solely because of their handicapping condition. This is, in effect, a civil rights law to protect the handicapped minority (Clelland 1978; Barbacoui and Clelland 1978).

## Concerns for handicapped involvement

There are three major issues related to handicapped involvement in early educational opportunities. First, the earlier intervention is begun, the more likely a child will overcome the handicapping condition (Caldwell 1970). Not only will greater success be achieved in overcoming the handicapping condition, but acceptance of the child's differences by peers is more likely to occur with earlier exposure to those differences (Hayden and Dmitriev 1975).

A second concern is that early childhood programs must be geared to meeting the needs of those handicapped children who are enrolled. The needs of each child should be considered in the program; however, the importance of planning in this way is intensified with the introduction of handicapped children.

A third concern is that the handicapped

are a significant portion of the potential work force, representing as much as 10 percent of the total population (Educational Research Service 1977). Employment of the handicapped in an early childhood setting must be carefully planned. Job demands and safety implications of each position will dictate what kinds of handicapping conditions can be accommodated in order to best serve the interests of both the employee and the program. The ability to put one's talents and skills to work, regardless of constraints, is an important concept for the young child to experience.

## Facility accessibility

Facilities and physical space contribute to the quality of early childhood programs. While facility accessibility has not received widespread attention, new preschool facilities or those being renovated should meet current standards.

Some of these standards that are appropriate for the handicapped adult and older student are inappropriate and even hazardous for young children. For example, many styles of wall-mounted handrails in hallways may be a disadvantage in an early childhood center since such projections may be hazardous and might foster dependence rather than self-reliance for mobility. Projections at head height can be especially dangerous for very active young children and for handicapped children learning to walk. With encouragement and a variety of appropriate gross motor experiences, many nonambulatory children can learn to walk. Thus, the supporting hand of an adult may provide a better temporary aid than the use of handrails. Handrails installed in such a situation should be chosen to meet the appropriate standards in a safe and useful way.

Another example of an inappropriate regulation relates to the height of sinks. Current regulations regarding sink and toilet heights are relevant only to the adult bathroom. Early childhood educators have long recommended child-height sinks and toilets, and these standards would also apply for handicapped children.

## Using the accessibility checklist

Only a limited number of regulations relate directly to facility accessibility for handicapped children. The accessibility checklist included here is applicable for facilities serving both adults and children and draws heavily from the ANSI standards.

The checklist has several uses. It could be used to evaluate an existing facility in an effort to determine the current level of accessibility. Such an evaluation might be an initial step in planning renovations. The checklist might also be helpful to a prospective buyer while evaluating a facility. Parents or guardians of a handicapped child could use the list to assess the appropriateness of a facility for their child's needs. Architects can use the checklist as they develop plans for early childhood facilities. A review of the list can sensitize children and staff to accessibility concerns.

Emergency exits for the handicapped are not dealt with in the checklist. Local, state, and federal fire codes and guidelines have adequate provisions for emergency exits but often do not mandate that they be accessible for the handicapped. It is critical that an emergency evacuation plan be developed and practiced to insure safe exit of each handicapped child and employee. Achieving accessibility under normal conditions as outlined in the checklist may not result in accessibility in a crisis situation.

The checklist can be used in any early childhood facility, including programs with minimal funds for facility modifications. In these settings, the checklist can be used to cultivate an awareness of the needs of handicapped students; then, as regular maintenance and repair occurs, modifications can be made to facilitate accessibility for the handicapped child.

---

### Accessibility for the Handicapped Checklist

Name of building _____

Address _____

Person completing checklist _____ Date _____

| | Yes | Not appli-cable | No |
|---|---|---|---|
| I. Site | | | |
|   A. Grading | | | |
|     1. Is the site graded to allow the handicapped entrance to the facility? | ___ | ___ | ___ |
|     2. Is the site graded to allow access to outside play areas? | ___ | ___ | ___ |
|   B. Parking lots | | | |
|     1. Are not less than 2 percent of the parking spaces set aside for the handicapped and located near the building entrance? | ___ | ___ | ___ |
|     2. Are designated parking spaces arranged so that the handicapped need not pass behind parked vehicles to reach the facility? | ___ | ___ | ___ |
|     3. Is each parking place for the handicapped identified with a sign? | ___ | ___ | ___ |

    4. Are designated parking spaces at least 12 feet wide to allow for wheelchairs between cars? _____ _____ _____

C. Walks and curbs

    1. Are all walks at least 48 inches wide? _____ _____ _____

    2. Are all walks continuous and free from steps and abrupt level changes? Do walks have a gradient of not more than 5 percent? _____ _____ _____

    3. Do all walks have nonslip surfaces? _____ _____ _____

    4. Are there common levels at all points where walks, drives, parking lots, or streets meet? (Curbs need not be eliminated because they provide a safety feature for some, especially the blind. Curbs simply need to be ramped where walks join other surfaces. Curbs typically should not exceed 7 inches.) _____ _____ _____

    5. Do walks leading to doorways have a level platform at the door that is (a) at least 5 × 5 feet if the door swings out toward the walk? or (b) 3 × 5 feet if the door swings into the building? _____ _____ _____

    6. Does the platform extend 1 foot beyond each side of the doorway (both inside and outside)? _____ _____ _____

II. General interior considerations

A. Levels of facility and ramps

    1. Are all levels of the facility accessible to the handicapped? _____ _____ _____

    2. Do ramps inside the building have a gradient no greater than a 1 foot rise in 12 feet? _____ _____ _____

    3. Does each ramp have a handrail 32 inches above the ramp surface for adults and a lower set appropriate to the size of the children served? _____ _____ _____

    4. Do the handrails extend 1 foot beyond the ends of the ramp in a nonhazardous way? _____ _____ _____

    5. Does each ramp have a platform every 30 feet and at all turns? _____ _____ _____

    6. When a ramp meets a door, is a platform provided that is (a) at least 5 × 5 feet if the door swings toward the ramp? or (b) 3 × 5 feet if the door swings away from the ramp? _____ _____ _____

    7. Does the platform extend 1 foot beyond each side of the doorway (both inside and outside)? _____ _____ _____

    8. Are ramp surfaces smooth, yet nonslip? _____ _____ _____

    9. Is there a 6-foot, straight clearance at the bottom of each ramp? _____ _____ _____

B. Entrances, doors, and doorways (provisions apply to both interior and exterior doors)

    1. Is at least one entrance accessible? (Ideally, all should be accessible since entrances also serve as emergency exits.) _____ _____ _____

    2. Do all doors have a clearance of at least 32 inches wide? _____ _____ _____

    3. Are doors operable with a single effort? _____ _____ _____

    4. Do doors have kickplates covering the bottom 16 inches

to withstand use of canes, crutches, and wheelchairs?

5. Are door handles sufficiently high to present no hazard and designed to be used by the disabled? (Doors that open and close on a time-delay system are preferable; automatic doors are desirable.)

6. Are thresholds level? (Floor on inside and outside of a door should be level for a distance of 5 feet and extend 1 foot on either side of the door.)

7. Are door mats greater than ½ inch in thickness recessed into the floor?

C. Stairs

1. Is step edge neither square nor abrupt?

2. Is there a 1-inch strip at the edge of tread nosing of a contrasting color to increase visibility?

3. Are two sets of handrails available on each side of the stairs at a height of 32 inches for adults and at an appropriate lower height for children? (measured from the tread at the face of the riser)

4. Do handrails safely extend 18 inches beyond the top and bottom step and run continuously around a landing?

5. Are risers no more than 7 inches high?

D. Corridors and floors

1. Are corridors at least 5 feet wide?

2. Are all protrusions (e.g., signs and lights) into the corridor at least 7 feet above the floor?

3. Are floor surfaces nonslip?

4. Wherever utility covers or access panels are in use, are barricades set up?

E. Telephones

1. Are public telephones or designated office phones always available for the handicapped?

2. Do(es) phone(s) for handicapped have equipment required for use by the hearing impaired and sight impaired? Are they also located at heights accessible to people in wheelchairs?

F. Water fountains

1. Are water fountains for the handicapped designed with spouts and controls in front, 36 inches from the floor, and accessible to the wheelchair handicapped?

2. Are provisions for drinking water accessible to handicapped children (fountain 26 inches from the floor or paper cups available next to the sink)?

III. Specific areas within buildings

A. Toilet facilities for adults

1. Is at least one toilet on each floor available to each sex and modified for handicapped use?

2. Does each toilet stall for the handicapped have (a) a space that is 3 feet wide and 5 feet deep? (b) handrails on each side that are 1½ inches in diameter, 33 inches high, located 1½ inches from the wall, and fastened at the ends and the center? (c) a toilet seat 20 inches from

|  | Yes | Not applicable | No |
|---|---|---|---|

the floor? and (d) doors that swing out and have a 32-inch clearance? ____ ____ ____

3. Do sinks have narrow aprons mounted at standard height so that wheelchairs can roll under the sink? (Hot water pipes must be wrapped to prevent burns to legs of individuals in wheelchairs.) ____ ____ ____

4. Are accessories such as mirrors, soap and towel dispensers, and shelving mounted no more than 40 inches from the floor? ____ ____ ____

5. Are all faucet handles and controls of the lever type? ____ ____ ____

6. Do toilet rooms have sufficient floor space (at least 60 × 60 inches) for wheelchair traffic? ____ ____ ____

7. Are wall urinals (for the male handicapped) mounted with the opening 19 inches from the floor? Are floor urinals mounted level with the floor? ____ ____ ____

B. Toilet facilities for young children

1. Is there an appropriate number of toilets available for handicapped pupils? ____ ____ ____

2. Are the heights of toilet seats appropriate (12-17¾ inches) for orthopedically handicapped children? (Young children in braces and wheelchairs need higher toilet seats than the nonhandicapped.) ____ ____ ____

3. Is there an appropriate number of sinks available for use by handicapped children? ____ ____ ____

4. Are the heights of sinks for orthopedically handicapped children 29-34 inches from the floor? ____ ____ ____

5. Do sinks have lever-type controls? ____ ____ ____

6. Are pull-up bars located near the toilet and sink for handicapped children? ____ ____ ____

7. Is a towel dispenser or hand dryer located beside each sink and mounted no higher than 30 inches from the floor? ____ ____ ____

8. Is there a full-length wall mirror mounted just above the baseboard? ____ ____ ____

IV. Controls, identification, and warning system

A. Controls

1. Are all controls and switches (e.g., for lights, windows, and alarms) not more than 48 inches from the floor? ____ ____ ____

2. To the extent reasonable, are controls either stick-type levers or toggle-type switches? ____ ____ ____

B. Identification

1. Are raised numbers and letters (a) used to identify rooms? and (b) placed 5 feet above the floor beside the door or entrance? ____ ____ ____

2. Is a second set provided for young children at a lower level? ____ ____ ____

3. Are doors to dangerous areas identified by knurled handles? (Knurl by applying plastic abrasive coating, beads, or Velcro to handles.) ____ ____ ____

C. Warning signals

1. Are all warning signals both audible and visual? ____ ____ ____

This checklist was developed largely from the ANSI standards. It has been modified and restructured to be applicable to an early childhood setting.  ◹

---

## References

American National Standards Institute. *Specifications for Making Buildings and Facilities Accessible To, and Usable By, the Physically Handicapped.* New York: American National Standards Institute, 1961.

Barbacoui, D. R., and Clelland, R. *Special Education in Transition.* Arlington, Va.: American Association of School Administrators, 1978.

Caldwell, B. M. "The Rationale for Early Intervention." *Exceptional Children* 36, no. 10 (1970). 717-726.

Clelland, R. *Section 504: Civil Rights for the Handicapped.* Arlington, Va.: American Association of School Administrators, 1978.

Educational Research Service. *Barrier-Free School Facilities for Handicapped Students.* Arlington, Va.: Educational Research Service, 1977.

Hayden, A. H., and Dmitriev, V. "The Multidisciplinary Preschool Program for Down's Syndrome Children at the University of Washington Model Preschool Center." In *Exceptional Infant: Assessment and Intervention Vol. III,* eds. B. Friedlander, G. M. Sterritt, and G. E. Kirk. New York: Brunner/Mazel, 1975.

National Association of State Directors of Special Education. *The Rehabilitation Act.* Washington, D.C.: National Association of State Directors of Special Education, 1977.

Nigent, T. *The Problem of Access to Buildings for the Physically Handicapped.* Farmington, Conn.: Stanley Works, 1978.

U.S. Department of Health, Education and Welfare. *Your Responsibilities to Disabled Persons.* Washington, D.C.: U.S. Government Printing Office, 1978.

Marce Verzaro-O'Brien, Denise LeBlanc, and Charles Hennon

# Industry-Related Day Care: Trends and Options

The next decade will be characterized by an increased need for child care options in the United States (Hofferth, Moore, and Caldwell 1978; Moore and Hofferth 1979). By 1990 it is predicted there will be 23.3 million children under six, 10.4 million (about 45 percent) with working mothers (Hofferth 1979) who will need child care. As child and family advocates plan for this projected need, the specific nature of the demands which could be made on the caregiving system will have to be determined. An examination of current needs and trends is a necessary first step in the process.

## Current day care trends

Two distinct types of caregiving systems have emerged: *individual and small group care*, which is home-based; and *group care* which is either home- or center-based. Individual care encompasses in-home care by a parent, relative, sibling, or baby-sitter, as well as out-of-home care by a sitter. Also included are family day care homes, where a caregiver has 5 or fewer children in her or his own home. Group care refers to programs for larger numbers of children, both in a home (6–12 children) and in a center (12 or more children) (Hofferth 1979). Group care can be sponsored by nonprofit and proprietary corporations, governmental agencies, and individuals.

Individual and small group care have been used more extensively than group

care (Low and Spindler 1968; U.S. Bureau of the Census 1976; U.S. Department of Health, Education and Welfare 1978). In 1977, there were approximately 18,300 day care centers with an enrollment of 900,000 children (Abt Associates 1978). It must be noted however, that many working mothers depended on several types of caregiving arrangements and these change frequently (Moore and Hofferth 1979).

The data on family preferences for types of caregiving are sparse. Working mothers may perceive individual care as similar to that which their child would receive within the family (Unco 1975). However, a different preference pattern has emerged from the 1978 *Family Circle* survey (Women's Bureau 1979). The results, while skewed in the direction of middle- and upper-middle-class families, suggested that previous studies may have missed important child care realities. As few as 10 percent of working mothers indicated that their first preference was to leave their children with a relative, and only 20 per-

**Marce Verzaro-O'Brien**, Ph.D., is Assistant Professor of Early Childhood, State University of New York College at Buffalo. **Denise LeBlanc**, M.S., is Lecturer, Human Development and Family Living, University of Wisconsin-Stout, Menomonie, Wisconsin. **Charles Hennon**, Ph.D., is Assistant Professor and an extension specialist, Family Resources and Consumer Sciences, University of Wisconsin-Madison.

cent now used relatives for caregiving, as opposed to 46.3 percent in 1965 (Low and Spindler 1968). Only 17.5 percent would choose individual and small group care if they could pick the arrangements they want for their children. In contrast, 44 percent would select group care, with well-

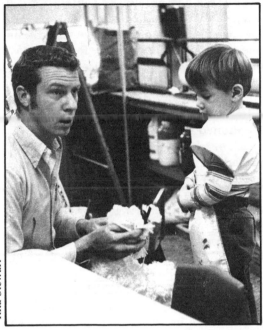

Benefits of industrial child care include easier recruitment of new employees, low absenteeism, and more positive attitudes toward work.

trained staff and balanced and stimulating daily programs. While parents were willing to pay for group care, cost and availability remain key issues in the final selection of the type of caregiving. Thus, the historical non-utilization of group care may be a reflection of factors other than parental choice, such as the lack of available programs at a reasonable cost.

Other data also lead to the prediction of an increased need for group caregiving. Hall and Weiner (1977) demonstrated that female-headed families and small families are most likely to select group care. In the last decade, there has been an increase in the number of single-parent families, that parent most often being female (Ross and Sawhill 1975). Further, while more families will have one or two children, fewer

will have three or more children (U.S. Bureau of the Census 1977). Thus, group care may be in greater demand as we move toward the 1990s.

Locating individual care providers may become increasingly difficult (Moore and Hofferth 1979). Although little is known about these people, their pay is low (Hall and Weiner 1977). Hence they may choose to enter the work force outside of their homes, or they may begin to charge more than families can pay (Shortlidge and Brito 1977). As the availability of individual care decreases, there may be a corresponding increase in the demand for group care.

Because the need for child care arrangements may well increase, so too may the demand for group caregiving escalate. What are the available means by which group care could be expanded? Discussion of options often has focused on governmental response to this perceived need. Existing programs such as Head Start, Title XX, WIN, and AFDC day care payments already provide a scattered system of governmental involvement in caregiving. In the 1970s, three national child and family service bills were proposed to provide funding for an expanded range of federally-supported child and family services, but all were defeated. The cost of such solutions as universally available, public-sponsored day care, extension of Head Start to all eligible families, and the expansion of the child care tax credit have been estimated (Congressional Budget Office 1978); but comparatively little discussion has centered on the role of labor and business in the sponsorship of group day care. If the projections of an increased need for group care are accurate, it is important to consider whether industry-related day care could be an option for that expansion.

## A new response to day care?

Industry-related sponsorship of day

care is not a new phenomenon. Prior to World War II, the day care involvement of business and labor was limited to health, and other scattered industries. During World War II, as more than 3 million married women entered the work force, child care became imperative. Public programs for day care were supplemented by child care programs in defense plants. The most extensive wartime day care operation was that of Kaiser Shipbuilding Corporation, who operated two centers in Portland, Oregon from November 1943 to September 1945, and served more than 4000 children. Although little has been written about these centers, their existence demonstrated that quality industry-based child care can be provided if there is a recognized need for and commitment to the task (LeBlanc and Hennon 1979).

After World War II, the interest in day care by industry and labor remained. Although descriptions of recent industry-related day care efforts are few, the Women's Bureau survey (1971) indicated that in 1970, at least eleven companies operated day care centers, with nine of them providing detailed information on their operations. Five of these companies manufactured textile products and had predominantly female work forces. The survey also found some caregiving commitment from unions (e.g., the Amalgamated Clothing Workers of America and the United Federation of Teachers), from hospitals, and from the federal government (as an employer). LeBlanc and Hennon (1979) found two of the eleven programs were still operating, but these were privately run and hence, independent of the company. All other programs had closed for these reasons: community day care filled the employee need (2); a low employee turnover led to an absence of age-eligible children (2); day care was a financial loss to the industry (1); the facility did not meet licensing regulations (1); the space was needed for business expansion (1); and unknown (2).

LeBlanc and Hennon (1979) contacted 48 other industries to ascertain their past, present, or future commitment to day care. In-depth interviews were conducted with personnel managers of 21 businesses who employed home economists—professionals who might have a commitment to children and families. None of the businesses had a day care center, nor did any of them intend to start one. Many of the personnel managers gave more than one reason for this decision. Reasons most often given were: the service was too expensive (4); no space was available (7); and the company did not claim responsibility for this type of service (9). Reasons mentioned only once included: there was a lack of employee interest; emphasis was placed on other service projects; state licensing standards are restrictive; and there was a need to retain funds for employee profit-sharing plans. In 6 businesses, employee leave was provided in order to care for a sick child, but none of these businesses provided payments for child care at other facilities.

In a comprehensive analysis of industry-related day care, Perry (1978) identified 9 day care centers sponsored by industries, 7 sponsored by the Amalgamated Clothing and Textile Workers Union, 14 sponsored by government agencies, and 75 sponsored by hospitals. The 1978 estimated enrollment in the employer-sponsored day care centers was: industry (545); labor union (1445); government agency (825); and hospital (5604). Also mentioned were facilities located on military installations. Identified by branches, the number of centers included: Army (50); Air Force (89); Navy (46); and Marine Corps (15). Estimated enrollment in military centers was 25,059 children.

Perry (1978) found differences between centers regarding years of operation, enrollment, and type of staff. Generally, military centers had been in operation the longest. Among civilian centers, hospitals had the longest history. Military-sponsored day care programs had larger enrollments than did civilian centers. The latter had more teachers with college degrees and utilized more full-time staff. Benefits reported by 72 of the centers included the following: new employees were easier to recruit (53); absenteeism of employees was lower (49); employees developed a more positive attitude toward their work (40); employees developed a more positive attitude toward the sponsoring organization (38); and the job turnover rate of employees was lower (34).

Eighteen of the centers surveyed had closed. Reasons for this decision were: there were not enough employees wanting the service to fill the center (11); the high cost of employer subsidies (9); the center was not needed to attract and keep a steady work force (4); administrative problems (4); the facility was needed for other uses (3); and employees were unwilling to pay costs (3).

While there may have been a major effort by business and labor in the late 1960s and early 1970s to explore day care as a fringe benefit, these sectors may be phasing out their concern for the reasons highlighted above. In light of this trend, it is important for child and family advocates to decide upon the feasibility of pursuing the expansion of industry-related day care.

## The future of industry-related day care

One approach to making this decision is to evaluate the advantages and disadvantages of industry-related day care.

### Advantages

If families are to thrive, the current separation of work place from family members must be altered (Bronfenbrenner 1976). The distance between work and home prevents young children from making connections with the adult work world and deprives them of a variety of adult role models (Urban Research Corpo-

ration 1970). Child care facilities located in a parents' work place might help young children to better understand their parents' roles outside the home. Children's tours of the industry, shared lunch hours, meeting parents' co-workers and supervisors, and learning about the types of jobs performed at the parents' work place could preserve some measure of family and community integration.

Industrial child care could preserve some measure of family and community integration.

Dual-career families, where both wife and husband have an equal commitment to their work, impose a unique challenge for work-family connections, especially in child care arrangements (Holmstrom 1973). These parents may have less time to spend with their young children. Availability of on-site child care could provide increased interactions during lunch hours and the commuting time to and from work.

Industry may be undergoing important changes. For example, as increased numbers of women enter the labor force, there may be concurrent changes in worker priorities and needs. Also, Bell (1973) has suggested that America may be moving into a post-industrial society, when future economic enterprises will focus upon their socializing functions (quality of life) as well as upon their economic functions (profit making). Such changes will require creative responses from businesses and unions, one of which could be sponsored day care.

Businesses and unions both could benefit from potential decreases in worker absenteeism and tardiness which result when transient and unpredictable caregiving arrangements create daily problems for families. Stable quality child care can also reduce employee turnover. Further, a child care commitment from a business could lead to greater worker loyalty and dedication to that business. There may be tax advantages for capital expenditures with which businesses develop day care centers (Women's Bureau 1979).

Conservation of gas and other energy sources could result if parents did not have to travel extra distances to drop off and pick up their young children. Conservation of family members' time would be another important savings.

## Disadvantages

Businesses may not be amenable to any pressures to include day care as a part of their commitment. In a needs assessment of 24 day care centers, Krantz, Vasquez, and Shimek (1971) found a clear consensus among businesses that, in a period of a high rate of unemployment, supportive services for employees were both unprofitable and unnecessary. Employees could be found who would neither need nor demand ancillary services such as child care. LeBlanc and Hennon (1979) found similar responses from businesses.

The day care tradition of cooperative management between parents and staff may not be as feasible in an industrial

day care center. Krantz, Vasquez, and Shimek (1971) found that companies would want complete operational control of the child care services and would not seek any form of community involvement.

Unions may not see child care as a major bargaining issue when salaries, health, and retirement benefits barely keep pace with the cost of living. Only those unions with predominantly female membership may be interested in pursuing discussions of sponsored day care, because other benefits have a higher priority for many union members. The low priority given to the child care issue by unions may be particularly critical in light of the LeBlanc and Hennon (1979) finding that businesses would only consider child care benefits if they were proposed by the union.

Regardless of sponsorship, it is possible that the placing of centers near industrial areas may be detrimental to the well-being and development of young children. The increasing evidence of the negative long-term impact of industrial pollution may outweigh the value of proximity to parents' work places. Further, it may be difficult to find suitable caregiving facilities in an area zoned for industries and businesses. The costs of renovation may be prohibitive for industry.

Parents who use buses, subways, and trains to get to work may not wish to have their young children using these modes of transportation during busy hours. Also, parents may wish to spend their work breaks socializing with friends or doing home-related errands and not with their young children.

## Options

Several choices are available to early childhood educators who want to become involved in industry-related child care. One role would involve serving as a resource person for both businesses who want to explore direct sponsorship of a child care program, as well as their employees. This would require knowledge of the various tax incentives available to businesses, such as the options in depreciation and amortization of child care facilities (CCH Editorial Staff 1980). Also important would be a monitoring of current Internal Revenue Service Rulings and federal tax regulations that are pertinent both to the sponsoring business and its employees.

For example, it is important that the relevant portions of the recently passed Economic Recovery Tax Act (1981) be explained, especially Section 129, which states that the gross income of an employee does not include amounts paid for or incurred by the employer for child care assistance, provided that assistance meets certain requirements described in the legislation. Further, employers will need to know that if they pay part or all of employees' child care fees, such expenses are perceived as ordinary and necessary business expenses, just as are insurance plans and other benefits. As such, all or portions of the fees are allowable as tax credits, under IRS Ruling 73-348. A similar tax credit or tax deduction may be available from various state revenue services.

A second role of child and family advocates is to work on behalf of proposed federal and state legislation that would provide additional incentives for businesses and unions to sponsor employee child care. As Goodman (1981) notes, the recent Metzenbaum-Hawkins amendment to the tax bill contained several important provisions that would have increased the tax deductions to businesses that assisted their employees in payments for child care. By advising employers and employees of pending legislation and ways to influence its passage or modification, advocates could help to insure a more favorable climate for industry-sponsored child care.

For some businesses and unions, investment in child care facilities may be appropriate. Child and family advocates should offer their expertise to these efforts. Because the value of industry-sponsored day care is related to so many factors, creative options to direct provision of child care need to be explored. For locations where creation of centers is not feasible, other vehicles for industrial commitment are available.

Business and union leaders could serve as catalysts in conducting community-based child care needs assessments, leading to a variety of available caregiving options. Financial donations could be made to facilitate child care planning and for center start-up costs. Companies or unions could provide a staff member who assists employees in locating suitable child care. In addition, a business or union might use a voucher system, in which the employee is issued a certificate worth a specified amount toward fees for child care. The employer or union could reserve a certain number of spaces in a day care center and could contribute to the cost of care. Personnel policies could be altered to provide a greater variety of personal leaves, sabbaticals, or Flexi-time schedules, all of which would assist employees in meeting family responsibilities.

These options may well have a higher probability of success than would advocacy only for industry-sponsored day care facilities. Adopting policies such as Flexi-time, day care vouchers, and placement assistance would permit what Liljeström (1978) describes as the synchronization of family members' careers within a labor market economy. Child and family advocates should initiate contact with industry and delineate the range of available options by which business and labor can assist families to find suitable child care arrangements. Such contact may well sensitize business and union leaders to their responsibilities in maintaining family strengths, as well as to the benefits that industry can gain from its demonstration of human concern. This task presents a creative challenge for child and family advocates.

## References

Abt Associates. *National Day Care Study: Preliminary Findings and Their Implications.* Cambridge, Mass.: Abt Associates, 1978.

Bell, D. *The Coming of the Post-Industrial Society.* New York: Basic Books, 1973.

Bronfenbrenner, U. "The Roots of Alienation." In *Raising Children in Modern America,* ed. N. Talbot. Boston: Little, Brown, 1976.

CCH Editorial Staff. *Tax Incentives for Employer-Sponsored Day Care Programs.* Chicago: Commerce Clearing House, 1980.

Congressional Budget Office. *Child Care and Preschool: Options for Federal Support.* Washington, D.C.: U.S. Government Printing Office, 1978.

Economic Recovery Tax Act of 1981. *Public Law 97-34.* Washington, D.C.: United States Congress, 1981.

Goodman, E. "Public Policy Report. The Transfer-And-Pray Theory." *Young Children* 37, no. 1 (November 1981): 71–73.

Hall, A., and Weiner, S. *The Supply of Day Care Services in Denver and Seattle.* Menlo Park, Calif.: Stanford Research Institute, 1977.

Hofferth, S. L. "Day Care in the Next Decade: 1980-1990." *Journal of Marriage and the Family* 41 (1979): 649-657.

Hofferth, S. L.; Moore, K. A.; and Caldwell, S. B. *The Consequences of Age at First Childbirth: Labor Force Participation and Earnings.* Washington, D.C.: The Urban Institute, 1978.

Holmstrom, L. *The Two Career Family.* Cambridge, Mass.: Schenkman, 1973.

Krantz, M.; Vasquez, A.; and Shimek, R. *An Investigation of Local Community Needs and Resources with Reference to Twenty-Four Child Care Services.* Milwaukee, Wis.: Milwaukee Christian Center, 1971.

LeBlanc, D., and Hennon, C. B. "On-Site Child Care and Other Child Care Policies of Business Firms and Their Impact on Everyday Life." Paper presented at the annual meeting of the National Council on Family Relations. Boston, October 1979.

Liljeström, R. *Integration of Family Policy and Labor Market Policy in Sweden.* New York: Swedish Information Service, 1978.

Low, S., and Spindler, P. *Child Care Arrangements of Working Mothers in the United States.* Washington, D.C.: U.S. Government Printing Office, 1968.

Moore, K. A., and Hofferth, S. L. "Women and Their Children." In *The Subtle Revolution,* ed.

R. Smith. Washington, D.C.: The Urban Institute, 1979.

Perry, K. "Survey and Analysis of Employer-Sponsored Day Care in the United States." (Doctoral dissertation, University of Wisconsin-Milwaukee, 1978).

Ross, H., and Sawhill, I. V. *Time of Transition: The Growth of Families Headed By Women.* Washington, D.C.: The Urban Institute, 1975.

Shortlidge, R. L., and Brito, P. *How Women Arrange for the Care of Their Children While They Work: A Study of Child Care Arrangements, Costs and Preferences in 1971.* Columbus, Ohio: The Center for Human Resources Research, 1977.

Unco, Inc. *National Day Care Consumer Study.* Chicago: Unco, 1975.

U.S. Bureau of the Census. *Daytime Care of Children: October 1974 and February 1975.* Current Population Reports, Series D-20, #298. Washington, D.C.: U.S. Government Printing Office, 1976.

U.S. Bureau of the Census. *Fertility of American Women: June 1976.* Current Population Reports, Series D-20, #308. Washington, D.C.: U.S. Government Printing Office, 1977.

U.S. Department of Health, Education and Welfare. *The Appropriateness of the Federal Interagency Day Care Requirements.* Washington, D.C.: U.S. Government Printing Office, 1978.

Urban Research Corporation. *Proceedings of the Conference on Industry and Day Care.* Chicago: Urban Research Corporation, 1970.

Women's Bureau. *Day Care Services: Industry's Involvement.* Washington, D.C.: U.S. Department of Labor, 1971.

Women's Bureau. *Community Solutions for Child Care.* Washington, D.C.: National Manpower Institute, 1979.

Reprinted from *Young Children*, Vol. 37, No. 2, January 1982. Copyright © 1982, National Association for the Education of Young Children,

Verzaro-O'Brien, LeBlanc, and Hennon

Karen Zimmerman and Judith Herr

# Time Wasters: Solutions for Teachers and Directors

Are you suffering from teacher burn out? Do you plan your time so that you may provide a quality learning environment for young children? Do you always complete your teaching responsibilities? Do you find yourself handling more routine classroom chores than actively teaching? Are you able to complete necessary reports by the deadline? If you have problems in any of these areas, this article is written for you!

Time is a critical resource for the early childhood educator. Examining how teachers and directors use time can be revealing, because loss of time in teacher-child interaction can affect children (Davidson 1980).

Effective early childhood education programs have certain common goals:

- provide a quality learning environment designed to meet the needs of children;
- plan and organize a developmental curriculum emphasizing social, intellectual, physical, and emotional development;
- provide quality teacher-child interactions.

Patience, wisdom, skill, knowledge, and time are required to achieve these goals. Our talents as educators can be nurtured and developed, but we must still budget our time.

We conducted an informal survey of 250 early childhood education teachers and directors to determine how they use their time during the working day. Each professional listed six time wasters related to their current position (MacKenzie 1975). The most frequently identified time wasters and possible solutions follow.

## How to handle time wasters

Teachers and directors shared their solutions to these problems. You may want to see whether they will help solve your problems with time.

### Telephone interruptions

A school or center telephone policy enables teachers to have more uninterrupted and productive time to interact with children and work toward program goals. We suggest that each professional set aside a specific period to receive and respond to calls. Parents and staff must be informed of this telephone policy for this suggestion to work. Accepting and returning calls at specified hours of the day allows for more quality teacher-child interactions.

**Karen Zimmerman,** Ph.D., is Professor and Department Administrator, Human Development, Family Living and Community Educational Services, University of Wisconsin-Stout, Menomonie, Wisconsin. **Judith Herr,** M.S. is Director, Child and Family Study Center, University of Wisconsin-Stout.

## Meetings, scheduled and unscheduled

If meeting dates are set on a regular basis, staff can more productively plan their schedules. Effective meetings usually have a predetermined agenda, and starting and ending times. Centers employing large staffs may distribute written announcements at the meeting. Another time saver is to cancel a regularly scheduled meeting if it is not needed.

## Unscheduled interruptions by visitors, parents, or staff

Some early childhood centers provide specific times either at the beginning or end of the day to meet with parents, visitors, and staff. Being continuously available to others simply does not make it possible to meet program goals and be somewhat objective about one's work.

## Routine and detail that should be delegated

Routines and details need to be examined in terms of who can best complete the task and profit from doing so. Involving children in routine tasks such as setting tables, cleaning cubbies, etc., can help them acquire more independence and responsibility (Mugge 1979). Delegating tasks to staff members, volunteers, parents, and children can promote their growth and abilities.

## Socializing/idle conversation

Chatting and socializing during work time was one of the most frequently named time wasters by teachers and directors. Possible solutions to this problem involve resisting interruptions during program hours, saving questions for other

*Providing specific times either at the beginning or end of the day to meet with parents, visitors, and staff limits the number of interruptions.*

Rick Reinhard

Zimmerman and Herr

Richard A. leFande

*Paper work can be better managed by developing a filing system, handling each piece of paper only once, and using the wastebasket liberally.*

staff members until the end of the day, and limiting the time spent having morning coffee and/or socializing.

## Cluttered work areas and personal disorganization

Paper work can be better managed by developing a fast, accurate, and simple filing system (Lakein 1973). He recommended handling each piece of paper only once, filing once a week, and using the wastebasket liberally.

## Disorganization of classroom and storage

Classroom and storage organization saves time and energy for teachers and staff (Minnichsoffer and Zimmerman 1978). Graphic symbols can be made to assist children in returning materials to the appropriate places if adequate time is provided during transitions.Children's cloth-

ing can be labeled to avoid confusion.

Carrying a pocket notebook or index cards to jot down a "to do" list of learning experiences, resources, etc., is one effective method to utilize spare moments and help teachers and directors organize their ideas and plans.

## Lack of or unclear communication

Whenever possible, center and board policies, minutes from meetings, notices, and suggestions for teachers should be posted. Letters to parents, on a regular basis, are another way to help ensure clear communication.

## Attempting too much at once and underestimating the time required to do it

If overall goals and objectives are established, then tasks can be assigned priorities. It is helpful to differentiate between tasks which are urgent (immediate) and those which are important (lead toward program goals).

A flexible daily schedule allows staff sufficient time to meet the unexpected demands that occur frequently in the classroom. MacKenzie (1972) suggested keeping 20 percent of the day flexible to meet these unanticipated demands.

## Fatigue

Adequate nutrition, regular exercise, and good sleeping habits are important to help teachers maintain their energy level, enthusiasm, and health. By observing your body clock and adjusting your key planning time according to when you are most alert, it is possible to accomplish more. By varying your tasks and pace during the day, you can make more efficient use of your time.

## Lack of objectives, priorities, and deadlines

Long-range program goals and the subsequent related short-range objectives can be planned and communicated. Deadlines can be used as a vehicle to achieve program priorities (Herr and Gill 1978).

## Indecision and procrastination

Self-imposed deadlines are effective for some teachers. This allows you to manage by choice, not by chance.

The Swiss cheese method is another useful technique for teachers and directors who are overwhelmed by a big project (Lakein 1973). By breaking the project into smaller tasks that can be completed in short periods of time, the work becomes more manageable.

## Failure to set up clear lines of responsibility and authority

Written job descriptions assist in clarifying roles of employees and volunteers in early childhood programs. An organizational chart aids employees and volunteers by indicating the lines of responsibility and authority within the setting.

## Summary

Teachers and directors who have successfully implemented time management suggestions have selected and concentrated on *only one* or *two* time wasters. After they have mastered management skills necessary to overcome those time wasters, they may revise their goals to include other skills.

Through the development of effective time management, teachers can affect the quality of education, the lives of young children, and increase their own satisfaction with their personal and professional lives. Time management can be an important key in providing quality early childhood programs and services.

### References

Davidson, J. "Wasted Time: The Ignored Dilemma." *Young Children* 35, no. 4 (May 1980): 13-21.

Herr, J., and Gill, S. "Planning a Child Development Laboratory for Secondary Schools." *Illinois Teacher* 22, no. 2 (1978): 96-101.

Lakein, A. *How to Get Control of Your Time and Life.* New York: Signet Books, 1973.

MacKenzie, R. A. *New Time Management Methods for You and Your Staff.* Chicago: Dartnell Corp., 1975.

MacKenzie, R. A. *The Time Trap: Managing Your Way Out.* New York: AMPOOM, 1972.

Minnichsoffer, E., and Zimmerman, K. "43 Ways for Home Economists to Save Time." *Illinois Teacher* 22, no. 2 (1978): 105-106.

Mugge, D. J. "Taking the Routine Out of Routines." In *Administration: Making Programs Work for Children and Families,* ed. D. W. Hewes. Washington, D.C.: National Association for the Education of Young Children, 1979.

# How to Choose a Good Early Childhood Program

*Administering Programs for Young Children* begins and ends with indicators of high quality programs for young children. The Criteria beginning on page 3 are intended for programs to use in evaluating themselves.

Parents also seek guidance when they select care for their child. NAEYC's highly regarded brochure is reprinted here because it is based upon the Criteria for High Quality Early Childhood Programs. Parents considering enrolling their child in your program and others in your community may welcome this professional assistance. Ordering information appears at the end of this section.

A good early childhood program can benefit your child, your family, and your community. Your child's educational, physical, personal, and social development will be nurtured in a well-planned program. As a parent, you will feel more confident when your child is enrolled in a suitable program, and the time your family spends together will be more satisfying as a result. Early childhood education plays an important role in supporting families, and strong families are the basis of a thriving community.

If you are thinking about enrolling your child in an early childhood program, you probably have already decided upon some of your basic priorities, such as location, number of hours, cost, and type of care that best suits your child. If you feel that a group program is appropriate, you can obtain a list of licensed programs for young children from your local licensing agency. Then you can call several programs for further information, and arrange to visit the programs that seem best for you and your child so you can talk with teachers, directors, and other parents.

**What should you look for in a good early childhood program?** Professionals in early childhood education and child development have found several indicators of good quality care for preschool children. You will especially want to meet the adults who will care for your child—they are responsible for every aspect of the program's operation.

## Who will care for your child?

*1. The adults enjoy and understand how young children learn and grow.*

Are the staff members friendly and considerate to each child?

Do adult expectations vary appropriately for children of differing ages and interests?

Do the staff members consider themselves to be professionals? Do they read or attend meetings to continue to learn more about how young children grow and develop?

Do the staff work toward improving the quality of the program, obtaining better equipment, and making better use of the space?

*2. The staff view themselves positively and therefore can continually foster children's emotional and social development.*

Do the staff help children feel good about themselves, their activities, and other people?

Do the adults listen to children and talk with them?

Are the adults gentle while being firm, consistent and yet flexible in their guidance of children?

Do the staff members help children learn gradually how to consider others' rights and feelings, to take turns and share, yet also to stand up for personal rights when necessary?

When children are angry or fearful are they helped to deal with their feelings constructively?

*3. There are enough adults to work with a group and to care for the individual needs of children.*

Are infants in groups of no more than 8 children with a least 2 adults?

Are two- and three-year-old children in groups of no more than 16 with at least 2 adults?

Are four- and five-year-olds in groups of no more than 20 children with at least 2 adults?

*4. All staff members work together cooperatively.*

Do the staff meet regularly to plan and evaluate the program?

Are they willing to adjust the daily activities for children's individual needs and interests?

*5. Staff observe and record each child's progress and development.*

Do the staff stress children's strengths and show pride in their accomplishments?

Are records used to help parents and staff better understand the child?

Are the staff responsive to parents' concerns about their child's development?

## What program activities and equipment are offered?

*1. The environment fosters the growth and development of young children working and playing together.*

Does the staff have realistic goals for children?

Are activities balanced between vigorous outdoor play and quiet indoor play? Are children given opportunities to select activities of interest to them?

Are children encouraged to work alone as well as in small groups?

Are self-help skills such as dressing, toileting, resting, washing, and eating encouraged as children are ready?

Are transition times approached as pleasant learning opportunities?

*2. A good center provides appropriate and sufficient equipment and play materials and makes them readily available.*

Is there large climbing equipment? Is there an ample supply of blocks of all sizes, wheel toys, balls, and dramatic play props to foster physical development as well as imaginative play?

Are there ample tools and hands-on materials such as sand, clay, water, wood, and paint to stimulate creativity?

Is there a variety of sturdy puzzles, construction sets, and other small manipulative items available to children?

Are children's picture books age-appropriate, attractive, and of good literary quality?

Are there plants, animals, or other natural science objects for children to care for or observe?

Are there opportunities for music and movement experiences?

**3. Children are helped to increase their language skills and to expand their understanding of the world.**

Do the children freely talk with each other and the adults?

Do the adults provide positive language models in describing objects, feelings, and experiences?

Do the staff plan for visitors or trips to broaden children's understandings through firsthand contacts with people and places?

Are the children encouraged to solve their own problems, to think independently, and to respond to open-ended questions?

## How do the staff relate to your family and the community?

**1. A good program considers and supports the needs of the entire family.**

Are parents welcome to observe, discuss policies, make suggestions, and participate in the work of the center?

Do the staff members share with parents the highlights of their child's experiences?

Are the staff alert to matters affecting any member of the family which may also affect the child?

Do the staff respect families from varying cultures or backgrounds?

Does the center have written policies about fees, hours, holidays, illness, and other considerations?

**2. Staff in a good center are aware of and contributes to community resources.**

Do the staff share information about community recreational and learning opportunities with families?

Do the staff refer family members to a suitable agency when the need arises?

Are volunteers from the community encouraged to participate in the center's activities?

Does the center collaborate with other professional groups to provide the best care possible for children in the community?

## Are the facility and program designed to meet the varied demands of young children, their families, and the staff?

**1. The health of children, staff, and parents is protected and promoted.**

Are the staff alert to the health and safety of each child and of themselves?

Are meals and snacks nutritious, varied, attractive, and served at appropriate times?

Do the staff wash hands with soap and water before handling food and after changing diapers? Are children's hands washed before eating and after toileting?

Are surfaces, equipment, and toys cleaned daily? Are they in good repair?

Does each child have an individual cot, mat, or crib?

Are current medical records and emergency information maintained for each child and staff member? Is adequate sick leave provided for staff so they can remain home when they are ill?

Is at least one staff member trained in first aid? Does the center have a health consultant?

Is the building comfortably warm in cold weather? Are the rooms ventilated with fresh air daily?

**2. The facility is safe for children and adults.**

Are the building and grounds well lighted and free of hazards?

Are furnishings, sinks, and toilets safely accessible to children?

Are toxic materials stored in a locked cabinet?

Are smoke detectors installed in appropriate locations?

Are indoor and outdoor surfaces cushioned with materials such as carpet or wood chips in areas with climbers, slides, or swings?

Does every staff member know what to do in an emergency? Are emergency numbers posted by the telephone?

**3. The environment is spacious enough to accommodate a variety of activities and equipment.**

Are there at least 35 square feet of usable playroom floor space indoors per child and 75 square feet of play space outdoors per child?

Is there a place for each child's personal belongings such as a change of clothes?

Is there enough space so that adults can walk between sleeping children's cots?

## For more information

For further information about how to select a good program, consult your state licensing agency, local resource and referral agency, or contact NAEYC. A division of NAEYC, the National Academy of Early Childhood Programs accredits high quality child care centers and preschools throughout the country. Contact the Academy at NAEYC for more information about accredited centers in your area.

*Accreditation Criteria and Procedures of the National Academy of Early Childhood Programs,* NAEYC, 1834 Connecticut Avenue, N.W., Washington, DC 20009. Paper $6.00. 1984.

*Choosing Child Care: A Guide for Parents,* by S. Auerbach. Institute for Childhood Resources, 1169 Howard Street, San Francisco, CA 94103, or from E. P. Dutton through any bookstore. Paper $7.25; hardcover $15.00. 1982.

*The Day Care Book: A Guide for Working Parents to Help Them Find the Best Possible Day Care for Their Children,* by G. Mitchell. Stein and Day, Scarborough House, Briarcliff Manor, NY 10510. $10.00. 1979.

*Quality Day Care: A Handbook of Choices for Parents and Caregivers,* by R. C. Endsley and M. R. Bradbard. Prentice-Hall, General Book Marketing, Special Sales Division, Englewood Cliffs, NJ 07632. $5.95. 1981.

# List of Articles

## reprinted from *Young Children*

Alger, H. A. "Transitions: Alternatives to Manipulative Management Techniques." 39, no. 6 (September 1984): 16–25.

Almy, M. "A Child's Right to Play." 39, no. 4 (May 1984): 80.

Aronson, S. S. "Injuries in Child Care." 38, no. 6 (September 1983): 19–20.

Axelrod, P.; Schwartz, P. M.; Weinstein, A.; and Buch, E. "Mobile Training for Directors of Day Care." 37, no. 3 (March 1982): 19–24.

Brooks, K. W. and Deen, C. "Improving Accessibility of Preschool Facilities for the Handicapped." 36, no. 3 (March 1981): 17–24.

Cataldo, C. Z. "Infant-Toddler Education: Blending the Best Approaches." 39, no. 2 (January 1984): 25–32.

Catron, C. E. and Kendall, E. D. "Staff Evaluation That Promotes Growth and Problem Solving." 39, no. 6 (September 1984): 61–66.

Denk-Glass, R.; Laber, S. S.; and Brewer, K. "Middle Ear Disease in Young Children." 37, no. 6 (September 1982): 51–53.

Halpern, R. "Surviving the Competition: Economic Skills and Arguments for Program Directors." 37, no. 5 (July 1982): 25–32, 49–50.

Hegland, S. M. "Teacher Supervision: A Model for Advancing Professional Growth." 39, no. 4 (May 1984): 3–10.

Hyson, M. C. " 'Playing with Kids All Day': Job Stress in Early Childhood Education." 37, no. 2 (January 1982): 25–32.

Katz, L. G. "The Professional Early Childhood Teacher." 39, no. 5 (July 1984): 3–10.

Kelly, F. J. "Guiding Groups of Parents of Young Children." 36, no. 1 (November 1981): 28–32.

Kendall, E. D. "Child Care and Disease: What Is the Link?." 37, no. 5 (July 1983): 68–77.

Koblinsky, S. and Behana, N. "Child Sexual Abuse: The Educator's Role in Prevention, Detection, and Intervention." 39, no. 6 (September 1984): 3–15.

Miller, J. B. and Miller, K. M. "Informed Purchasing Can Stretch Short Dollars." 35, no. 6 (September 1979): 15–20.

Readdick, C. A.; Golbeck, S. L.; Klein, E. L.; and Cartwright, C. A. "The Child-Parent-Teacher Conference: A Setting for Child Development." 39, no. 5 (July 1984): 67–73.

Scott, L. C. "Injury in the Classroom: Are Teachers Liable?" 38, no. 6 (September 1983): 10–18.

Stevens, J. H., Jr., "Everyday Experience and Intellectual Development." 37, no. 1 (November 1981): 66–71.

Verzaro-O'Brien, M.; LeBlanc, D.; and Hennon, C. "Industry-Related Day Care: Trends and Options." 37, no. 2 (January 1982): 4–10.

Voignier, R. R. and Bridgewater, S. C. "Allergies in Young Children." 36, no. 4 (May 1980): 67–70.

Wishon, P. M.; Bower, R.; and Eller, B. "Childhood Obesity: Prevention and Treatment." 38, no. 1 (November 1983): 21–27.

Ziajka, A. "Microcomputers in Early Childhood Education? A First Look." 38, no. 5 (July 1983): 61–67.

Zimmerman, K. and Herr, J. "Time Wasters: Solutions for Teachers and Directors." 37, no. 3 (March 1981): 45–48.

# Index

# Information about NAEYC

## NAEYC is . . .

. . . a membership-supported organization of people committed to fostering the growth and development of children from birth through age 8. Membership is open to all who share a desire to serve and act on behalf of the needs and rights of young children.

## NAEYC provides . . .

. . . educational services and resources to adults who work with and for children, including

• *Young Children, the* journal for early childhood educators

• **Books, posters, brochures,** and **videos** to expand your knowledge and commitment to young children, with topics including infants, curriculum, research, discipline, teacher education, and parent involvement

• An **Annual Conference** that brings people from all over the country to share their expertise and advocate on behalf of children and families

• **Week of the Young Child** celebrations sponsored by NAEYC Affiliate Groups across the nation to call public attention to the needs and rights of children and families

• **Insurance plans** for individuals and programs

• **Public affairs information** for knowledgeable advocacy efforts at all levels of government and through the media

• The **National Academy of Early Childhood Programs,** a voluntary accreditation system for high-quality programs for children

• The **National Institute for Early Childhood Professional Development,** providing resources and services to improve professional preparation and development of early childhood educators

• The **Information Service,** a centralized source of information sharing, distribution, and collaboration

**For free information about membership, publications, or other NAEYC services . . .**

• call NAEYC at 202-232-8777 or 1-800-424-2460,

• or write to the National Association for the Education of Young Children, 1509 16th Street, N.W., Washington, DC 20036-1426.